EDITED BY

SCOT McKNIGHT *AND* JOSEPH B. MODICA

JESUS IS LORD

CAESAR IS NOT

EVALUATING EMPIRE IN NEW TESTAMENT STUDIES

IVP Academic

An imprint of InterVarsity Press
Downers Grove, Illinois

InterVarsity Press
P.O. Box 1400, Downers Grove, IL 60515-1426
World Wide Web: www.ivpress.com
E-mail: email@ivpress.com

InterVarsity Press® is the book-publishing division of InterVarsity Christian Fellowship/USA®, a movement of students and faculty active on campus at hundreds of universities, colleges and schools of nursing in the United States of America, and a member movement of the International Fellowship of Evangelical Students. For information about local and regional activities, write Public Relations Dept., InterVarsity Christian Fellowship/USA, 6400 Schroeder Rd., P.O. Box 7895, Madison, WI 53707-7895, or visit the IVCF website at <www.intervarsity.org>.

Excerpt on p. 14 from "To Mock Your Reign" by Fred Pratt Green. © 1973 Hope Publishing Company, Carol Stream, IL 60188, www.hopepublishing.com. All rights reserved. Used by permission.

Cover design: David Fassett
Interior design: Beth Hagenberg
Images: Christ mosaic: public domain/Wikimedia Commons
   paper background: © toto8888/iStockphoto
   Augustus von Prima Porta: © Till Niermann/Wikimedia Commons
   golden wreath: © Ivana/iStockphoto
   Jesus Christ: © ihsanyildizli/iStockphoto
   Statue of Caesar: © arne thaysen/iStockphoto

ISBN 978-0-8308-3991-9

Printed in the United States of America ∞

Library of Congress Cataloging-in-Publication Data

Jesus Is Lord, Caesar Is Not : Evaluating Empire in New Testament Studies / edited by Scot McKnight and Joseph B. Modica.
    pages cm
  Includes bibliographical references and index.
  ISBN 978-0-8308-3991-9 (pbk. : alk. paper)
    1. Christianity and politics—Biblical teaching. 2. Bible and politics. 3. Politics in the Bible. 4. Church history—Primitive and early church, ca. 30-600. 5 Bible. N.T.—Criticism, interpretation, etc. I. McKnight, Scot, editor of compilation. II. Modica, Joseph B., editor of compilation.
  BS2545.P6J47 2013
  225.6'7—dc23

                                                                        2012045944

P	20	19	18	17	16	15	14	13	12	11	10	9	8	7	6	5	4	3	2	1
Y	30	29	28	27	26	25	24	23	22	21	20	19	18	17	16	15	14	13

for

Dwight N. Peterson

Friend, Scholar, Follower of Jesus

Here's to lattes, biscotti and the world to come . . .

CONTENTS

FOREWORD

Andy Crouch

The signs of empire are everywhere. In the most prosperous places, the empire's name is found engraved on items in every home; in the poorest places, the empire and its representatives build infrastructure, initiate trade and dictate military policy—ideally, as with all empires, ruling as much by indirect suggestion as by direct command. As the world's largest economy, it is able to dictate favorable terms wherever it goes; as a military power that invests vast sums in new technology, it can shape the course of world affairs. Its rise to power has delivered untold wealth to some of its citizens (and generous benefits to its allies and vassals) while leaving many needy. Gleaming new buildings and thoroughfares coexist with rural and urban poverty.

Portions of the empire's elite embrace a Christian faith, marked by evangelical fervor, that seems able to coexist with deeply rooted nationalism and ethnocentrism. Others among its ruling class are determined skeptics who believe monotheism is for weaklings. What all the elites have in common, whatever their faith, is their conviction that the empire's reign is inevitable and laudable—a conviction all the more powerful because it is held at a level deeper than reason or argument can reach.

You may find echoes of Rome in this description, or nineteenth-century Britain may come most quickly to mind, or perhaps late-twentieth-century America—but the empire I have in mind is China. If not every feature of this description is yet fulfilled, there are good reasons to believe that most or all of the previous two paragraphs could be true of China in our lifetime.

This, at least, is seeming increasingly likely: whatever the exact magnitude of the role China plays in the world of the twenty-first and twenty-second centuries, Christian believers will play a major part in its story. Already they number at least 50 million. Their biological and spiritual children will speak the language spoken by more people than any other language on earth; they will have been inducted from birth into its incomparably rich cultural history and heritage; they will, like all of the latter generations of empire, increasingly take their nation's stature in the world for granted. If present trends continue, a disproportionate number of these Christians will come from the relatively educated and urban elite—as seems to have been the case among the first Christians in the cities of the Roman imperium—and will be consciously and unconsciously shaped by that status. And they, like Christian believers in empires before them, will largely read the Scriptures in a way that confirms, not challenges, most of their assumptions. Yet they will also be challenged by the Bible's story. Perhaps they too, like Christian believers in empires before them, will ask whether the story told by their nation is entirely true.

I don't bring up the possible rise of a Chinese imperial age to stoke xenophobic or declinist fears among Western readers. (I should say, of course, *another* Chinese imperial age, since China has played imperial roles for good portions of millennia, and that longevity may be its greatest difference from any other empire in history.) Rather, the possibility that the "empire" that our children's children will most readily think of will be ruled in Mandarin, not English, is a helpful reminder of several fundamental truths.

We will always have empires. By *empire* I suppose we mean a political and economic order that succeeds in subsuming previously disparate nations and economies under a rule that can call on both the "hard power" of military might and technological achievement and the "soft power" embedded in deep structures of ideology, philosophy and theology. Every empire worthy of the name combines visible, tangible instruments of enforcing the will of its elites with invisible, intangible systems of thought that, for those within the reach of the empire, make sense of the world. Ultimately these systems of thought are the true source of imperial power, for they not only legitimate the use of hard power but take up their dwelling in the secret places of the heart. They become taken for granted, defining the horizons of the possible and thus existing beyond the reach of ordinary challenges and change.

Empire—this combination of hard and soft power extended over previously disparate territory—seems to be a recurring and near-permanent feature of human history. At different times the forces at work may be geographic, demographic, technological, ideological or even psychological (at least in the short term—think of Alexander "the Great"). But consistently, at least since human beings emerged from the age of nomadic hunting and gathering, certain societies have acquired enough of a durable advantage over their neighbors, and enough yearning for expansion, to construct an empire. For a brief time after the fall of the Soviet Union, it seemed to a few observers as if this long history might be at an end—in the sense that the deep structures of "Western" thought might permanently settle into the aspirations of people in every part of the globe, perhaps even rendering the "hard power" of major military conflict between states unnecessary. Three decades later it is abundantly clear not only that there is nothing eschatologically settled about a Western-style commitment to liberal democracy. Rather other powers are rising, animated by systems of thought that are just as compelling to their adherents, while being by no means similar to Western ones, and showing every promise of having access to sufficient hard power to rival anything the West can muster.

So it seems reasonable to assume that we will have empires, or at least aspiring imperial powers, as long as we have complex human societies. This should not be surprising to biblical people. For the biblical writers themselves consistently give voice to the essential yearning that empires embody: that the human race might simultaneously be fruitful and multiply, filling the earth and subduing it, while also being reconciled to one another in one cohesive system of life, work and worship. These twin human drives, expansion throughout the world and reconciliation with one another, are from the biblical point of view rooted in our image-bearing, however distorted they may become. It should be no surprise that whenever image-bearers acquire sufficient collective power, they pursue something like empire—nor that the hope of both Testaments of the Bible is that the now divided and warring nations will come to one mountain, bowing before one king, to offer a symphony of praise.

Empires always end. Every empire seems eternal. This is an essential asset in the storehouse of imperial soft power. But just as myriad factors give rise to empire, so empires can erode or collapse for any number of reasons—perhaps most commonly, the rise of an even more well-integrated, powerful and ambitious rival. These moments are aptly compared in Scripture to "the end of the world"—stars falling from the heavens, the earth being shaken, just as even today we can refer to an economic or political revolution as "earth-shaking"—because for those living within the horizons that empires create, that is exactly what they are. Since all human beings depend on comprehensive systems of meaning for an inhabitable world, the loss of empire is profoundly disorienting—even for the empire's least willing subjects.

And yet empires are inherently precarious. They are precarious by definition, because what it means to be an empire is to cross boundaries of culture, holding together disparate "nations" (in the biblical sense of distinctive and durable cultural traditions). The end of the Soviet empire in recent decades has reminded us of just how much ethnic pride and hostility, how much pent-up hope and conflict, was held in check by Soviet power and communist ideology. Empires depend on a false or at least premature reconciliation of the tensions in the human story—they claim more than they can ever achieve. For this reason all empires contain at least the seeds of idolatry, a promise of transcendence that can never be fulfilled.

So the Western consensus, birthed from American power in two world wars and rooted in a secularized democratic liberalism, far from being the end of history, will itself come to an end in history, if the Lord tarries. This is not to say that the American nation will dissolve any time soon—China, again, reminds us of just how durable a nation can be—just that its sway over world affairs will diminish sooner or later, perhaps because of the rise of another more powerful rival or simply the tensions of its own internal and irresolvable contradictions. And the same will be true for whatever empire succeeds the American one—China may have millennia of history, but only in some eras has it been able to exert significant power beyond the borders of the Han nation. Its time may come in the twenty-first century, but its time will also pass.

About this rising and falling of empires the biblical writers are surprisingly ambivalent. The great apocalyptic visions always predict a succession of empires, but while sometimes they cheer ("Fallen, fallen is Babylon the great!"), at other times they mourn or simply narrate dispassionately the Holy One's view of history. This ambivalence seems congruent with the nuanced judgment that God's prophets pronounce on the nations of the world—just as nations can reject God's purposes (think of Babel) or repent and fulfill them (think of Nineveh), so empires can be instruments of God's work or obstacles to his reign. The end of an empire is never entirely surprising to the biblical writers, and it is never something to shake the faith of God's own people. But nor is it a cause for gloating—when Daniel foretells the end of Nebuchadnezzar's reign, he is deeply troubled and prays that the vision might apply not to the king but to his enemies. Daniel's loyalty to the occupier of his homeland seems to exemplify a consistent biblical view that emperors, and empires, are responsible agents within history, subject both to prophetic judgment and to priestly counsel. Indeed, an emperor can even be called "Messiah" with a straight face (Cyrus, in Is 45:1) when he puts his power at the service of God's anointed people.

And this leads to our third observation:

Not all empires are alike. The word *empire* is much in use these days among Christians, and it is almost always used in an imprecatory manner, as with a tweet that arrived as I was drafting this essay: "We haven't really begun 'doing' justice or preaching Jesus until we've unsettled the Powers of the Empire." In this habit of thought, which may owe more than we'd like to admit to George Lucas's Star Wars trilogy, Empire (with that ominous capital letter) distills institutionalized, implacable evil. It exists to be unsettled and ultimately undone, as my Twitter friend suggests, by the proclamation of the gospel and the doing of justice.

And of course this is true of Empire. But it is true of every single human cultural institution or artifact with a Capital Letter—that is, every created thing that sets itself up in the absolute and ultimate place reserved for the Creator. Every idol capitalizes itself (with the possible exception of a supremely powerful commercial empire, Apple, Inc., which prefers a lowercase *i* for its ventures in godlikeness). But every idol is the simultaneously exalted and degraded form of a good, created thing. Evil has no resources of its own but must colonize the good. And while Empire, by definition, is idolatrous (and our moment in history, like all past moments, provides plenty of examples of such idolatry), the much more complex reality of empire (just like the much more complex reality of emperors) always contains within it some elements of genuine good, however residual they may be.

All this is to say that empires differ in the extent to which they partake in the idolatry of Empire. One need only compare the colonial enterprises

of the various European powers—shot through with sin as they all were—
to see that the Belgian empire was of a vastly different and more destructive
character than the British one, with divergent consequences for the Belgian
and British colonies that continue to the present day. Likewise, the Soviet
empire was different and more destructive than the NATO alliance, even
though the latter shared many of the features of a modern empire with the
former. Indeed, the Soviet empire was implicated much more deeply in
destructive idolatry (which always leads directly to injustice, the robbing
of God's creation of its proper dignity and destiny) precisely because of its
hostility to any transcendent reality that might sit in judgment of the
empire itself.

Consequently, the question is really not whether we will have empires
(we will) or whether they will endure (they will not), but what *kind* of
empires we will have in this time between the times. Will our empires
succumb entirely to the idolatry of power and the lust for domination
that comes when human beings explicitly cast off their accountability to
the Creator God? Or will they be chastened by the vision of a tree, "great
and strong, so that its top reached to heaven and was visible to the end of
the whole earth, whose foliage was beautiful and its fruit abundant, and
which provided food for all, under which animals of the field lived, and in
whose branches the birds of the air had nests"—yet which could be
chopped down in a moment by the judgment of the Most High (Dan
4:20-21 NRSV)? Note that the tree itself is described in wholly positive
terms—it serves the good purposes of empire, to use its strength to
provide for a rich diversity of creatures, reconciling them under one
canopy. It is only when the Most High is scorned or forgotten that
judgment comes, "until you have learned that the Most High has sovereignty over the kingdom of mortals, and gives it to whom he will" (Dan
4:25 NRSV). And even then, as Isaiah prophesied over God's own wayward
people, there is a stump still left in the wasteland, with a shoot yet to come
forth even from the most desolate relic of disobedience.

The ethicist Oliver O'Donovan makes the perceptive observation that
the resurrection of Jesus, vindicating him as King of kings and Lord of lords,
does not spell the end of political rule in history—and we might add that,
empirically at least (noting the pun!), it has not spelled the end of empires.
But it *has* put an end to the claim of rulers to provide *salvation*—rescue from
the conditions of sin and death. And none too soon, because these claims

were always faintly pathetic and frequently became frighteningly demonic—there is a reason the world cheers at the fall of "Babylon the Great." We no longer need to invest our political structures with hopes of eternal rescue from the abyss of chaos—that has been done and dealt with by Christ. Instead, we grant them humbler status, befitting mere creatures—indeed, creatures of creatures, our own cultural creations meant to serve the purpose of image-bearing. They are meant to secure certain kinds of liberty and to provide, as in Daniel's vision, for the flourishing of all. They can only do so when they are chastened by the proclamation of the world's true Ruler, the one who truly is the Beginning and the End, who has triumphed over death and hell.

I believe this explains what, to me, is the clearest finding of this book: the dog that didn't bark. After all the scholarly examination is done, even with a stiff tailwind of intellectual fashion propelling the quest for signs of anti-imperial sentiment, it seems that the only fair conclusion is that there is a surprisingly small place in the New Testament writers' attention for denunciations of Caesar, explicit or otherwise. When the clerk at Ephesus says, "They are neither temple-robbers nor blasphemers of our goddess," he is simply telling the truth—even though the proclamation of Christ surely would put an end to the legitimacy of idols like Artemis and put her temple out of business sooner or later (in the timescale of history, it turned out to be sooner). The way of Jesus' first followers was not to blaspheme Artemis or to denounce Caesar—it was to proclaim Jesus.

To put it another way, to say "Jesus is Lord" does not seem actually to entail *saying* "Caesar is not [Lord]." Rather, it entails *not saying* "Caesar is Lord." This minute grammatical distinction, simply a matter of where the negation is placed, seems to me to explain so much about the New Testament witnesses. The affirmation "Jesus is Lord" requires not so much a strident denunciation of earthly lords as a studied silence concerning their pretensions. The answer to Caesar's inflated claims of significance is further proclamation of Jesus the Messiah's real significance.

Of course, *saying* "Jesus is Lord" does require *believing* that Caesar is not Lord—with, as we would say today, a capital *L*. But in this case saying does not seem to be the same as believing. Not once does a New Testament writer or character deny Caesar's status as *kyrios* outright. For in fact, *Kaisaros* (the human being) is *kyrios* (the "lower-case" political role), lord for the moment of that which has been entrusted to him, and accountable to the

King of kings and Lord of lords for his stewardship of it all. Rather, what Jesus and the first followers do is simply insist that Jesus is Lord. "Give to Caesar what is Caesar's." No less and no more. To be sure, if Caesar, aspiring to apotheosis, demands more than is his due, the followers of the world's true Lord will not play his game. They—we—will not say "Caesar is Lord," especially when that phrase is accompanied with the libations of worship and the sycophantic cries, "A god and not a man!" But neither will they preoccupy themselves with announcing that "Caesar is not Lord." That is the negative way of cynics who have not been granted a vastly greater hope, the resurrection whose positive proclamation and genuine revelation of power renders all mere critique of earthly powers scanty and small.

So let the naming of the world's true Lord expose what is genuine in Caesar's lordship and what is false. Let the bold proclamation of King Jesus lead to audiences with procurators and proconsuls, or to stocks and chains— be that as it may. The task of Christians is not to denounce Caesar but to exalt Jesus, in whose image Caesar is made and from whose authority Caesar derives whatever just authority he may possess. Let the chips fall where they may—we are placed in this world not to condemn the world but to proclaim the way by which the world may be saved.

And let us pray that the followers of Jesus might be found everywhere, in the far-flung and forgotten corners as well as in Caesar's household, amid the perhaps-fading empires of the West and amid the perhaps-rising empires of the East and South, to bear the good news—the justice-bearing, idol-withering news—that "though empires rise and fall, / [Christ's] kingdom shall not cease to grow / 'til love embraces all."[1]

---

[1] From the hymn "To Mock Your Reign," by Fred Pratt Green.

INTRODUCTION

Scot McKnight and Joseph B. Modica

The King James Bible (1611) was an empire-drenched Bible. Officially approved by the Church of England, its translators were tasked with providing a Bible that was simultaneously faithful to Savior and to Sovereign, attentive to the Greek and Hebrew while being careful to undergird the legitimacy of monarchy and episcopacy. Understandably, they were quick to endorse the divine right of kings from such passages as God's grand promise to David of an everlasting dynasty (2 Sam 7). Others, however, had claimed that the Bible proclaims every king's rights are subordinate to King Jesus, particularly in the church. This was made abundantly clear in the marginal notes of the Geneva Bible (1560), the preferred Bible of Presbyterians and Puritans—the popular Bible which King James was attempting to replace.

This, of course, is not the official story any of us heard if you grew up as I (McKnight) did—reading, memorizing and publicly reciting the King James Bible. Nor by the 1960s in the heart of America's Midwest did the divine right of kings, or empire for that matter, concern us. Not too many of us thought the Vietnam conflict, not to mention World War I, II or the Korean War, had anything to do with what the Bible said about empire.

But neither the royal tranquility of King James nor the imperial naiveté of mid-twentieth-century Americans are as stable as they once were. In fact, there is a growing method in biblical studies, found in the European but especially the North American academy, called "empire criticism," and while we might be able to trace its roots to a number of early voices in scholarship, the relentless work of Warren Carter, now at Brite Divinity School, is what has pressed empire criticism onto the main stage of biblical studies.

Empire criticism, though, is not just for the academics when they gather at conferences to read papers to one another. Due in part to the skilled pens of Tom Wright and Richard Horsley, this work has now reached anyone who cares to read anything above populist literature. A notable example of empire criticism is the InterVarsity Press book by Brian Walsh and Sylvia Keesmaat, *Colossians Remixed: Subverting the Empire*. This book combines judicious study of Paul's letter with trenchant social critique, all framed in empire criticism.

So what is empire criticism? In short—and this book is devoted to both description and evaluation of this method—it refers to developing an eye and ear for the presence of Rome and the worship of the emperor in the lines and between the lines of New Testament writings. One example here will suffice. A simple reading of Luke 2 reveals Luke using the following terms for Jesus—*Savior* and *Lord*, and alongside those terms are the terms *good news* (gospel) and *peace*. Now it so happens that empire critics call to our notice that these are the precise terms used of Caesar in Rome, the very terms broadcast throughout the empire on declarations and in letters and on countless inscriptions visible in all major cities in the empire. The implication of Luke 2, empire critics claim, is that Luke was not just imparting spiritual goods about the Christian faith. Instead, his words were laced with criticism of Rome—to say Jesus was Lord and Savior or to say Jesus was the one who brings peace and good news is at the same time, in a covert way, to say Caesar was not Lord and not Savior, and that his good news and peace ring hollow. The language of Luke 2 then was coded for anyone with a good first-century ear. It is only our distance and comfort with modern empires that deafen us to the sounds.

Empire critics claim most Bible readers, especially those in the established and wealthy parts of Western culture, are not far from the desired readership of King James himself: he wanted his readers both to affirm the divine right of kings and to not even notice they were doing so. Empire criticism is minimized when one doesn't see the issues at hand. What empire critics want us to see is what the Geneva Bible's editors wanted their readers to see and then put into practice: the empire, including James, must bow before King Jesus. Well, that's a rough and ready analogy that can serve our purpose. In brief, then, empire criticism asks us to listen closer to the sounds of the empire and the sounds of challenging empire at work in the pages of the New Testament.

This method has now extended to all books in the New Testament, and not just to Revelation, where it has played a role among scholars for longer than scholars care to count. It asks us to stand up and notice that the message of the gospel was at once spiritual and subversive of empire, that it was both a powerful redemptive message and a cry for liberation. Moreover, the New Testament, if we care to listen, is at times an assault on Caesar and calls the Christian to form an entirely different society—one that listens to Jesus as its King and takes its orders not from Caesar or his laws but from Jesus and his moral vision, shaped by a cross that breeds sacrifice and self-denial. It calls us to worship King Jesus and not Caesar.

This approach, if right, is breathtaking in its implications.

Which is just the problem: Is it, many are asking, right? Are we reading Rome and Caesar *into* the New Testament or are we reading *what is actually there*? If you insert the theme, the theme will suddenly appear everywhere. Is it just insertion? These are the questions *Jesus Is Lord, Caesar Is Not* seeks to answer.

In advance of the various authors' forays into empire criticism, we (the editors) want to offer a brief on *how empire criticism actually works*. It appears to work on a spectrum from the obvious—does anyone wonder if Rome is in mind in Revelation 18?—to the implicit. We propose, then, the following five methods at work in empire criticism.

First, some statements in the Bible are overtly and directly anti-empire and anti-imperial worship. We find this in Acts 14:14-18.

> When the apostles Barnabas and Paul heard of this, they tore their clothes and rushed out into the crowd, shouting: "Friends, why are you doing this? We too are only human, like you. We are bringing you good news, telling you to turn from these worthless things to the living God, who made the heavens and the earth and the sea and everything in them. In the past, he let all nations go their own way. Yet he has not left himself without testimony: He has shown kindness by giving you rain from heaven and crops in their seasons; he provides you with plenty of food and fills your hearts with joy." Even with these words, they had difficulty keeping the crowd from sacrificing to them. (NIV)

Here the apostle Paul says the idols of the Roman city are "worthless," and the citizens need to turn instead to the one true and living God. This is direct criticism of some religious practices at work in the Roman Empire.

Second, sometimes a passage has more than one term that has distinct and notable uses in the Roman Empire's official ideology and even emperor cult. We previously brought out the evidence in Luke 2. It is not a stretch of anyone's imagination to contend that these terms are at work in the imperial cult, and so it is worth pondering whether Luke was not at least implicitly criticizing Rome (or he was naive to a fault).

Third, it now gets tricky. Some empire critics observe texts where Rome is clearly present—say Romans 13—and explain such texts not as a blanket endorsement but instead as a backhanded way of saying "Sure, go along with the emperor, as long as he does not transgress proper boundaries." Implicit is the argument that the original listeners of Romans 13 will have seen the critique because they will have seen Romans 13 as much critique and leveling of the emperor's authority as affirmation of Rome. The argument pushes further: it is only blinding ideology that blocks our seeing empire criticism in a text such as Romans 13. Alongside such conclusions from those with sensitive ears is the explanation that any text criticizing idolatry necessarily implies criticism of emperor worship. More often than not, in fact, empire critics see a hidden criticism of empire in criticism of idolatry more than a direct criticism of pagan religious worship.

Fourth, empire critics indulge in the claims of the sensitive historian. That is, their assumptive knowledge of both the texts of earliest Christianity and the Roman Empire makes them particularly sensitive to hear things others don't hear. Just as when Dan Brown published *The Da Vinci Code* and many Christians were caught totally unaware of how the New Testament canon was formed and how the Nicene Creed actually came about (and then had to do some quick research to discover he had hoodwinked many), so also good Roman historians caught many Bible readers unaware. If a century ago good Bible readers knew their Roman history and customs well, today's Bible readers are often much more informed of the Jewish context but much less so of the Roman context. Few serious Bible readers can read Latin anymore. So when someone who knows far more than they do about Roman religion and something called the "imperial cult" points out some Roman item at work in a text, many feel like a cow on ice—they've lost all traction and can be pushed wherever the farmer wants the cow to go.

So it is with some empire critics: study Rome, learn customs about Rome, get some facts about Caesar and the imperial cult under your belt, and then open up your New Testament and you can find connections. Such an armed empire critic will draw our attention to Paul's entrance into Italy in Acts 27, observe that this sure sounds like an emperor's staged parade into Rome with his retinue, and then infer that Luke is mocking Rome in describing Paul. To the one who knows nothing about Roman customs, such a connection can't be made. The game works both ways, though: if you play this hand too often, it gets suspicious. In fact, the empire critic might begin to resemble the lobbyist in Washington, DC. This assumptive approach has to do its job well.

Fifth, we will not be the first to observe, for many have been saying this and some in the pages of this book will say it again, that at times empire criticism *sounds too much like one's personal progressive, left-wing, neo-Marxist, or whatever, politics.* It has to be observed that it is probably not accidental that empire criticism became most popular during the Bush years, when the same academics were up in arms about colonialism and empire. I (McKnight) read a piece from a disinterested New Testament scholar in the United Kingdom who simply observed that empire criticism is a North American, university-shaped method designed to critique American international policies. He then moved on to another topic. Anthony Thiselton, long ago, chronicled the development of sociopragmatic hermeneutics, and his sketch of feminist and Marxist hermeneutics revealed what was clearly confessed by its practitioners: they read the Bible to use the Bible for their own uses. As Brian Blount openly admits in his stunningly interesting *When the Whisper Put on Flesh*—sections of which one of us (McKnight) assigns to his students to experience an honest-to-goodness African American liberation approach to the ethics of the Gospels—that he is in search of themes for liberation, so empire critics need at times to admit that the first foot in their dance is a sociopragmatic hermeneutic that finds in Western democracies an imperialism that deserves critique. The issue, of course, is how much of this is sociopragmatics and how much of it is history.

In the pages that follow we will attempt to sort this out.

Here's how this book is organized. We have asked an expert on Rome, David Nystrom, now provost at Biola but formerly a colleague of Mc-Knight's at North Park University, to sketch how Roman religion and the imperial cult worked. This piece is masterful, even if concise and restricted by space. Then Judy Diehl, New Testament professor at Denver Seminary, provides a wide-ranging sketch of who is saying what in empire criticism. Judy has now authored three long articles on empire criticism for *Currents in Biblical Research*, and we are grateful she has reduced that longer survey into something briefer. With these done, we proceed to specific studies on New Testament authors and books: Joel Willitts, North Park University, examines Matthew; Dean Pinter, Eton College in Canada, does Luke; Christopher Skinner, Mount Olive College looks at the Gospel of John; and the book of Acts is examined by Drew Strait, a PhD student at Pretoria University, South Africa, who is doing his research on anti-empire rhetoric in the Jewish and Roman worlds. In turning to Paul, we asked Michael Bird, Crossway College in Brisbane, Queensland, Australia, to tackle Romans, a book that has now some of the most complete empire critical studies ever done. Then Lynn Cohick, Wheaton College, an expert on the history of the Mediterranean, examines Philippians, and Allan Bevere, an expert on Colossians, puts Walsh and Keesmaat's study to the test. We finish this part of the book with a study by Dwight D. Sheets, Evangel University, on Revelation, and Sheets offers a breathtaking set of suggestions that turns against one of the critical assumptions of empire criticism in Revelation. A highlight of this book is that we asked Andy Crouch, whose book on culture (*Culture Making: Recovering Our Creative Calling*) has been given a wide hearing and whose forthcoming book (*Playing God*, both from InterVarsity Press) researching power in the church and society, to examine these essays from a wider lens and offer his assessment in a foreword.

It might be asked if the editors or authors were driven by an agenda, and in this postmodern age it would only be a fool who would claim total objectivity. Before we answer this a brief word: I (McKnight) am an Anabaptist inclined to believe every instance of empire criticism that could be found. That is, I'm inclined to apply Thiselton's sociopragmatics and to join the empire critics. Yet from the very beginning I felt a historical unease with the empire critics while I was convinced their sociopragmatics would still be of use. I (Modica) have sought to interact deeply with the question What is the gospel? namely, that Jesus' message (and salvation history in general) addresses the redemption of fallen persons in "fallen" history. Hence, I have a particular interest in the hermeneutical implications (and at times "gymnastics") of those espousing empire criticism. We asked our authors only to find and describe what empire critics were saying about their New Testament book and then to evaluate it. We did not ask them to take a negative or a positive stance, and we are happy to say that we find their studies convincing if not also compelling. There is some balance and some diversity in the studies that follow; not everyone would agree with each other's studies, but we are satisfied that empire criticism is here put to the test. We leave it to our readers to judge for themselves.

1

We Have No King But Caesar

Roman Imperial Ideology and the Imperial Cult

David Nystrom

Beginning in 327 BC, the Roman state went to war eighty of the next eighty-five years.[1] Incessant bellicosity, observed Cicero, was the expected norm. Glory and an empire could thereby be won.[2] Following the Roman victory at Pydna in 168 BC, Polybius, forcibly transplanted to Rome, became an ardent admirer of his conquerors.

> There can surely be no one so petty or so apathetic in his outlook that he has no desire to discover by what means and under what system of government the Romans succeeded in less than fifty-three years in bringing under their rule almost the whole of the inhabited world, an achievement unparalleled in human history.[3]

The Athenian empire survived thirty years. Alexander's began to unravel within minutes of his death. The Romans forged an empire that lasted centuries.

---

[1] See William V. Harris, *War and Imperialism in Republican Rome, 327-70 BC* (Oxford: Clarendon Press, 1979), p. 10.
[2] Cicero, *De Officiis* 2.45.
[3] Polybius, *Histories* 1.1.

The Roman Achievement

This achievement required a complex and vibrant ideological matrix that was already decades old when Augustus came to power. He did not fundamentally alter it by assuming the trappings of personal supremacy, but rather magnified it by directing Roman tradition through the prism of his own story. Like his republican forebears, Augustus was able to anneal the vanquished to the Roman cause by blending power with service and reward. What were the salient features of this ideology? How did Augustus shape it? What did it mean to worship Augustus or to call an emperor "king"?

Ordained by the gods. The Romans claimed a divine commission to conquer and to civilize.

> Rome is a land nourished by all, and yet parent of all lands, chosen by the power of the gods to make even heaven more splendid, to gather together the scattered realms and to soften their customs and unite the discordant wild tongues of so many people into a common speech so they might understand each other, and to give civilization to mankind (*humanitatem homini*), in short to become the homeland of every people in the entire world.[4]

Pliny asserts the divine commission was not so crass as mere conquest, but through conquest to proffer *humanitas* to all peoples and thereby fashion a type of new humanity.

Just. The Romans bore the conviction that their rule was just. The epic poem Virgil crafted to laud Augustus pressed into service this theme. The Roman project was to "submit the whole world to the rule of law": *totum sub leges mitteret orbem.*[5]

Fundamental to the education of Roman elites was the belief that rule over others demanded self-mastery.[6] Roman law was a codified expression of this belief. To bring sober and restrained government to others was the Roman idea. "You, Roman, be certain to rule the world (be these your arts), to crown peace with justice, to spare the vanquished and crush the proud."[7]

Roman militarism was defended on the basis of justice. The Romans wished to believe they stood for order and sobriety in public life, that they were quick to display clemency to the supine but resolved to confront the

---

[4]Pliny, *Natural History* 3.39.
[5]Virgil, *Aeneid* 4.231.
[6]See Peter Heather, *The Fall of the Roman Empire* (Oxford: Oxford University Press, 2006), p. 19.
[7]Virgil, *Aeneid* 6.851-853.

obstinate.[8] Undergirding this was a belief that *Romanitas* was superior to other forms of human culture.[9] Cicero records the view that Rome is greater than Greece because Rome stands alone as the home of virtue, imperial power and dignity (*domus est virtutis, imperii, dignitatis!*).[10] Rome is marked, he avers, by the wisdom of its laws and the vastness of its empire. These make Rome glorious beyond all others.

Vast. Cicero once lauded Pompey and Caesar for so expanding the arena of Roman domination that its borders "are fixed not by limits of the earth but by limits of the sky."[11] Two centuries after Cicero, Aelius Aristides wrote, "You have caused the word 'Roman' to belong not to a city but to be the name of a sort of common race, and this not one out of all the races, but a balance to the remaining ones."[12]

Of course the Romans could also display xenophobic passions. Juvenal wrote he hated a Rome full of Greeks and lamented that "the Syrian Orontes has long since flowed into the Tiber."[13] Cicero could be equally caustic. He disparaged Mysians and Phrygians and opined that the Jews were among several peoples born for slavery (*nationibus natis servituti*).[14] In a delightfully pregnant passage Juvenal writes: "Leave that sort of lie to the equites from Asia, Bithynia and Cappadocia too, and the powerful that were imported with bare feet from New Gaul."[15]

Access to power in the capital was extended slowly, offered first to Latin speakers in the west.[16] By the early second century several emperors were of non-Italian origin (e.g., Hadrian was born in Spain), and citizenship, once rarely enjoyed by non-Italians, was in AD 212 extended to all free persons within the bounds of the empire.

Stratified. Roman society was hierarchical and featured a dizzyingly steep social pyramid. Wealth, class, ancestry and location were only the most salient factors that together conveyed status. Seneca observed, "how

---

[8]Livy, *Histories* 33.12.7, observes that when dealing with the Carthaginians the Romans were magnanimous in victory.

[9]*Romanitas* is a term used by historians to refer to Roman culture. The term was not used by the ancients.

[10]Cicero, *De Oratore* 1.196.

[11]Cicero, *In Catilinam* 3.26.

[12]Aelius Aristides, *Orations* 26.63.

[13]Juvenal, *Satires* 3.60-63.

[14]Cicero, *Epistulae ad Quintum Fratrem* 1.1.19; Cicero, *De Provinciis Consularibus* 10.

[15]Juvenal, *Satires* 7.14-16. The reference to "bare feet" indicates those who were once slaves.

[16]For example, at the direction of Claudius (AD 41-54) the Aedui, one of the most docile of the Germanic tribes, were made eligible for the senate.

vast is the majority of the poor."[17] Aggressively class conscious, the Romans took active steps to reinforce social stratification in even the smallest of cities.[18] Roman attitudes regarding class were vividly expressed. Martial claimed that sexual relations with a free woman were preferable to sexual relations with a freedwoman.[19] Augustus closed the ranks of the senatorial order and restricted intermarriage between classes.[20] Tacitus complained of the marriage of a woman of senatorial standing to an equestrian whose grandfather was from a town other than Rome.[21] Varro considered rural slaves equipment and classified them with farm tools.[22] In a passage that reveals cascading levels of honor among cities, Cicero relates Anthony's barb directed at Octavian: "He charges that Caesar's mother is from Aricia, as if it were the same as Tralles or Ephesus!"[23] For Cicero even a magnificent provincial city like Ephesus was beneath comparison to an Italian city.

The distinction between the "best sort" of people and the "lesser sort" is commonly represented in Latin literature,[24] and appears casually in this bit of Tacitus concerning the year of chaos following the death of Nero:

> The worst element were delighted but the best citizens scandalized (*bonos invidiae*) by the act of Vitellius in erecting altars on the Campus Martius and sacrificing to the shades of Nero (*inferias Neroni fecisset*). The victims were killed and burned in the name of the state. The torch was applied to the sacrifices by the Augustales, a sacred college which Tiberius Caesar had dedicated to the Julian gens.[25]

In the fourth century the Roman diplomat Symmachus described the senate as *pars melior humani generis*, "the better part of humankind."[26] The distinction was a key element in the Roman strategy of imperial stability.

---

[17]Seneca, *De Consolatione ad Helviam* 12.1, "*quanto maior pars sit pauperum.*" See Mk 14:7.

[18]See Pliny, *Epistles* 10.112-113, for examples of divisions by wealth set by the emperor.

[19]Martial, *Epigrams* 3.33.1.

[20]Augustus set entrance into the senatorial order on three factors: personal integrity, military service, a personal fortune of HS1,000,000. The intermarriage restriction is either the *lex Iunia* of 17 BC or the *lex Norbana* of 19 BC. A detailed account of Augustan social legislation is to be found in P. A. Brunt, *Italian Manpower* (Oxford: Clarendon Press, 1971), pp. 558ff.

[21]Tacitus, *Annals* 6.27.

[22]Varro, *Rerum Rusticarum* 1.17.

[23]Cicero, *Philippics* 3.15.

[24]Perspective, of course, counts. As seen earlier, a senator from an impoverished family might seem "better" than a nouveau-riche freedman. A household slave, however, might wish for riches more than honor.

[25]Tacitus, *Histories* 2.95.

[26]Symmachus, *Letters* 1.52.1.

Aelius Aristides remarked approvingly,

> You have divided all of the men in your empire, and by this I mean of
> course the entire inhabited world, into two parts, and everywhere you
> have made citizens of all who are the more accomplished, and noble, and
> powerful of people, even if they maintain their own cultural proclivities,
> while those who are left you have made the subjects.[27]

True civilization, apparently, could only be realized by elites.

Urban and material. The Roman Empire was an urban phenomenon.
Supreme among all cities was Rome. Italian cities typically enjoyed a privileged status relative to cities outside Italy. Many cities were *colonia* or colonies, technically extensions of the city of Rome itself. These were often
populated with retired soldiers. Other cities were *municipia.* Some *municipia* outside of Italy possessed Italian rights (*ius Italicum*), a favored status
that conveyed exemption from certain taxes. The East was already highly
urbanized by the time the Romans arrived, and where possible the Romans
blended in Latin forms.[28] In the nonurbanized West the Romans founded
cities in order to spread *Romanitas.*[29]

Trier on the banks of the Moselle River, originally a military camp,
became a Roman city replete with circus, palace, basilica, hot and cold
baths, and a gymnasium. Similar cities could be found from Britain to
Africa and Asia Minor. The political life of cities was pressed to conform to
the Roman pattern. The Lex Irnitana (constitution of Irni) discovered in
1981 outside of Seville suggests that by the late first century a basic constitution crafted in Rome was available for adoption by towns throughout the
empire.[30] It stipulated qualifications for election to the town council, the
responsibilities of council members and what sorts of legal cases could be
handled locally. The conquered had lost political rights and perhaps material wealth. The route open to restore their fortunes was to learn to play by
Roman rules. The Romans could not, of course, force the conquered to
accept *Romanitas,* but they could render acceptance of Roman ideology at-

---

[27]Aelius Aristides, *Orations* 26.59.

[28]The Augustan colony at Beirut, Colonia Julia Augusta Felix Berytus, was founded with traditional Etruscan rites, laid out in a grid with hippodrome, forum and amphitheater.

[29]The success of this enterprise can even be seen in the gradual displacement of porridge by
bread in Roman Gaul. See also D. J. Mattingly, "Vulgar and Weak 'Romanization,' or Time
for a Paradigm Shift?" *Journal of Roman Archaeology* 15 (2002): 163-67.

[30]See J. Gonzales, "The Lex Irnitana: A New Copy of the Flavian Municipal Law," *Journal of
Roman Studies* 76 (1986): 147-243.

tractive. Savvy provincials quickly realized that adopting a Roman constitution was a first step to securing Latin rights and eventually citizenship.

Informal with power centered at the top. The letters of Cicero and Pliny
indicate that informal personal ties characterized the Roman ruling elite. It
was by use of these ties of patronage that the Romans held sway over a vast
empire of some forty provinces with an administration that was both nu-
merically meager and essentially amateur.[31] Among the Romans a patron or
benefactor was a person who provided protection, financial assistance or
political influence. The recipient of this largesse was the client. The client
was expected to honor and at times serve the patron. "To fail to repay a
favor is not permitted to a good man," wrote Cicero.[32] "Homicides, tyrants,
thieves, adulterers, robbers, sacrilegious men, and traitors there will always
be; but worse than all these is the crime of ingratitude," wrote Seneca.[33] This
system, he opined, is the glue holding society together.[34] Effective use of
these relationships depended on not only fame (what was said about one)
but also *gloria* (the notoriety that results from effective self-promotion).

The Romans expected and practiced self-promotion. Tacitus once wrote,
nam contemptu famae contemni virtutes (to fail to cultivate one's reputation
is to lose respect for one's virtues).[35] Only by boasting of their own exploits
could there be a record for the moral instruction of future generations.
Gloria was necessary to advance a career during which great deeds could be
attempted and placed before the arbitriment of history. So Cicero wrote,
optimus quisque maxime gloria ducitur (the better the man the more committed to glory).[36] There were limits of course. Cicero in a letter begged
Lucceius to make his name "illustrious and renowned" by being so prof-
ligate with the truth as to test the limits of its elasticity. Embarrassed, Cicero
nonetheless noted, "a letter cannot blush."[37] This pattern concentrated
power in the hands of a relatively small group of people. With Augustus this
changed. Instead of dozens of great patrons all enjoying similar levels of

---

[31]Provincial officials typically stayed in office for only a few years, had little or no diplomatic
   training and brought with them a small staff dominated not by professionals but by their
   friends. During the early imperial period these figures were often *equites* at times designated
   "a friend of Caesar," a practice that points to the idea of patronage.
[32]Cicero, *De Officiis* 1.48.
[33]Seneca, *De Beneficiis* 1.10.4.
[34]Ibid., 1.4.2.
[35]Tacitus, *Annals* 4.3.5.
[36]Cicero, *Pro Archia* 26.
[37]*epistula enim non erubescit*, Cicero, *Epistulae ad Familiares* 5.12, 1.

prestige, Augustus towered above the others. He became patron par excel-
lence and so focused the narrow of beam of glory on the Julian house that
it was without serious rival.

Religion as compact. In AD 180 a group of Christians brought to trial so
frustrated the official before whom they were arrayed that he declared, "We,
too, are a religious people" (*Et nos religiosi*).[38] The story illustrates the difference between pagan and Christian experiences of religion. Jason Davies
notes there are two questions to ask about Roman religion: What did they
think? and What did they do?[39] The first is seldom ventured; the second, he
avers, is important but yields answers that do not satisfy. Scholars have
rightly avoided the idea of "faith" in regard to Roman religion even while
asserting that to regard Roman religion as mere "public participation" is to
relegate it to the status of a shade. There is more there, but how to get at it?

Paganism can be described as a collection of cult acts. There was no creed.
Sacrifice of animals, grains or the pouring of libations was common. The-
atrical performances and processions accompanied festivals honoring the
gods.[40] There was no conversion in paganism. More room could always be
made on the shelf for another god. There was no sense of sin in paganism.
Difficulty or misfortune was the result of an offense against a god or a group
of gods. The trick was to discern which ones and then seek to placate them.
For this reason the Romans prized the *pax deorum*, the peace with or of the
gods. The Romans believed the favor of the gods rested upon them because
of their acts of fealty. Livy records the misfortune that occurred when an official mishandled a prayer. The prayer had to be recited again and this time
without stumble.[41] The Romans understood their dominance as attributable
to this compact. One might argue that the Romans saw victory in war as
evidence that the right man, the one chosen by the gods, was at the top. This
helps to explain the many coins struck with images that combine imperial
piety with victory.[42] Closely tied to the *pax deorum* was the *mos maiorum*,
the tradition of the ancestors. In Roman homes were depictions of the ancestors on display, and these were carried in funeral processions as if to say,

---

[38]*Acts of the Scillitan Martyrs*, 9-11.
[39]Jason Davies, "Review of *Religion in Republican Italy*, and *Roman Religion and the Cult of
Diana at Aricia*," *Journal of Roman Studies* 99 (2009): 245-47.
[40]See Bruce Chilton, *Rabbi Paul* (New York: Doubleday, 2004), p. 11.
[41]Livy, *Histories* 41.16.
[42]See Andrew Wallace-Hadrill, "Image and Authority in the Coinage of Augustus," *Journal of
Roman Studies* 76 (1986): 71, for the combination of the laurel leaves of victory with symbols
of piety.

"This is what our family has done, this is who we are, this is how we should act." Careful adherence to the patterns of the past was of signal importance for the good of the state. In Roman paganism the chief magistrates also functioned as the chief figures in religion. The Christian notion of faith was largely alien to paganism. Within the compass of antiquity faith was considered among the lower orders of mental activity. Excessive faith, *superstitio*, was to be avoided as a type of unhealthy credulity. When on trial early Christians could prove their loyalty not so much by proclamation of belief as the performance of certain acts, such as pouring libations to the emperor.

From the earliest period of their history the Romans practiced sacrifice to the dead. The Romans called these shades *di manes* (the spirits of the dead), *di lares* (guardian spirits associated with the crossroads) and *di penates* (spirits of the inside of the house or spirits of the family ancestors). The three are sometimes conflated and by the time of Virgil could refer to an individual as well as the collective whole. *Di penates* were also associated with the genius or spirit of the *paterfamilias* and the national cult of the ancestors of the Roman people.[43] The Romans, therefore, evinced a belief in something like the spirits of the dead as well as the genius of the living. Public worship of the living generally linked the living person with one or more of the gods, such as picturing an emperor in the guise of Jupiter.[44] Private worship involved prayers for the genius of the person in question. From exile Ovid tried to mollify Augustus with claims of remorse and piety (*nec pietas ignota mea est*). He wrote that at dawn he "offers incense and words of prayer" to his household images of Augustus, Livia, Tiberias, Germanicus, Julius Caesar and Drusus.[45] When a group of Christians were brought before him, the proconsul Saturninus said "we swear by the genius of our lord the emperor (*genium domni nostri imperatoris*) and we offer prayers for his health" and he then advised them to do the same.[46]

AUGUSTUS AND IMPERIAL IDEOLOGY

After Actium the future Augustus stood alone on the pinnacle of Roman power. While he retained the preeminent place won in war, he chose to avoid the trappings of supreme power, instead electing to embrace the tra-

---

[43]When Augustus was declared Father of the Country (*pater patriae*) by the senate in 2 BC he was declared head of a vast household.
[44]This is true both in terms of statuary and coinage.
[45]Ovid, *Ex Ponto* 4.9.105-12.
[46]*Acts of the Scillitan Martyrs*, 9-11.

ditions of the past. To this end Augustus produced several intentional attempts to shape how and what others thought of him, including the *Res Gestae* and the Augustan forum.

Augustus and his legacy. The *Res Gestae* (things done) was left with the Vestal Virgins to be read in the senate after the death of Augustus. It recalls the shaping events of Roman history, while highlighting no individual apart from Augustus. It is a record of all that he as benefactor had done for the Roman people, coupled with the insistence that all was done within the normal compass of Roman public life. Three copies of the *Res Gestae* have been found, all in Asia Minor. The most complete text, with Greek translation, is at Ancyra. The others are found in temples at Apollonia and Pisidian Antioch.

A second attempt to shape his legacy was a series of inscriptions in his new forum, the Forum Augusti. The focal point of the forum was to be the temple to Mars Ultor (Mars the Avenger) but placed within the forum were a series of statues of the great men of Rome's past accompanied by inscriptions summarizing each man's achievements.[47] The point is to teach the story and character of Roman history. In the center was to be a statue of Augustus himself, riding in a chariot with the title "Father of his Country." The point is to demonstrate that Augustus is the greatest in a long line of Roman political figures. He is the greatest, but he is still a part of that line and is therefore the supreme example of *Romanitas*. Any claim to kingship would invalidate the essential features of *Romanitas*.

The historical Augustus is an enigma. Even the basic question of whether he restored the Republic or constructed the Principate is hotly debated. What we do know is that he routinely turned aside entreaties on the part of the senate to invite him to occupy positions of power,[48] he refused to use personal power to secure land needed for his forum,[49] he proclaimed that the Romans should evaluate future leaders according to the standard of Roman history,[50] he studiously avoided any reference to himself as king,[51] and he was allergic to entreaties to offer him worship.

---

[47]Virgil's *Aeneid*, 6, contains a litany of the achievements of the famous men of Roman history.

[48]After 23 BC he refused the plan that would guarantee him annual reelection to the consulship, for instance.

[49]Suetonius, *Augustus* 56.2, *Forum angustius fecit non ausus extorquere possessoribus proximas domos* (He limited the expanse of his forum rather than risk forcibly dispossessing the owners of the adjacent houses).

[50]Suetonius, *Augustus* 31.8.

[51]It was not until the third century that the use of *basileus* became a usual designation for Caesar. The Latin *imperator* was not commonly used of emperors until after Vespasian.

This pattern was followed by his successors. Tiberius turned down the request of the two consuls in AD 14 to assume the third chair to match the pattern to which Augustus reluctantly agreed. When in AD 25 the Spanish province of Baetica proposed to construct a temple to Livia and to himself, Tiberius refused. Suetonius provides a description of the restraint of Tiberias:

> He forbade the decreeing to himself of temples, flamines and priests, and even of statues and representations without his permission, and he permitted them only on the condition that they should be set, not among the images of the gods, but among the decorations of the temple.[52]

With the exceptions of Caligula and Commodus, the emperors were careful to avoid official deification while alive. On his deathbed the famously humorous Vespasian said, *puto deus fio* (I think I am becoming a god).[53]

Patronage. The largesse of Augustus was unparalleled.[54] This meant that for senators, equestrians and provincial elites, social position depended largely on their standing in the sight of the emperor. Pliny says the basic job of an emperor is to be a good paternal protector and benefactor, not so much to be a good administrator.[55] Augustus bestowed favors on many, and government positions were divvied up based not on skill but on personal relationship. Augustus and his successors artfully linked their largesse with the benefits offered by the empire. "No mere sample of milestones can do justice to the experience of walking a Roman road: a series of such inscriptions, recording the emperor who built it and the emperors who repaved the road . . . boasting their ancestry and their conquests . . . (is) itself a history of one's empire."[56] Imperial generosity annealed provincials to the

---

Imperium means "command," and *imperator* was the term soldiers gave to their victorious field commander. Translators do not always understand this, and can obscure as well as illumine. In Lk 3:1 the word *hegemonia* (= Latin *principatus*) appears, and ought to be rendered "government" or some close cognate. But the NEB translates the passage "In the fifteenth year of the Emperor Tiberias," thus anachronistically associating the family name "Caesar" with the term *emperor*. See E. A. Judge, "'We Have No King But Caesar.' When Was Caesar First Seen As King?" *Papers of the Macquarie University Continuing Education Conference for Ancient History Teachers* (1986): 108-19.

[52]Suetonius, *Tiberias* 26.
[53]Suetonius, *Vespasian* 23.
[54]The personal wealth of Augustus was often used to supplement the state treasury. The sources are unclear as to the difference between the state treasury (*aerarium*), the imperial treasury (*fiscus*) and the personal treasury of the emperor (*patrimonium* but often called his *fiscus*).
[55]Pliny, *Panegyric* 2.21.
[56]Clifford Ando, *Imperial Ideology and Provincial Loyalty in the Roman Empire* (Berkeley: University of California Press, 2000), p. 322.

state, and against such a catalogue of beneficence clients could not offer fair recompense. What could be given was deference, and offers to establish cults to Augustus should be so understood. Donors whose largesse was used to erect temples and statues to Augustus could hope to be noticed by the emperor, and benefactors responsible for other projects could hope for appreciation and fame forever to be attached to their names. In 27 BC Mytilene on Lesbos voted a series of honors on Augustus and sent an embassy to Rome proudly to announce this. There are a host of reasons. A prominent one was to attempt to curry favor with the emperor. If a city could attract the attention of the emperor, then it could secure a more favored position in the imperial patronage chain. Donating funds to support the imperial cult provided urban elites with the opportunity to pursue social, economic and political advantage.

In the first centuries of the Christian era cities, particularly in the East, vied with one another for prominence in part to attract imperial attention. Ephesus and Smyrna competed for the title "First and Greatest Metropolis of Asia," historically assumed by Ephesus but envied by Smyrna. Later Pergamum joined in, but was forced to be content with the title "Metropolis of Asia and first city to be Twice Temple-Warden."[57] By the early second century Trajan was so worried that he felt compelled to send a personal emissary to investigate the wretched fiscal condition of some of these cities. Pliny, the legate in question, found city after city in Bithynia mired in public debt due to extravagant building programs such as theaters, baths, aqueducts and even excessive road maintenance.[58] Festivals, shrines and public works could mean economic benefits for cities and offered residents a basis for civic pride, but were often fiscally ill-considered.

Augustus and religion. The title *divus Julius* (divine Julius) assumed by Julius Caesar was a formal title of divinity. The odiousness of this claim led directly to his discomfiture. Caligula's claim to be a god struck his contemporaries as evidence of instability. The title *divi filius* (son of the divine) by which Augustus was worshiped during his lifetime was not a formal title of divinity. It was not until after his death that he was accorded *caelestes honores*. Nonetheless, honors came his way. By 36 BC Italian cities had begun to grant him a place in their temples, acknowledging that he was worthy of worship. Beginning in 30 BC his birthday was declared a public

[57]*Corpus Inscriptionum Graecarum* 3538.
[58]Pliny, *Epistles* 10.19; 38.42.

holiday, and various forms of worship (pouring of libations, public honoring of Augustus at meals) began to take place. In 29 BC he granted permission for temples to be dedicated to divine Julius and Roma at Nicaea and Ephesus, and temples dedicated to Roma and Augustus at Nicomedia and Pergamum. That same year his name was included in the list of the names of the gods in various hymns. In 27 BC his genius was linked with the name of Jupiter and *di Penates*. None of these equals deification, however. The Romans had long worshiped the genius of others without conveying the idea of divinity.

Jakob Munk Højte's study of imperial statuary (or more precisely the dedicatory bases of some 2,300 imperial statues) shows that for decades cities in Greece and Asia Minor erected statues to the emperor and his family, usually with a spike in the first two years of reign of any given emperor.[59] They were often in response to some action of imperial favor. People felt the need to worship the genius of the current emperor. The emperors learned to use these spontaneous actions to advance the cause of *Romanitas*.

The imperial cult. Early in the reign of Augustus and without imperial prompting, cities began to erect temples dedicated to the worship of the emperor and his family. Only rarely was the imperial cult imposed. Among these rare examples is the altar of the three Gauls in Lugdunum (Lyon) erected by Drusus in 12 BC after an unsuccessful revolt. On it are displayed the names of some sixty Germanic tribes brought under the sway of the Romans. The altar helped to establish Roman rule in these newly conquered territories by associating Roman rule with the person of Augustus.

The temples were typically located in a prominent place, the one in Athens on the acropolis and the one built by Herod over the harbor in Caesarea dominated the town. The temples vary and can display architectural hybridity, indicating participation by local elites in the Roman experiment. The Sebasteion at Aphrodisias included a relief sculpture complete with depictions of more than fifty ethnic peoples from around the Roman Empire. Brittania subdued appears as Penthesilea before Achilles at Troy.

In 25 BC Pisidian Antioch was annexed by Rome, declared a colony and veterans from Legions V and VII were settled there. The locals lost most of their political rights and the newly arrived veterans immediately became the political elite. The displaced elite quickly joined forces with the settled

---

[59]Jakob Munk Højte, *Roman Imperial Statue Bases: From Augustus to Commodus* (Aarhus: Aarhus University Press, 2005).

veterans, and together they undertook the task of building a temple complex dedicated to the emperor Augustus and his family, a temple completed while Augustus was still alive.

Most of what we know about the sanctuary is due to the work of W. M. Ramsay and D. M. Robinson and their team working from 1913-1924. The temple was constructed high on the east side of the acropolis, affording a marvelous vista of the surrounding region. The complex included a copy of the *Res Gestae* and a triple arched propylon studded with sculptures of Augustus, his family, a statue of the goddess *Roma* and depictions of captive barbarians. The fragmentary dedicatory inscription names Jupiter, indicating the divine commission for the Romans to conquer. Augustus, acting as the agent of the divine purpose, had done so, offering to the conquered the benefits of Roman civilization. The many inscriptions proclaiming the largesse of donors indicates that some of the provincial elites had gotten the message. The Augusteum was dedicated by Eueius and his son.

On holidays the people of Antioch and the surrounding countryside would gather for a festival, offer prayers and sacrifices on behalf of the emperor and his family, and to witness the mysteries, usually the unveiling of images of the emperor himself. Also associated with the festival would be gladiatorial games, animal sacrifices, processions and feasts. The rituals were intended to reinforce social hierarchy and to grant a sense of place and security within the compass of Roman civilization. Many fragments of imperial statuary have been found at the site, and it seems likely that these were purchased by locals and visitors as a way of demonstrating their loyalty to the emperor and his family.

CONCLUSIONS

The Roman Empire was vast, and the means of administration available to the emperors were few. Rather than rely on brute force and the markers of personal ascendancy, the imperial strategy was to link the traditional ideology of Roman rule with the imperial house. Coins, statuary and the imperial cult all thrust the emperor before the people in ways that evoked continuity with this ideology.[60] People worshiped Augustus as they worshiped their family ancestors, and they thought of him as lord and king, but he was

---

[60]Andrew Wallace-Hadrill, "Image and Authority in the Coinage of Augustus," *Journal of Roman Studies* 76 (1986): 70-71. From 31 BC on almost no coins appeared without the image of Augustus.

careful to link his role with traditional symbols and patterns of power. As lord he stood for more than himself. He stood for the entire compass of Roman civilization. His image and story conjured not simply his own person but the empire as an ordered world community that offered benefits to those who participated in its life. It was ordained by the gods. It favored might and the exercise of power. It offered a life of virtue as it fashioned a type of commonwealth that prized social hierarchy and stability. It was worldwide and intentionally stratified, affording benefits to conquered elites but little to the "lesser sort." It prized tradition and its glory was linked to the self-adulation of its elites. It prized honor and offered material reward to satiate that desire. It was a vast household existing under the benign and generous influence of an emperor who symbolized the Roman way. While there are spectacular exceptions, such as Caligula, Augustus and his successors employed the imperial cult not to fuel some megalomania but to instruct provincials on the patterns and benefits of *Romanitas* and so further the Roman project.[61] The message of the New Testament conjures a kingdom at variance with the Roman project at many points. The identity of the true King and Lord is the chief among them, as it at once implies the others.

BIBLIOGRAPHY

Ando, Clifford. *Imperial Ideology and Provincial Loyalty in the Roman Empire.* Berkeley: University of California Press, 2000.

Brunt, P. A. *Italian Manpower.* Oxford: Clarendon Press, 1971.

Chilton, Bruce. *Rabbi Paul.* New York: Doubleday, 2004.

Davies, Jason. "Review of *Religion in Republican Italy,* and *Roman Religion and the Cult of Diana at Aricia.*" *The Journal Roman Studies* 99 (2009): 245-47.

Gonzales, J. "The Lex Irnitana: A New Copy of the Flavian Municipal Law." *Journal of Roman Studies* 76 (1986): 147-243.

Harris, William V. *War and Imperialism in Republican Rome, 327-70 BC.* Oxford: Clarendon Press, 1979.

Heather, Peter. *The Fall of the Roman Empire.* Oxford: Oxford University Press, 2006.

Horsley, Richard A., ed. *Paul and Empire: Religion and Power in Roman Imperial Society.* Harrisburg, PA: Trinity Press International, 1997.

---

[61]Caligula famously said, "Let there be one Lord, one king" (Suetonius, *Gauis Caligula* 22), after which he demanded to be treated as a god and began appearing in public dressed as various deities. He once ordered a statue of himself erected in the temple in Jerusalem (Philo, *On the Embassy to Gaius* 30.203).

Højte, Jakob Munk. *Roman Imperial Statue Bases: From Augustus to Commodus.* Aarhus, Denmark: Aarhus University Press, 2005.

Judge, E. A. "'We Have No King But Caesar.' When Was Caesar First Seen As King?" In *Papers of the Macquarie University Continuing Education Conference for Ancient History Teachers*, pp. 108-19. Sydney, 1986.

Mattingly, D. J. "Vulgar and Weak 'Romanization', or Time for a Paradigm Shift?" *Journal of Roman Archaeology* 15 (2002): 536-40.

Price, S. R. F. *Rituals and Power: The Roman Imperial Cult in Asia Minor.* Cambridge: Cambridge University Press, 1984.

Wallace-Hadrill, Andrew. "Image and Authority in the Coinage of Augustus." *Journal of Roman Studies* 76 (1986): 66-87.

2

Anti-Imperial Rhetoric in the New Testament

Judith A. Diehl

First-century Romans venerated, honored and revered the emperor so much it is said that they worshiped him as a god. The words of this ancient dedication reveal this high esteem:

> Because mankind addresses him thus as *[Sebastos]* in accordance with their estimation of his honour, they revere him with temples and sacrifices over islands and continents, organized in cities and provinces, matching the greatness of his virtue and repaying his benefactions towards them.[1]

The title "Sebastos" (from *eusebeia*) is the Greek equivalent of the ancient Latin title of "Augustus," which meant "divine favor." The Latin title was given to the first emperor, Octavius, whom we now refer to as Augustus Caesar. The use of the Greek title Sebastos insinuates to a greater extent the reverence and religious honor granted to the emperor by his human subjects. This inscription may be shocking to contemporary readers who reserve such superlative words, titles and honors for the divine figures of our Christian faith alone. Yet, for many people in the Roman Empire, the em-

---

[1]Nicolaus of Damascus, quoted in Graham Stanton, *Jesus and Gospel* (Cambridge: Cambridge University Press, 2004), p. 26. Nicolaus of Damascus was writing about Roman emperor Augustus.

peror was considered to be a divine figure, an exalted benefactor and a savior of people across the immense empire.

What, then, were the early Christians thinking when they confessed Jesus as their Lord or King or Messiah? Did they have one eye on Rome when they uttered a declaration of Jesus as their Lord? Were they looking over their shoulders when they spoke about the "kingdom of God"?

The present volume surveys current scholarship that suggests that the New Testament authors used anti-imperial rhetoric; that is to say, when the New Testament authors professed that "Jesus is Lord," they also meant "Caesar is not!" Each contributor in this volume investigates what is happening historically, ideologically or literarily at the time of the New Testament writings, with the intent of exposing possible latent themes that can be perceived in the ancient documents. Those scholars who think that the first-century authors were criticizing Rome's imperial ideology by confessing "Jesus is Lord" also contend that, at the same time, the earliest Christians were also defiantly saying "Caesar is not!" Scholarly interest in this topic is growing rapidly and is focused on the specific events, occasions, political and social circumstances as well as ideologies that were present across the Roman Empire during the first and early second century CE.

A cursory review of the New Testament writings reveals an abundance of direct references to the people and culture of the Roman Empire, many of which have become so familiar to modern readers that little thought is given to them: Roman soldiers, centurions, proconsuls, guards, kings and kingdoms, rulers, councils, and governors. We recall Caesar's taxes, tax collectors, customs and decrees, Roman roads, palaces and prisons, Roman power, authority, and citizenship. There is a constant challenge to the famous but frail Roman peace (*pax Romana*) in the land of Israel. The New Testament provides us some information (but perhaps not enough) about Roman gods, goddesses, idols, shrines and ideology, as well as imperial persecution, arrests, executions, severe economic conditions, famine, courts, trials and crucifixion.

But indirect information teases us and pushes us to closer examination. We begin to ask questions like these: Since Caesar was considered a god, what did that mean for the earliest Christians who gave allegiance to "another" God (the God of Israel and his Son)? For the earliest Christians, was the confession of Jesus as Lord just another deity added to the religious options? Or, within the imperial milieu, was the deity of Jesus Christ seen as a rivalry to the reigning Roman emperor? Were the New Testament books formed as a conscious reaction to the Roman imperial authority and emperor worship in the empire? Does the New Testament encourage the recipients to acquiesce or to resist the Roman rulers and authorities? One of the most important questions we will ask in this book is: Did the historical situation of the early Christians create the necessity of written literary features such as "hidden language" and "codified messages" for the political protection of the readers, as well as the authors? The answers to such questions not only give us insight into the historical world of the Roman Empire but also give us a clearer picture of the culture, society and setting in which the New Testament was written.

The historical-critical approach to the New Testament writings dominated at the turn of the nineteenth and into the twentieth centuries as it relates to the Roman Empire. The texts of the Bible were read in the context of the historical Roman world. Scholars were in a quest for connections between the Bible and Rome. Still, historical data alone proved to be inadequate to answer all of our questions with great certainty. A shift began to take place in the twentieth century, when theoretical concepts of human nature and culture began to reframe the historical data. Theoretical approaches such as "colonial" criticism and "empire" criticism, defined and discussed in this chapter, proved to be suggestive and even radical. Increasingly, biblical scholarship has been highly influenced by the concepts and methods of sociology, political and cultural anthropology. In effect, such approaches led to attempts to answer *why* (or more theoretical) instead of the more historical *what* questions. This does not mean that present scholarship ignores or disparages historical and cultural criticism; rather, the historical context remains a necessary, basic building block for researching and interpreting the ancient writings. The biblical writings were not created in a vacuum but were ardent, conscious messages intended to be shared with people who were living, working, worshiping, hurting and healing amid real circumstances, not unlike the readers of today. For this reason, and for many others, scholars began to look beyond the evidential historical circumstances to newer interpretive horizons.

In addition to the more social-scientific methods, twentieth-century scholarship began to analyze the biblical documents using various literary approaches to the text. Narrative, rhetorical and linguistic approaches shed new light on old manuscripts. Key observations have been made about the literary sources, redactions, forms and functions of the texts. These observations led to the conclusion that the written communications of the ancient authors may indeed include elusive messages, cryptic language, figurative words and unusual forms of literature that spoke clearly to the original audiences, but may elude modern readers. The prime example is the New Testament book the Revelation of John, where the apocalyptic genre (or type) of literature is easily misunderstood and misinterpreted, but where there is clear evidence that the author has his eye on Rome and on its manifold idolatries.

Weaving together history, social and cultural awareness, and distinctive literary features, biblical scholars are becoming increasingly aware of numerous passages in the New Testament that can be interpreted and understood as anti-imperial rhetoric. One of the most recent developments is the topic of this book: as a result of newer methods and approaches to the New Testament documents, many readers see a flourishing anti-imperial dimension to earliest Christianity. Consequently, if the New Testament does contain a latent anti-imperial message, there is great significance for the church today, not only in how we interpret the text but how we apply the text to contemporary social situations. This introductory chapter unpacks each of these three aspects of the texts—historical, theoretical and literary—while highlighting select biblical passages that exemplify the application of these aspects. In addition, a number of scholars are introduced (although all relevant scholars cannot be cited) who represent the advancement of various approaches of scholarship with respect to anti-imperial rhetoric.

HISTORY

The first century (CE) of the Roman Empire can be divided into two parts. The first part actually begins with the reign of Julius Caesar, who met his death in March 44 BCE. At that time the Roman senate officially recognized Julius Caesar as divine. After his assassination, the ruling authorities inaugurated the customs related to the imperial cult, though various succeeding emperors played down their acclaimed divinity. This led to emperor "worship" on the part of the people in Rome and also by the people in the conquered, outlying provinces of the vast empire. After Julius and Augustus Caesar, this line of emperors included Tiberius (14-37 CE), Gaius (37-41), Claudius (41-54) and Nero (54-68). Each of these four is connected by birth or by adoption to Julius and Augustus Caesar. The reign of the Julio-Claudians, then, continued in the empire until the Roman Empire's civil wars of 68-69 CE.

After the Julio-Claudians, the second part of the first century was ruled by the Flavians. Swift changes were initiated by Galba, Otho, Vitellius and then by the military leader Vespasian, who began the siege of Jerusalem in 68 CE. He was followed by his son Titus. After Titus, the notably malicious Domitian ruled; the weaker Nerva and stronger Trajan finished the century. The seeds of autocracy in the Roman Empire were sown by the last of the Julio-Claudians, Emperor Nero, and they reached fruition during the decades of the ruling Flavians.[2] It was the early biographers such as Tacitus (*Annals, Dialogus*) and Suetonius who grant modern readers the most historical information about the first-century Roman emperors, famous and infamous.

By the first century CE, the city of Rome was, in every way, the center of the known universe. It was the hub of a huge empire, the epicenter of government and culture. The emperor and the leading citizens wielded power and prestige over millions of people spread over a massive geographical area. In addition, the populated urban areas of the empire were major centers of philosophical and intellectual thought. Philosophy functioned as the primary intellectual driving force of the ruling society. While esteemed philosophers held the highest rank as supporters of the emperors, others played a role as the emperor's greatest enemies, philosophically challenging his every move and even acting as conspirators in assassination plots for the betterment of the empire. The clash of absolute power and human philosophy is evident from history: from the time of Augustus Caesar (about 14 BCE) to the end of the first century (96 CE), only one out of ten Roman emperors died a natural death.[3] The job of Caesar, it seems, was not an easy one; even acclaimed as a ruler sent from the gods, or as god himself, the dictator of the empire collected many enemies.

Somehow, within this extraordinary time and region, the budding Christian church grew and blossomed. Geographically, the Christian movement broadened relatively rapidly from its beginnings in Jerusalem and Palestine through Asia Minor and into the Achaian peninsula. Historically, while its roots were in Judaism, the movement spread throughout a region populated primarily by Gentiles, all of whom were under the subjugation of the emperor in Rome. As a result of their immediate social, religious and political situations, the New Testament authors wrote their versions of a biography (the Gospels), as well as concerned epistles and an

---

[2]Barry Baldwin, *The Roman Emperors* (Montreal: Harvest House, 1980), p. 115.
[3]Ibid., pp. 2-8.

apocalyptic document, within a very volatile environment. Such writings could have been perceived as another new and arguable philosophy, or as political challenges to the ruling authorities, or both. *In an empire where leaders had absolute power and in an increasingly hostile environment, explicit language and direct antigovernment or anti-emperor literature would have been quite dangerous; such writing could have resulted in the death of the ones communicating opposition to the ruling authorities and/or the audience to whom they wrote.*

One important writer who gave us a cultural picture of the Roman Empire was the Jewish historian Flavius Josephus. As an apologist and historian Josephus is representative of early witnesses in the Jewish nation during the Roman period. Josephus comments on complicated social movements within that time and culture; he also provides critical information concerning some Roman officials named in the New Testament, such as Pilate and Herod. Then again, modern scholars continue to debate the reliability of the writings of Josephus as accurate historical aids that help us to understand the Roman period and first-century Judaism. While Josephus employed literary conventions common for his time, his view of history and his recording methods would be unacceptable by today's standards. In spite of his discrepancies and manipulations, Josephus does provide one vision of the events of the first century. In the shadow of the historical events themselves, we have one outlook that attempts to "walk a tightrope" between the Jewish perspective on important events and the perspective of the Roman imperial government, which had authority over many such events.

By the twentieth century the historical and cultural background material of the Roman Empire was of considerable interest to historians, Bible readers and theologians. On the one hand, scholars emphasized the power, the glory, the preservation and pleasures of the Roman Empire, in addition to the internal and external strife that resulted in extensive wars and bloody assassinations. Historians have observed how the Roman Empire greatly influenced later European life and culture even centuries after its decline; it left a heavy mark on later politics, laws, speech and rhetoric. Yet other twentieth-century scholars stressed the economic hardship, religious persecution and social ostracism caused by Rome's strict social-class divisions. There is little doubt historically that boldly practicing Christian believers within the first-century Roman Empire were subjected to persecution and social exclusion.

SOCIAL MILIEU

Investigations into the first-century social milieu of the Roman Empire reveal a sizable gap between the wealthy elite class of people and the general populous or the nonelites. The extensive empire was hierarchical, and a small, elite group of about 2-3 percent of the population held most of the power and positions. These elites fashioned the political, cultural and social experiences of the entire empire. They controlled the wealth and enjoyed an elevated status and quality of life. Both power and position were hereditary in the empire, and this status was highly protected. It was also an agrarian society, with agriculture supporting the economy and wealth of the people. The elites owned the valuable land and consumed about 65 percent of its production, thus allowing the landowners to exploit the hired laborers.[4] In fact, the aristocrats dominated the lower classes of people in all aspects of society: in political authority, land ownership, trade and labor agreements, slavery, taxation and tributes, military power, social relations, religious rites, rhetoric (or what we might call "the media"), the judicial system, and city management.[5]

In addition to the emperor himself, the elite class of people helped maintain the empire with the Roman army. Over a period of time Roman military leaders had firmly established and steadily expanded the power and authority of Rome until an entirely new framework of imperial politics, economics and culture was created. This Romanization, which began with the reign of Augustus, spread throughout the empire through local agents such as King Herod of the New Testament Gospels.

EMPEROR WORSHIP

The reigning emperor maintained a tight grip on the empire. His duties included financial and military matters as well as diplomatic responsibilities; he was accountable for preserving and protecting the governmental authority and wealth across the vast empire. The emperor became the "Father of the Fatherland" (*pater patriae*), a competing idea to the Jewish and Christian belief that God is the "Father" of all. As such, the emperor was the essence of the strong, male-dominated, male-centered, orderly society.[6]

---

[4]Warren Carter, *The Roman Empire and the New Testament: An Essential Guide* (Nashville: Abingdon Press, 2006), p. 3.
[5]Ibid., p. 14.
[6]Ibid., p. 4.

Moreover, each emperor had to show that he was the recipient of divine favor from the recognized gods of the local provinces. Amazing signs and wonders, and strategic battles and victories were all understood to be the gods' endorsements of a successful ruler. Essentially, the imperial cult was the recognition of the gods' blessings on the emperor and the empire. Worship of the emperor was conducted in numerous impressive temples, involving statues, decrees, rituals, incense and sacrifices. Sacrifices were given in honor of the leader, as expressions of submission to the emperor by his devoted, loyal subjects.[7]

Participation in the imperial cult, in local feasts, festivals and celebrations was not obligatory for most people. Cultic worship was most crucial for the elite men and women who served as temple priests and personnel, because they could afford to sponsor such celebrations. Their exterior worship was a symbol of their own status and their faithful loyalty to the emperor. As a result, those who could afford to do so were given elevated status, prestige and power because of their outward devotion to the emperor and to other local deities. Proper worship, then, was connected to one's privileged birth, wealth and social standing in the immediate community.[8] Certainly public worship could not be understood as devotion to an "unseen God" and to his agent, a peasant Jew who was crucified as a criminal by the Roman authorities. Thus, the Christian faith was subjected to both scrutiny and sanction.

CHRISTIAN PERSECUTION

There is a well-known passage in the writings of Tacitus, in which Emperor Nero tries to transfer the blame for the devastating fire in Rome (64 CE) on to the Christians of the city. At that time, Nero's persecution of Christians may have been totally irrational, but it illustrated that he, as well as many other leaders, held a very low estimation of the Christians. According to Tacitus, Nero's attack on the Christians was not the inauguration of a prolonged and orderly assault on Christians. Scholar N. T. Wright declares that the worst oppression and persecution of Christians does not appear to be full-blown until about a hundred years after Jesus' time on earth. This dating is presumed to be well past the time of the writing of the New Testament. There may have been rumblings in the first century, but the New

---

[7]Ibid., p. 8.
[8]Ibid.

Testament texts were written before the Christian communities began to face severe opposition from the pagan authorities, some of which was no doubt horrendous.[9]

Although the peak of sustained persecution and the slaughter of Christians in the Roman Empire may have come well into the second century CE, history does relate that by the time of the martyrdom of Bishop Polycarp (c. 155 CE), Christianity was viewed as a seditious sect in the empire. Trials and executions of Christians were already considered to be a regular occurrence, though apparently there were no official imperial edicts or official methods for punishment of the Christians. Generally, Christians were accused of the same charge of atheism that was directed at the Jews because they believed in an invisible God. In particular, the Christians resisted allegiance to the reigning Caesar and refused to swear by his "genius." In this sense, Roman officials viewed Christ as a rival monarch, a king in direct conflict with the dictatorship of the emperor. Beyond the recognized practices of Judaism, it was the supremacy of Christ that defined Christianity over against the state and religious deities of the Romans.[10]

Further, as a result of their practice of celebrating the Lord's Supper, the first-century Christians were accused of cannibalism. They were placed under a prohibition against "corporate ritual meals." Christians "ate the body" and "drank the blood" of a crucified criminal; both strict Jews and educated Gentiles cringed at such beliefs and behavior. The mysterious actions and ambiguous language of the Christians were in opposition to the accepted Roman sociocultural practices. While the Christians were generally cautious, law-abiding citizens within the empire, their bold devotion to Jesus Christ as Lord and King put them in grave danger with the authorities.[11]

GOSPELS AS HISTORICAL ACCOUNTS

The Gospel of Mark, generally accepted as the first of the canonical Gospels, records historical data of the life and ministry of Jesus. During a time of intense struggle and uncertainty in the city of Rome, the writer of Mark's Gospel may have thought that it was necessary to put into writing a document to encourage and support the struggling Christian communities in the region. To be sure, Mark's Gospel is Jewish in nature and contains no

---

[9]N. T. Wright, *The New Testament and the People of God,* Christian Origins and the Question of God 1 (London: SPCK, 1992), p. 346.
[10]Ibid., pp. 347-49.
[11]Ibid., p. 350.

references to Greek philosophy or quotations from Greek literature. Yet this Gospel uniquely gives a voice to ordinary people, particularly peasants and villagers in Galilee and the eastern parts of the Roman Empire. This is a story that touched those people, in their subjected position, over and against the Roman emperor and the Roman system of authority.[12] More than objective history, Mark's ancient biography was intended to be an encouragement to the readers, reminding them of the solid foundations of their faith.

The Christians in Rome were not only suffering from their own particular trials, but also from the hardships experienced by the other residents of Rome. By the early 60s CE, there was increasing anxiety by the general population over the poor economic conditions and political unrest in the empire. A crack was beginning to open in the most powerful empire in the known world. The split between the rich aristocracy (who were increasingly self-indulgent) and the poorer, ordinary people (who experienced increases in taxation and food shortages) was getting wider and wider. There were reports of military losses, shocking defeats, famines and a disgruntled army across the empire. Between the middle of 68 to the end of 69 CE, Rome experienced five leaders; Galva was murdered, and Otho was forced to commit suicide. Furthermore, Rome suffered another tragic event, a flood, which led to the collapse of many physical and social structures. The historical evidence points to a fractious and demoralized empire burdened with political, economic and military failures.[13]

But at least some good news reached the city of Rome at this time, when Vespasian's forces crushed the region of Judea. Perhaps the time of punishment by the Roman gods was over; perhaps the power of the empire was restored. The victory of Vespasian and Titus was celebrated in Rome in mid-71. Vespasian was declared the "savior of the Roman peace"; the conquering general Titus became the "destroyer of the Temple of Yahweh." The victory was both political and religious; it began a new regime and gave birth to new hope in Rome. General Titus, with his father Vespasian, would forever be remembered as the ones who annihilated the Jewish race and destroyed the city of Jerusalem.[14] A good example of the intensity of the resolve can be seen today from the top of Masada in Israel. Anyone who

---

[12]Richard A. Horsley, *Hearing the Whole Story: the Politics of Plot in Mark's Gospel* (Louisville: Westminster John Knox, 2001), pp. 41-51.

[13]Brian Incigneri, *The Gospel to the Romans: The Setting and Rhetoric of Mark's Gospel,* Biblical Interpretation Series, ed. R. Alan Culpepper and Rolf Rendtorff (Leiden: Brill, 2003), pp. 156-58.

[14]Ibid., pp. 162-63, 177.

ascends the ramp to that last Jewish holdout can see the Roman encampments that were built below Masada, a living testimony both to Jewish resistance as well as to the pragmatic determined resolve of the Romans to extract defeat, regardless of expense and effort.

Modern scholarship has recognized the importance of the Jewish revolt of 66-70 CE against Rome, and its devastating effects on the Jerusalem temple and on the Jewish people. Their heritage, land and temple were utterly destroyed at the hands of the Roman army. The early Christians and Jews were forced to flee their land and scatter across the empire, no doubt wondering how they could maintain their religious faith after such devastation. The military victor, Vespasian, became emperor in late 69 CE (after Vitellius). Seldom do we ponder these events from the Roman point of view, but a military victory validated the reigning emperor in his role as the political and religious absolute ruler of the conquered peoples. If the Gospel of Mark was written down at some point in the middle of the first century, it predated the Roman desolation of Jerusalem. Yet if a later date for this account is presumed, we may surmise that the intention of the author of Mark's Gospel was to counteract the Vespasian reports of victory over the Jews. With these issues in mind, a close reading of Mark's Gospel reveals features that imply that it was written in the shadow of the long arm of the Roman imperial power.[15] It is valuable to consider two examples which suggest that we look at Mark's Gospel in light of the Roman world; these cases in point serve to demonstrate the anti-Roman, anti-imperial views at work in today's scholarship.

As a prime example, Mark's use of divine and royal titles is revealing. The Greek word *kyrios* (Lord), commonly used for a Roman emperor, is not used by Mark as an explicit title for Jesus. Mark is the only writer of the four Gospels that avoids this title for Jesus. The title "Lord" was used for the Emperor Nero (*Nero kyrios*); so, it may have been advantageous not to employ such a title for Jesus. Josephus relates that when Vespasian returned to Rome, he was hailed as "their Benefactor and Savior."[16] Mark never entitles Jesus as "Savior," although he does imply that Jesus, and not a human emperor, "saves" (Mk 5:23, 28, 34; 6:56; 10:26, 52; 13:13; 15:30-31). There is an implied ambiguity in the words of the Roman centurion in Mark 15:39, who witnesses the death of Jesus and calls him the "Son of God," a title commonly used for the Roman emperors. Another title that was used for Nero

---

[15]Ibid., p. 172.
[16]Josephus, *Jewish War* 7:71.

("the Good God," *agathō theō*) is used in Mark 10:18; yet, with subtle irony, Jesus responds to a rich man that "God alone is good." Mark's selection of titles may indicate that he was highly aware of the need to be cautious about referring to Jesus by the same titles that were used for the Roman leaders.[17]

Second, specific events in Mark's Gospel emphasize the power of Jesus over the perceived powers of the emperors. Mark is the only Gospel that has Jesus using "spittle" for healing, and he does so twice. In both instances, the unusual healings occur just before the critical question of "Who do you say that I am?" (Mk 7:32-37; 8:22-26). Ancient historians (Tacitus and Suetonius) relate that Emperor Vespasian healed with spittle in full view of an amazed crowd of people, "proving" his power and authority. However, Jesus removes the afflicted people away from the crowd and then instructs them not to tell anyone about the healing (Mk 7:36; 8:26). The perplexing, hidden actions of Jesus take on new meaning as a contrast to the public, self-centered display by Vespasian. Tacitus also reports that Vespasian "heals" a man by stepping on his withered hand. In Mark's account, Jesus heals a man's withered hand merely by speaking (Mk 3:1-6), with God-like authority and power (Gen 1). In addition, Tacitus reports that when the accused, degraded Emperor Vitellius was led away at night to his public execution, it was to the taunts and mockery of the crowd. One of the emperor's supporters actually approached and cut off an ear of the soldier that was guarding him.[18] If the readers of Mark's Gospel knew of these events, they would have understood the striking parallel to Mark's scene of the arrest of Jesus in Mark 14:47. Mark seems to make an intentional comparison between the victorious spectacle of Vespasian and Titus and his depiction of Jesus as "king" (Mk 15:26).[19] Thus, the "gospel" (*euangelion*) of Jesus Christ (Mk 1:1) is a strong contrast to the "good news" announced in the city of Rome as a result of human power and spectacle.

HISTORICAL ACCOUNT OF ACTS

In past decades Acts has been seen as a record that overtly and intentionally defends the possibility that the Roman government and the early Christian movement should exist together in peace and harmony.[20] Numerous New Tes-

---

[17]Incigneri, *Gospel to the Romans,* p. 169.
[18]Tacitus, *Histories* 3.84.
[19]Incigneri, *Gospel to the Romans*, pp. 171-76.
[20]C. Kavin Rowe, *World Upside Down: Reading Acts in the Graeco-Roman Age* (Oxford: Oxford University Press, 2009), pp. 53-54.

tament scholars dating back to 1720 have maintained this positive view of the book of Acts with little adjustment over the years.[21] The traditional scholarly view understands Acts to be an apologetic, defending the relatively harmless Christian movement that was ignored by the Roman government. In other words, Acts wants to defend the (Jewish) Jesus movement as a *religio licita*, or a legally legitimate religion within the empire. However, C. Kavin Rowe has edited a recent volume on the book of Acts that argues for the presence of anti-imperial ideology and the clash of cultures in the ancient world.

Accordingly, in its attempt to form communities that witness to God's plans and purposes, Luke's second volume is a politically and theologically incriminating document against Rome. Modern readers should be aware of a "profound tension" as we interpret the book of Acts. From one angle the Christian movement was a real and competing presence within the Roman pagan culture. From another angle Luke attempts to narrate the spread of Christianity in such a way as to eliminate any threat to the Roman government. While Luke's goal is the creation of a totally new pattern of life and an entirely new culture that is fundamentally different from the most important aspects of the Gentile society, he must also demonstrate that Christianity is innocent of any type of treason and trouble-making.[22]

Acts 17:1-9 is one example that punctuates this "tension" created by the author. In this scene, Paul visits Thessalonica, where the Jews confront him concerning his proclamation. Here we see two critical actions that are considered rebellious: the believers declare that Jesus is "Lord of all," and they "are all defying Caesar's decrees, saying there is another king" (Acts 17:7). These two actions define Luke's overall cultural dream for the expanding Christian church. Further, Acts indicates that Paul will die in Rome as "an innocent man." Thus, the narrative in Acts continues and reframes the story of Jesus in the story of Paul: "So Jesus (in Jerusalem). So Paul (in Rome)."[23] Luke carefully provides his readers with the theological and cultural resources to proclaim their own innocence while they face persecution and possible death at the hands of the Roman state. For Rowe, there is little subversive language found in the book of Acts; the anti-imperial rhetoric is quite clear.[24]

It is also significant to observe the important narrative functions of the Roman and Jewish characters in the book of Acts. Because of their half-

---

[21]Ibid., pp. 3-4.
[22]Ibid., p. 91.
[23]Ibid., p. 89.
[24]Ibid., p. 92.

Jewish ancestry, there is a difference between the Herods (Antipas, Agrippa I and Agrippa II) portrayed in Luke-Acts and other pagan Roman governors. The tragedy, for Luke, is the ungodly, fraudulent nature of these "Jewish" rulers, who should have known better. As corrupt leaders, they were failures as the shepherds of God's people. Gentile, imperial rulers are, in Luke's presentation, merely pawns in God's greater plans of salvation history.[25] In summation, then, Luke's overall view of the Roman Empire is thoroughly negative; yet this conclusion is not based on the political oppression of God's people but on all humanity's failure to recognize the sovereignty of God and the lordship of Jesus Christ.[26]

PAUL THE JEW AND THE GENTILE WORLD

The contrast between the historical narrative in the book of Acts and the historical evaluations of Paul's letters is a contentious element in New Testament scholarship. Scholars have observed an apparent conflict between Luke's picture of Paul in Acts and the portraits of Paul that emerge from studies of his own letters. There is some question as to whether the Paul we see in Acts 22–28 is the same person who wrote all the epistles normally attributed to him. Is it possible that Paul's view of the Roman authorities changed as he grew older and progressed in his ministry? After being imprisoned "in chains" on a number of occasions under Roman authorities, did his view of the empire alter? Perhaps the nature and character of the various emperors affected a possible change in the way Paul regarded the empire. Such issues lead some scholars to question the historical reliability of the book of Acts, and they suggest that as readers, we must be cautious of how we connect the events and chronology of Acts with the epistles of Paul.

Unfortunately, neither historians nor biblical scholars can construct a precise, foolproof time line and travel itinerary of Paul's life and mission work. If we knew with certainty when a letter was composed and delivered, it would be easier to determine its audience and the precise conditions that precipitated the communication. If we could discern an accurate order and timing of Paul's letters, we could better judge if there is a change in his theology or rhetoric from one decade to the next. This makes it difficult to superimpose the letters attributed to him on top of the historical life of Paul

---

[25]Kazuhiko Yamazaki-Ransom, *The Roman Empire in Luke's Narrative*, Library of New Testament Studies 404 (New York: T & T International, 2010), pp. 199-201.
[26]Ibid., p. 202.

as seen in Acts. Such differences in timing, various omissions and a lack of clarity need to be reconciled if indeed they are obstacles in our understanding of Paul and his letters.

We are further reminded that in some scholarly views the Christian movement within the Roman Empire of the first century was relatively small and insignificant. It could be argued that Paul, the Jew, was allowed to speak boldly about himself and about his message of the Jewish Messiah as he traveled in the empire. For example, Paul speaks openly to Roman rulers Festus and Agrippa in Acts 25:1–26:32 about his gospel message, and he does not appear to be a major threat to the imperial system (Acts 26:30). We can note that in the book of Acts the Roman authorities actually aided and protected Paul in his conflict with the Jewish leadership in various cities: in Corinth (Acts 18:12-17), in Jerusalem (Acts 21:27-40; 22:22-30), in Caesarea (Acts chapters 23–25) and in Rome (Acts 28:17-20). Nevertheless, these accounts in Acts are quite early in the advancement of the Christian movement; in addition, the Roman authorities may have been merely attempting to maintain peace and order in chaotic situations rather than actually assisting and supporting the Christian mission (Acts 21:27-32).[27]

Historically and traditionally we can be fairly certain about key items of interest concerning the apostle Paul. First, even as a Jew by birth, Paul is considered to be the "apostle to the Gentiles" (Acts 13:46-47). He is almost an ironic selection for such a task. Second, we know that, as a Roman citizen (Acts 22:22-29), Paul traveled freely and extensively throughout the Roman Empire as a Christian missionary, teaching in synagogues, establishing churches and visiting those which he did not begin. We may assume that Paul was highly successful in attracting Roman Gentiles to the Jewish Messiah in pagan cities. Third, Paul was held "under house arrest" in the city of Rome for "two whole years" (Acts 28:30). This meant that Paul was a resident in the capital for a lengthy time and was allowed to continue his missionary work, right "next door" to powerful political opposition (Acts 28:31). Ultimately, history has it that Paul was imprisoned and executed in the city of Rome, under the authority of the Roman government, but there is still uncertainty as to how the Roman Empire affected Paul's thinking and his ministry. How did he navigate his way through such a powerful empire dominated by offensive, opposing cultures and religions?

---

[27]Richard Cassidy, *Society and Politics in the Acts of the Apostles* (Maryknoll, NY: Orbis, 1987), p. 2.

Though he was Jewish by birth and custom, perhaps it was the Romanness of Paul that allowed him to travel freely in the empire, to speak relatively openly about religion and to write with comprehension to Roman audiences. It is apparent that the combination of Paul's Jewish background and his Roman citizenship helped him advance the gospel message across Asia Minor. We know that not infrequently Paul and his message were rejected by the local Jews (Acts 22–23), and he was protected by the Roman public. Surrounded by hostility on all sides, Paul and his associates may have found it necessary to use "hidden" language so as not to incite the wrath of the Roman establishment or of the Jewish leaders. When he wrote to his fellow believers in the empire, caution was needed with his words and directions so that he did not place his recipients in danger of treason.

IMPERIAL CULT

The one specific historical practice that intersects the world of Rome and the world of Paul became known as the imperial cult. The gospel message of Paul and his fellow missionaries would have been in direct opposition to the customs associated with emperor worship. In a general sense Richard Horsley contends that the Roman imperial government, and specifically the imperial cult, is the main force that was shaping the world of Paul. It was primarily through the mission of Paul that the "crucified Christ" became the dominant emblem of the Christian movement. In spite of the fact that the Roman military employed crucifixion as a vehicle of terror against subjected people, it represented something entirely different to the early Christians. The Romans established shrines, images, temples and statues promoting emperor devotion; their symbols were reminders of the imperial power and the superior force of the conquerors. At the same time, the symbol of the cross spread, subversively, reminding Christians of the ultimate power and authority.[28] With some degree of irony, then, what the Romans publicized as an emblem of fear and terror (the cross) ultimately became a symbol of true power and supremacy for the Christian believers in the empire.

The worship of a human ruler was an inherited concept from an older Hellenistic (Greek) practice; familiar imagery and symbols were adopted and were easily integrated into the newer Roman system. Roman icons and idols

---

[28]Richard Horsley, introduction to *Paul and Empire: Religion and Power in Roman Imperial Society*, ed. Richard Horsley (Harrisburg, PA: Trinity Press International, 1997), p. 10.

proliferated and unified the appearances of the cities, not the least of which was the official Roman port, Ostia Antica. Thus, the devotion to the emperor and to other ruling authorities was a critical aspect of Romanizing the previously Hellenistic cities. Such visual expressions of the imperial cult served as reminders to all the people, while they gave the local authorities and aristocracy a vivid means of conveying and preserving their positions of power. Roman religion, then, was woven into the same cloth as the other vital aspects of the society, such as military might, economics and politics. The religion/politics of the imperial cult was such a part of all public life and culture that it penetrated all portions of society. Any alternative ideology or religion promoted to the people would necessarily have carried political implications as well. As N. T. Wright writes, "Who needs armies when they have worship?"[29]

There is recent debate as to the extent to which the people of Asia Minor were participating in the imperial cult at the time of Paul's letters. Recent archaeology, investigating the ruins of large cities in Asia Minor, has determined that the adoption of the imperial cult did not develop as rapidly as once thought. Colin Miller concludes that previous scholarship has not accounted for the lack of evidence of extensive dispersion of the imperial cult, at least in the cities known to Paul.[30] For example, cities such as Paphos, Lystra, Iconium, Derbe, Colossae and Laodicea do not reveal confirmation of the imperial cult in the first century CE. In Philippi there is no evidence of emperor worship before the second century. Verification of the imperial cult in Thessalonica appears to be late, dating from 238 CE.[31]

Confirmation of the imperial cult, or the physical evidence of the worship of the emperor, does emerge in some of the Pauline cities: Tarsus, Pisidian Antioch and other Galatian cities, Hierapolis, Ephesus, Athens, and Corinth. Particularly in Ephesus, there is abundant evidence: temples for the emperor date back to the time of Augustus's reign, imperial shrines were found in the agora, and an inscription from 29 BCE refers to a sanctuary for Augustus. A coin from 65-66 CE is inscribed with the title of Ephesus, *Epheson Neokoron*.[32] Certainly there were forms of emperor worship at Ephesus at the time of

---

[29]N. T. Wright, "Paul's Gospel and Caesar's Empire," *Center of Theological Inquiry*, Reflections: 1-13. http://ntwrightpage.com/Wright_Paul_Caesar_Empire.pdf.

[30]Colin Miller, "The Imperial Cult in the Pauline cities of Asia Minor and Greece," *Catholic Biblical Quarterly* 72 (2010): 322.

[31]Ibid., p. 321.

[32]Steven J. Friesen, "The Cult of the Roman Emperors in Ephesos," in *Ephesos, Metropolis of Asia: An Interdisciplinary Approach to its Archaeology, Religion and Culture*, ed. Helmut Koester (Valley Forge, PA: Trinity Press International, 1995), pp. 229-50.

Paul's ministry, but apparently nothing took supremacy over the revered city goddess Artemis. Ephesus remained "the city of Artemis," and its loyalty to the emperor was not exclusive, over and above other cults. In fact, the statuary implies a plethora of deities where the human emperor was only one among many.[33]

In Corinth, imperial cultic evidence is incomplete, but it is very likely that Paul encountered the cult in this city. It is quite possible that from an early date Julius Caesar was worshiped as the founder of the "new" city of Corinth. The city was named for him, "Colonia Laus Julia Corinthiensis," so there was a strong emphasis on the Roman emperor as the ultimate patron in Corinth. One inscription in Corinth honors the "high priest of the first provincial imperial cult of Achaia." If there was a "high priest," then there were other priests as well and the existence of a temple in the area.[34] However, as in Ephesus, the statuary in Corinth confirms a highly polytheistic city, where the imperial cult took its place, without exclusivity, among the other gods deemed crucial to city life.[35]

Perhaps the imperial cult was not as substantial at the time of Paul's writings as it would become in later decades. If historical evidence reveals only a minor presence of the imperial cult, modern readers should not conclude that all of Paul's missionary work and communications were done as a result of a pervasive culture of the imperial cult. Even so, in the days of Paul's ministry, there still could have been political, economic and cultural oppression experienced by the Christians to whom Paul was ministering. Such conditions, both historical and cultural, would have an effect on the language and the manner used by Paul to communicate to specific Christian communities.

LETTER TO THE ROMANS

Paul's epistle to the church at Rome is his most influential letter. Scholars have debated Paul's presentation of key theological issues in the letter that stood as foundational stones in the building of the Christian faith. Further, scholars noted the Jewish flavor of the letter, including Paul's allusions to the Old Testament and God's treatment of the nation of Israel (Rom 9–11), even though it was written to people living in a Roman city. In fact, relatively little was men-

---

[33]Miller, "Imperial Cult," pp. 327-28.
[34]John K. Chow, "Patronage in Roman Corinth," in *Paul and Empire: Religion and Power in Roman Imperial Society*, ed. Richard Horsley (Harrisburg, PA: Trinity Press International, 1997), pp. 105-6.
[35]Miller, "Imperial Cult," p. 331.

tioned about the influence of the Gentile context of the letter and the volatile political milieu of the Roman Empire on the church and on Paul himself.

In the opening three chapters of Romans, Paul narrows his focus on people who refused to honor God and embraced idolatry instead. So, Paul writes to the believers in Rome to warn them that outward appearances are not always what they seem to be; what may seem to be righteous and just in the empire is really nothing of the kind. Paul opens his letter by giving himself the title of a humble "slave [*doulos*] of Christ Jesus" (Rom 1:1), in stark contrast to the leading Roman orators and authorities. In Romans 3:10-18, Paul cleverly borrows passages from the Psalms (Ps 14:1; 53:1-3; 5:9; 140:3; 10:7; 36:1) as well as a portion from Isaiah (Is 59:7-8) to illustrate to his audience that both Jews and Gentiles can be deceptive. By making these Jewish allusions, while implying the application of such sayings to the leaders in power, Paul could vilify the Roman leadership without openly condemning their wickedness. Paul crafts a "battle of the empires" document by comparing the Roman Empire, which revolved around human authority, and the divine "kingdom" centered on Jesus Christ (Rom 1:18-23).

The notoriously contentious passage, Romans 13:1-7, is the pinnacle of perplexing rhetoric. The passage, which begins "everyone must submit himself to the governing authorities" (Rom 13:1 NIV 1984), is problematic exegetically, theologically and politically. The passage has been analyzed historically, socially, politically and legally. Is it an example of Paul's use of hidden or coded anti-imperial rhetoric? Is it surrender to Caesar or to the surrounding authorities in order to secure protection for the young church? Is it a tongue-in-cheek, subversive message or neutral comments about governments in general? Dilemmas abound. To begin, Paul does not explain his use of the phrase *governing authorities* (*exousiais hyperechousias*, literally, "superior authorities") in verse one. In contrast, he uses the term *rulers* (*archontōn*) or *leaders* in 1 Corinthians 2:6-8. Who are the "superior authorities" in Rome, and why would Paul urge his readers to obey them? What were the social and political factors that could fully explain Paul's positive accommodation of the Roman officials and their taxation? Why would Paul give such blatantly political directions to the Roman church, in view of the domination of the imperial rulers *in that very city*?

The responses that have been proposed by scholarship are attempts to neatly fit Romans 13 into history and into the rest of Paul's ideology and theology. Historically, there may have been an apprehension within the believing community between the Jewish Christians and the Gentile Christians. The letter may have been written to alleviate such tensions in a time and place where it was not favorable to be either one. Ideologically, perhaps Paul's positive experiences of being born and educated as a Roman citizen colored his thoughts and influenced his relationship with the Roman officials at that time (that is, before his personal interactions with the Roman prison system).

N. T. Wright proposes that while it is true that the emperor proclaimed himself to be sovereign and without rival in the divine as well as the human sphere, in this passage Paul claims that the Roman emperor remains answerable to the true God. By using careful, subversive language, Paul is able to diminish the transparent imperial superiority and self-importance while still not subjugating people to it. With one foot in the Roman Empire and the other foot in the kingdom of God, the Christian believers owe to the emperor "appropriate civil obedience," but not the worship devotion acclaimed by Caesar. Wright concludes that "the subversive gospel is not designed to produce civil anarchy."[36] In agreement, Stanley Porter notes that Paul has already told his readers that he is an opponent of the imperial reign (see Rom 1:1-6), and in Romans 13 he is demanding that the Roman leaders be "just" authorities. Christians are urged to obey "just" authorities, but at the same time, Roman "unjust" authorities are not even on Paul's radar screen.[37]

All of which leads to this: Romans 13:1-7 may appear to be a relatively *pro*-Roman government passage until we put it into the context of the entire letter. First, Paul recognizes the sinfulness of all humanity, the rulers and the ruled (Rom 3:22-24). He declares that "no one will be declared righteous . . . by observing the law" (that is, the Roman law or the Jewish law [Rom 3:20]). The peace, justice and righteousness of the Roman Empire falls short because it is of human construct. Instead, true righteousness is God's righteousness, apart from all human law, which "comes through faith in Jesus Christ" and not from human rulers (Rom 3:19-22). Further, Romans 15:7-13 is blatantly addressing Gentile believers, who are reminded that their hope is in Jesus and praise is for God, who "gives endurance and encouragement" (Rom 15:5). There is no question that Paul is urging the unity of the church, Jews and Gentiles, under the authority and the grace of God and of Jesus Christ. Particularly in this letter, considering all the features of

---

[36]Wright, "Paul's Gospel and Caesar's Empire," pp. 5-6.

[37]Stanley Porter, introduction to *Empire in the New Testament*, New Testament Study Series 10, ed. Stanley E. Porter and Cynthia Long Westfall (Eugene, OR: Pickwick, 2011), p. 11.

the historical and cultural milieu of the recipients, it is crucial for Paul to communicate not only boldly but carefully.

In short, it was necessary for the writers of the canonical Gospels and the book of Acts to actively engage with the pagan society around them. Moreover, the epistles of Paul cannot be fully comprehended without due consideration given to their respective historical settings. The book of Romans is a leading example of an intentional communication written to Christian believers living in the first-century Roman Empire. Each biblical document is situated in a specific historical setting and cultural climate as it spoke to real people in real life situations. In many respects our understanding of the biblical texts progresses with a greater and greater understanding of the historical and cultural aspects that "lie behind" the texts.

THEORETICAL APPROACHES

Beyond our historical thinking, contemporary theories and concepts about the nature of human beings and their culture affect our interpretations of the New Testament. Often these theories lie in front of the text and act as a grid through which we perceive the writings. Historical research is critical to our understanding of the Roman imperial context, while more recent sociocultural ideologies help us to understand the thoughts and forces that influenced the ancient writers. An imbalance of either history or theoretical ideas can skew our interpretations. It is important to consider the pressing social, religious and political notions of the time which demanded that the New Testament authors compose politically charged documents.

Colonialism and empire. In the latter twentieth century, scholars began to investigate a number of related concepts that fall into two categories: colonialism and empire. The concept of colonialism holds a negative connotation, describing conditions of economic exploitation of colonized people. Such people, of course, are those of one land dominated by the government of a distant land. The concerns reflected in the literature of colonized people include neglect, poverty, slavery, oppression, abuse, ostracism and worse. Ironically, the biblical documents have been used in modern times by the colonizing authorities to demand obedience and subjugate other nations, while the colonized peoples have employed the Bible for encouragement and examples of liberation and freedom.[38]

---

[38]Michael G. Smith, "The Empire Theory and the Empires of History—A Review Essay," *Christian Scholar's Review* 39, no. 3 (2010): 305-22.

After the nineteenth- and twentieth-century colonialism by European powers, historians realized that a key element of the concept of empire was oppression of the colonized peoples. This concept of oppression drives the theoretical model of empire. Further, it is difficult to define the term *empire* without implications of colonialism, imperialism and the cultural domination and political sovereignty of one nation over and against another (or others). This model is derived from a type of post-Marxist thought; it is specifically applied to human beings (both the powerful and the powerless) without regard for other divine powers or influence.[39] For scholars today, the real consequence of the concept of empire is more theoretical than it is historical. Not unlike the ideas related to colonialism, the accepted notion of empire is inherently evil, but for many reasons that are assumed and not necessarily demonstrated in history. The concept of empire is in direct opposition to national, ethnic and individual "self-determination."[40]

These concepts can be illustrated from the canonical letter of James. James addresses economic issues, including exploitation, materialism, poverty and normally accepted behavior in the Roman Empire. The "rich" (Jas 5:1) and the "humble" (Jas 1:9) are discussed, and common human trials are exposed—suffering, unequal patron-client relations, favoritism, unequal friendship and the selfish hoarding of wealth—all ingredients of the Roman Empire society. Seldom have scholars fully taken into account the letter's denunciation of the economic conditions and the social elites, of the landowners and the merchants (Jas 5:1-6; 4:13-17).[41]

Further, in a hierarchical system the dominant power can define or redefine the meaning and significance of common events and aspects of people's everyday lives. For example, language, or the power of speech, can be a vehicle and an expression of colonization. Across the Roman Empire, the concept of *pax Romana* was maintained by enforced tranquility, in words and in actions.[42] In contrast, the book of James urges the readers to seek true wisdom and "words of truth" from God, who gives his people "good gifts" and "does not change like shifting shadows" (Jas 1:16-18; 3:5-8). Thus,

---

[39]Ibid., p. 322.

[40]Ibid.

[41]Cynthia Long Westfall, "Running the Gamut: The Varied Responses to Empire in Jewish Christianity," in *Empire in the New Testament*, ed. Stanley Porter and Cynthia Long Westfall (Eugene, OR: Pickwick, 2011), pp. 232-33.

[42]Sharon H. Ringe, "The Letter of James," in *A Postcolonial Commentary on the New Testament Writings*, ed. Fernando F. Segovia and R. S. Sugirtharajah (New York: T & T Clark, 2007), p. 374.

James may be considered "a postcolonial voice," calling for a response to the imperial system, not by escaping from it but by demonstrating a power of God that is greater than Rome or any other human institution.[43]

Empire and Israel. It seems inappropriate to discuss the influence of the Roman Empire on the New Testament writings without some consideration of what the concept of empire meant to the ancient Jews and to the writers of the Old Testament. In the ancient Near East, the concept of empire was built on the assumption that a nation has the right to create an empire at the expense of other nations. To control foreign lands and subjugate the residents therein was a demonstration of the power of a strong ruler, and the entire conquering nation as well as the god of the conquerors.[44]

The Old Testament writings generally display a kind of resistance to the concept of a fallible human emperor who battles with the nation of Israel and with Yahweh God (i.e., Assyria, Babylon, Persia, Greece, Rome). Yet the rule of King David and King Solomon could well be considered empires because they were expanded as the result of warfare. Thus, we see the Old Testament scene of the "holy war" where a religious battle was fought by Yahweh himself. The goal of such a battle was the annihilation of an entire evil, godless culture, where God secures the victory for his people. We can perceive a direct conflict between the normally accepted concept of securing and expanding a pagan empire with a human ruler and the concept of the Old Testament holy war to the glory of an unseen God. Furthermore, we can recognize the theology behind the Old Testament holy war is the driving notion behind the concepts of the kingdom of God and the messianic expectations found in Second Temple Judaism.[45]

The book of Isaiah was designed to move the Israelites to be the people of God during a time when other human empires were attempting to take over the land and the people.[46] The prophetic vision of the ideal nation of Zion is based on the older traditions of Israel's imperial primacy among the nations, and to the reign of God as the one and only emperor. The book of Isaiah indicates that the Israelites did not willfully bring themselves into

---

[43]Ibid., p. 378.

[44]Douglas Stuart, "The Old Testament Context of David's Costly Flirtation with Empire-Building," in *Empire in the New Testament*, ed. Stanley E. Porter and Cynthia Long Westfall (Eugene, OR: Pickwick, 2011), p. 17.

[45]Ibid., p. 33.

[46]Mark J. Boda, "Walking in the Light of Yahweh: Zion and the Empires in the Book of Isaiah," in *Empire in the New Testament*, ed. Stanley E. Porter and Cynthia Long Westfall (Eugene, OR: Pickwick, 2011), p. 83.

compliance with the rule and reign of God. Isaiah, then, is an early theological reflection on one nation's struggle for identity in a world of powerful, dominating human empires.

The conquering mindset was also foundational for the related ideology prevalent within the Roman Empire. Powerful empires subjugated conquered peoples. This ideology is the basis of the rhetorical techniques that were used to convince the conquered people to accept their fate, and for the conquered people to adjust and adhere to the values of the conquering nation. It undergirds the rights and privileges of the powerful nation to maintain order and peace, and for the superiority of the powerful empire's deity (or deities). According to this mindset, the book of Isaiah serves as a paradigm of how the concept of empire pervaded the Old Testament, and how the Hebrew concept of empire provides a background for the concept in the New Testament writings.[47]

"Social gospel." It is helpful for modern biblical readers to attempt to bridge the huge gaps between ancient and modern social culture, concepts, philosophies and ethos. Representative of this notion is Bruce Malina, who has considered the proclamations and ministry of Jesus through the theories and models of sociology and cultural anthropology. Malina presents the gospel of Jesus as a "social gospel" that spoke to the inhabitants living in the Mediterranean area in the first century. While his approach has its foundations in the history and culture of the area, Malina uses social systems and paradigms to help explain the New Testament canonical stories about Jesus and the kingdom of God. In view of the existing social conditions, Jesus boldly proclaimed the coming of the alternative kingdom of God. What was wrong with the existing kingdom that motivated the people to listen to Jesus' promises? That is, what was it about the Jewish and the Gentile societies that made Jesus' gospel message of another kingdom so appealing?

The two key aspects of the society in the first-century Roman Empire were economics and religion. It was a society of great diversity in both of these aspects. As we have seen, there was a great gulf between the elites and the nonelites. Jesus' life and ministry unfolded within the eastern Mediterranean setting of the extremes of Roman prosperity and serious poverty, persons of high status and influence and people with little rank and worth. In the New Testament Gospels, Jesus declared a new kingdom in a setting of prevailing violence, oppression and inequity. In exchange for honor and

---

[47]Ibid., p. 85.

veneration of the emperor, the elite people gained position, wealth and security locally. In other words, it was a society where basically "the rich got richer and the poor got poorer."

One difficulty may have been rooted in the Jewish aristocracy, in the wealthy families living in the region of Palestine, who had adapted well to the Roman economic and political systems. The traditional religious theocracy of the Jews crumbled under the selfish, ambitious leadership of the upper classes of Jews in Jerusalem. In the agrarian society the wealthy landowners contracted with the laborers to work the land; in turn, the laborers received material goods, security and protection from their prosperous landlords. The accepted social system depended on the reciprocal exchange of goods and services, but the abuse and neglect of the lower-status workers (clients) by the socially higher patrons resulted in crises for the peasants.[48] This situation is reflected in the words and stories of Jesus which clearly show the division of the social roles (see parables in Mk 12:1-12; Lk 12:13-21; 16:1-15). Jesus' reference to loving "your neighbor as yourself" (Mt 19:19) is pronounced in the context of the questions of a "rich man" who may have personally experienced the disregard of the wealthy Jews toward the poorer Jews in the region.

In reaction to these conditions, the alternative kingdom of God announced by Jesus was the promise of a good and benevolent patron, God himself. He is portrayed as a Father who cares for his children, and not as an autocratic monarch who seeks his own affluence and influence. In the ancient social world, the father metaphor designated the patron half of the patron-client relationship.[49] Such an alternative kingdom was inaugurated by Jesus and welcomed by many people (both Jews and Gentiles) who were glad to receive such good news. In Jesus' socially upside-down kingdom, "the first will be last, and many who are last will be first" (Mt 19:30). Both the normally accepted (but corrupt) religious and economic systems of the controlling Roman Empire were threatened by the messages of Jesus found in the New Testament Gospels; his gospel intimidated both the Roman and the Jewish leadership.

Corinthian social divisions. The two canonical epistles addressed to the believers in Corinth may offer the best examples of social divisions found

---

[48]Bruce Malina, *The Social Gospel of Jesus: The Kingdom of God in Mediterranean Perspective* (Minneapolis: Augsburg Fortress, 2001), pp. 31-34.
[49]Ibid., p. 34.

in Paul's communications. Corinth was a capital city, located in the Roman province of Achaia. By the 50s CE the population in Corinth was perhaps between 80,000 and 130,000 people. Historians have substantially agreed that the city was ethnically and religiously diverse. A small group of wealthy families controlled the city's power and prestige, and the city was very typical in its hierarchical social and political structures.[50]

While the book of Acts relates a conflict that arose when Paul's message was rejected by the Jewish community in Corinth (Acts 18:6, 12-17), the 1 Corinthians letter does not reveal any such conflict with the synagogue or any disagreements between the Gentile and Jewish believers. On the contrary, the letter reveals that conflicts and divisions among the believers were rooted in loyalty to different church leaders (1 Cor 1:10-11) and to their positions in the community (1 Cor 11:19). The difficulties in 1 Corinthians were due to strong social divisions within the church, and a split between the wealthy and the poorer classes of people. The elite members were educated members of the church, and the "wise" belonged to the educated classes (1 Cor 1:26). As the prevailing majority in the Christian community, the wealthy may have been given an unequal amount of influence in the church.[51] Further differences became evident as the Corinthian believers celebrated the Lord's Supper, divided by the participants' ability to eat an accompanying meal (probably those with some wealth) and an inability to wait for other (probably working) members of the community (1 Cor 11:17-34). The divisions were not theological but social.

In the canonical second letter to the Corinthians, it is evident that Paul is having difficulties in reconciling groups of people holding to diverse viewpoints and interests.[52] In 2 Corinthians 2:14-16 Paul employs patent imperial imagery. Paul pictures the traditional "triumphant procession" of the military victor into a city. Certainly, such a spectacular procession would have been a familiar display of power to the readers of the letter, along with the devastating effects of the Roman military conquests. Yet, perhaps more than any other issue Paul addresses, the collection for the "poorer saints" of

---

[50]Warren Carter, *The Roman Empire and the New Testament: An Essential Guide* (Nashville: Abingdon Press, 2006), p. 56.

[51]Philip F. Esler, *The First Christians in their Social Worlds: Social-Scientific Approaches to New Testament Interpretation* (London: Routledge, 1994), p. 2.

[52]Richard Horsley, "The First and Second Letters to the Corinthians, " in *A Postcolonial Commentary on the New Testament Writings*, ed. Fernando F. Segovia and R. S. Sugirtharajah (New York: T & T Clark, 2007), p. 237.

Jerusalem (2 Cor 8–9) illustrates Paul's desire to create another value system to counteract the Roman imperial economic system. Paul was not only urging his readers to resist the accepted system of social divisions but was trying to form a new kind of order and community in spite of it.[53]

Patronage. The concepts of patronage and benefaction were relevant to the social systems present in the Corinthian culture. As protector of the citizens in Corinth, the Roman emperor was revered as the one who could bring peace, order and prosperity to the city. Honorable titles were used of the emperor: "patron, benefactor, savior, son of a god." When he visited the city of Corinth, Paul could not have missed all the images that displayed the power and presence of the Roman emperor, represented by coinage, statues, temples, monuments and inscriptions. It appears that in first-century Corinth this patron-client society was visible in all aspects of the culture, including trade associations, local officials, literary guilds and even in the common households, with slaves and masters. While some early Christians may have benefited from such relationships, generally the economics of the patron-client society worked against the lower, laboring class of people. As a result, these aspects of the economy and the society become a background for our understanding of the Corinthian church and the aggravating issues that confounded Paul in his ministry.[54]

Other New Testament letters. Other New Testament letters disclose negative appraisals of the familiar Roman social systems; however, in this introduction, only select, brief examples of these inferences are given attention. For example, the language in the first letter to the Thessalonians portrays the highly debated concept of the *parousia* (the promise of Christ's return to earth), bringing to the readers' minds the returning victorious Roman army, parading into the city: "the coming of the Lord . . . with a loud command . . . with the trumpet call of God" (1 Thess 4:15-16). Paul, however, gives a real hope to these believers in the form of Christ instead of the emperor.

Not unlike Mark's Gospel, Paul juxtaposed his proclamation about the good news (*euangelion*) about Christ with the other good news presented by those attempting to influence the Galatian readers (Gal 1:6-7).[55] To Roman citizens the language of "good news" and "glad tidings" functioned as announcements

[53]Ibid., p. 243.
[54]Chow, "Patronage in Roman Corinth," pp. 120-25.
[55]Mark D. Nanos, *The Irony of Galatians: Paul's Letter in First-Century Context* (Minneapolis: Fortress Press, 2002), pp. 284-85.

of important events concerning the divine ruler of the empire, such as a birth, an enthronement, speeches or decrees, or news of military victory. Such imperial announcements were aimed at reassuring the colonized people. In addition, the same terminology of "good news" was also meaningful in Jewish literature, especially at the time of the writing of the New Testament. It was not connected to a human benefactor but to God. In Galatians 3:8, for example, Paul uses the term in regard to the "good news in advance to Abraham." Therefore, the common concepts of good news are blended into one message of positive expectation for the Jewish and the Roman Christians alike. The claims of Israel's God, even from times that predated the Roman Empire, directly challenged the claims of Caesar. By announcing that God is king, the obvious implication is that the reigning Caesar is not.

Brigitte Kahl places Paul's Galatian letter in the context of the Roman viewpoint of "vanquished people," that is, those people who are counted among the nations conquered by the Roman Empire. In Galatians, Paul presents a more universal worldview that involves all the nations (the ruled and the ruling) in a move toward greater peace and justice, universal law and order, through the gospel message of Jesus Christ. Diverse politics, economics and theology are set as a background for Paul's argument with the Galatian believers and their progression away from the exclusive freedom found in only Christ. Thus, Kahl asks, what if Paul was ultimately more concerned with the Roman imperial laws than the "Jewish Torah"?[56]

The language of the "powers" of this world has been considered a major topic in the letter to the Ephesians. The author announces that Christ is absolute over the familiar "powers" in the empire. We have already noted how the ideology of the holy war and the role of the victorious warrior are rooted in the Hebrew Old Testament; such battle ideology may have been conveyed about the kings of Israel, as seen in Psalm 68 (Ps 68:11-14, 18) and cited in Ephesians 4:8. By using this psalm, the author of Ephesians modifies the Old Testament ideology and overlays the Roman image of the imperial triumph on top of the Old Testament concept. In a pagan city such as Ephesus, the readers would have grasped the concept of power, redesigned in a positive sense, to focus on Christ's power that transcends familiar human power.[57] In this letter Christ is the Conqueror, yet his empire has

---

[56]Brigitte Kahl, *Galatians Re-Imagined: Reading with the Eyes of the Vanquished*, Paul in Critical Contexts (Minneapolis: Fortress Press, 2010), p. 7.

[57]Matthew F. Lowe, "'This Is Not an Ordinary Death': Empire and Atonement in the Minor Pauline Epistles," in *Empire in the New Testament*, ed. Stanley Porter and Cynthia Long

been spiritualized; those people who understand the power of the spiritual realm do not need to be anxious about a system of unjust human rulers. The emphasis in Ephesians is the empowering of people who may appear to be intimidated by the Roman imperial system.[58]

In his letter to the Philippians, Paul uses the prison context to focus on three aspects of the Christian life: citizenship, peace and the crucifixion. The reference to heavenly citizenship in Philippians 3:20 assumes a certain amount of discontent with earthly Roman citizenship and presents an alternative. The "peace of God" (Phil 1:2; 4:7) is contrasted to the human concept of Roman peace. The memorable hymn of Philippians 2:6-11 is a masterpiece of irony. It contrasts Jesus' humble obedience to the imperial power over life and death. While the act of crucifixion was seen as a Roman curse and a dreadful execution, in the hymn it is translated into Jesus' exaltation and glory. In addition, the picture of Jesus' ascension in the hymn (Phil 2:9-11) vividly brings to mind the worship and esteem given to the emperor; yet it is Jesus, and not the Roman emperor, who is acclaimed as Lord (v. 11).[59]

The book of Colossians is a volatile and dissident letter written in the milieu of the Roman Empire.[60] Even as a prisoner Paul writes to these believers concerning another view of reality, articulating another way of life that was seditious to the authority of the empire (i.e., Col 2:6-8). The poem in Colossians 1:13-20 declares that a new and different kingdom exists, and that it is ruled by One who forgives, redeems, reconciles and establishes peace, not only on earth but also in heaven (v. 20). Greater than everything "visible and invisible," this Ruler surpasses all "thrones or powers or rulers or authorities" (vv. 15-16), and existed before any human ruler (v. 17). These are bold and risky words from a man already imprisoned in the empire (Col 4:10).

General Epistles. Like the Pauline Epistles, readers can analyze the other New Testament letters by using patterns from the social sciences, such as class divisions, economic and religious power.[61] Similar to Romans 13, 1 Peter also contains a debatable passage, to "submit yourselves for the Lord's sake to every authority instituted among men: whether to the king as

Westfall (Eugene, OR: Pickwick, 2011), pp. 204-6.
[58]Jennifer Bird, "The Letter to the Ephesians," in *A Postcolonial Commentary on the New Testament Writings*, ed. Fernando F. Segovia and R. S. Sugirtharajah (New York: T & T Clark, 2007), p. 278.
[59]Porter, introduction to *Empire in the New Testament*, p. 13.
[60]Brian Walsh and Sylvia Keesmaat, *Colossians Remixed: Subverting the Empire* (Downers Grove, IL: InterVarsity Press, 2004), p. 7.
[61]Westfall, "Running the Gamut," p. 231.

the supreme authority, or to governors who are sent by him to punish those who do wrong and to commend those who do right" (1 Pet 2:13-14). The 1 Peter author directs his readers to use their freedom correctly (though it is unclear what that looks like), and to "show proper respect to everyone . . . fear God and honor the king" (1 Pet 2:17). Is this subversive language or is the author suggesting that the readers acquiesce to the imperial authorities? Paradoxically, while the readers have one foot in God's world, as "a chosen people, a royal priesthood, a holy nation, a people belonging to God" (1 Pet 2:9), they have the other foot in the Roman Empire, as "aliens and strangers" in the world (1 Pet 2:11).

The Johannine Epistles can be understood as contrasts in moral principles and standards because they emphasize those of God's kingdom in contrast to those of a secular kingdom (1 Jn 5:3-5). The author of these epistles, like the author of the book of Revelation, helps his readers to understand that the root of human sin and wickedness is not so much the familiar human rulers; evil originates from deeper, satanic/supernatural powers (1 Jn 5:19; Rev 12:7-12).

The book of Hebrews challenges the Roman rules of empire by demonstrating the superiority of Christ over all human institutions.[62] It may be that the Jewish Christian communities provide the clearest resistance to the Roman Empire in the New Testament. Jewish Christianity occupied a far more difficult position as it fought for its existence, caught between the Roman Empire and traditional Judaism. The alienation that grew between the Jews and the Jewish Christians weakened the Christian resistance to the imperial dominance. Outside of Jewish protection the Christians suffered hardships (Heb 12:7) and encountered "strange teachings" (Heb 13:9-10). The author of Hebrews urges the readers to obey Christian leaders who "watch over" the believers, and not political leaders (Heb 13:17). In spite of persecution, the Christian believers found their true value and hope in the "kingdom of God" (Heb 6:16-20; 12:28).[63]

Postcolonialism. A relatively new ideology influencing biblical interpretation is postcolonialism. There is a distinction between postcolonial studies and empire studies, though the distinction may be a "porous one."[64] More difficult yet is to determine the differences between postco-

---

[62]Ibid. See also Porter, introduction to *Empire in the New Testament*, p. 14.

[63]Westfall, "Running the Gamut," p. 256.

[64]Stephen D. Moore, *Empire and Apocalypse: Postcolonialism and the New Testament* (Sheffield: Phoenix Press, 2006), pp. 19, 124.

lonial studies, empire studies, liberation and contextual hermeneutics. Many works in these latter two areas overlap with the former two categories, so it is not simple to place significant research into one or another rigid category. We separate them, then, only for convenience. Although postcolonial approaches commonly consider the ideology of human liberation and resistance to oppressing forces, they also consider the abilities (or the lack thereof) of the marginalized peoples to raise themselves out of oppressive situations.

Scholars have recognized an unmistakable postcolonial factor in the New Testament literature. The New Testament authors attempted to communicate truths to people despite the Roman control (or colonization) over the land and its inhabitants.[65] Recent scholarship has tackled key postcolonial concepts such as poverty, inequity, economic class and stratification within the Roman imperial system. A postcolonial reading of the New Testament epistles, for example, observes that Paul attempts to establish communities that are alternatives to and resistant to the accepted imperial society. The imperial power system crushed the subjected people's fundamental culture and social customs, and then imposed new forms of civilization on them. This is evident from numerous passages in the Pastoral Letters that reflect an alternative attitude to be adopted by the colonized people, such as the condition of slavery, the role of women, male leadership in the community and earthly wealth.[66]

LITERARY APPROACHES

Finally, we can identify the literary aspect of the texts that is valuable to gain a richer, fuller understanding of the biblical documents. We recognize that communication is the process of sending and receiving information, and as readers, we are constantly interpreting what another person has written. Many factors can manipulate or influence such a process. To approach the biblical texts as written communications necessarily coded by the ancient authors to the ancient readers raises a myriad of scholarly questions about this communicative process.

---

[65]Philip Esler, "Rome in Apocalyptic and Rabbinic Literature," in *The Gospel of Matthew in its Roman Imperial Context*, ed. John Riches and David Sim (New York: T & T Clark International, 2005), p. 9.

[66]Ralph Broadbent, "The First and Second Letters to Timothy and the Letter to Titus," in *A Postcolonial Commentary on the New Testament Writings*, ed. Fernando F. Segovia and R. S. Sugirtharajah (New York: T & T Clark, 2007), p. 323.

Subversive language. The first consideration has to do with words, language and symbolism. Subversion may be defined as reinterpretation or a new construal of established, commonly understood concepts, especially those expressed in images, words or symbols. That is, a word, a story, an image or a symbol used in one situation is consciously redefined or altered into a new significance.[67] As an example, the image of a temple would have been equally familiar to both Jews and Gentiles as a place of worship and sacrifice in the first century. Yet the New Testament authors redefine the use of this building image into the body of Christ (Jn 2:19-22; 1 Cor 3:16-17; Eph 2:19-20). Because diachronic words can reflect a broad interpretive semantic range, they can be used and reframed to reflect an innovative or uncommon meaning. The larger context in which a word appears creates a change or modification to the word. For example, the common word *crown*, used by Paul in 1 Corinthians 9:25, would evoke a particular image in the minds of readers who were familiar with the Roman and Isthmian athletic games. In the context of a "race" (1 Cor 9:24-27), the crown of victory generates the picture of the triumphant athlete, but Paul transforms the image into an eternal victory of the Christian life. The extraordinary race that Paul was running was far more important than the common, yet popular, competitive events. Thus, words used in an indirect, subversive (or hidden) sense may be chosen to relay a message that would otherwise be unacceptable to readers in a direct sense.

Familiar, acceptable patterns of language develop within a specific social system or within a close-knit group of people (as the early Christian communities).[68] The Gospel writers adapted subversive rhetoric that would allow the words and the story of Jesus to spread throughout the empire without putting the authors or the readers into a treasonous position. One interesting example is found in Matthew 10:17-31. In this discourse Jesus warns his disciples that they may be rejected, arrested and flogged by "local councils," "governors" and "kings" (v. 17). But the disciples are not to worry about this situation; they are not to be "afraid" (vv. 26, 28). Jesus says, "if the head of the house has been called Beelzebub, how much more the members of his household!" (v. 25). In this context the reference to "Beelzebub," considered to be the "prince of demons" (or Satan, see Mt 12:24), may be a

---

[67]Brian Godawa, *Word Pictures: Knowing God Through Story and Imagination* (Downers Grove, IL: InterVarsity Press, 2009), p. 115.

[68]Malina, *Social Gospel of Jesus*, p. 5.

coded reference to the Roman emperor expressed in terms that the Jewish followers would understand. In fact, Jesus is compared to Beelzebub by the Pharisees in Matthew 12:24-28; following this accusation, Jesus reveals the true nature of his Father's kingdom (Mt 12:25-28).

While the New Testament writers reinterpreted known Jewish imagery, they redesigned imagery from the pagan culture as well. Greco-Roman sources replicated in the New Testament include words from such writers as Sophocles, Plutarch, Aristotle and Seneca. This indicates that there is a considerable interchange with the common Greco-Roman culture, rhetoric and philosophers (see, e.g., 1 Cor 6:12-13). Thus, certain passages of the New Testament writings can be read as a subversion of the commonly accepted terminology, language and symbols of the Empire. By employing diachronic words and phrases, the New Testament authors redefined the pagan worldview in terms of Jesus Christ and the Christian perspective.[69]

Carter considers the New Testament writings to be "hidden transcripts." They were not intended to be public writings to the general populace of the Roman Empire. They were specific communications written by and for communities of people who were followers of a man (Jesus) who was crucified by the Roman government. The New Testament writings were intended to be aids that helped the followers of Jesus to "negotiate" life in the Roman world. On the one hand, the New Testament writers attempted to articulate alternative ways to be a Christ follower and still live in the Empire. On the other hand, they suggested ways of living that did not differ significantly from the patterns of the Roman world. Most often, the New Testament writers offered concrete ways of understanding the (often seemingly bizarre) pagan world, while still refusing to direct their readers to extreme positions of complete rebellion or total concession.[70]

Rhetorical-critical analysis. Language, of course, reflects the society that uses it; without social awareness, readers may misinterpret passages of literature. The use of rhetoric was everywhere in the Greco-Roman world, including speeches and debates that occurred in common public places such as the marketplace or the theater, as well as in the schools and law courts. The rhetorical methods of the time and culture were familiar even to those who did not attain a high education. While rhetorical writing and speaking were distinguished art forms during the Hellenistic time period,

[69]Godawa, *Word Pictures*, p. 121.
[70]Carter, *Roman Empire and the New Testament*, pp. 12-13.

the purposes and structures have been lost on modern audiences. Ancient handbooks on classical rhetoric serve as important resources for our modern study of very old literature.

Aristotle's *Art of Rhetoric* may have had the most influence on orators during the Roman, Hellenistic and Greek periods. Three basic genres of classic oration were recognized: epideictic, deliberative and forensic rhetoric. Epideictic rhetoric began in such public forums where speeches gave honor and praise of the virtuous people, and vilified others. Moving oratory reminded the audience of the value of virtuous living in order that social structure and culture could be maintained. This type of persuasive rhetoric moved quickly into other assemblies where a living person or a deceased person received high praise, such as a funeral speech.

Second, deliberative rhetoric was employed when important decisions had to be made with respect to a future action or engagement (e.g., in a political assembly). From the political arena, deliberative rhetoric trans-ferred easily into the other large gatherings, such as the Jewish synagogue and the Christian church. When addressing the Christians in his Galatians letter, Paul employs deliberative arguments in an attempt to counsel them in their decision-making process. Third, forensic rhetoric was first used in formal law courts and council gatherings. It was then employed outside of formal courtrooms when issues of blame or innocence were involved. A forensic topic can be observed when Paul found it necessary to answer charges brought against him concerning his authority and his genuineness (1 Cor 4). Certainly a combination of two or more types of rhetoric was skillfully used by orators to get their points across. Language is rarely limited to one type of speech. In a court of law, for example, the defender could employ epideictic rhetoric to picture the defendant, and forensic speech to argue his innocence.[71]

The use of rhetorical criticism has increased in the last few decades because scholars have realized that meaningful comparisons can be made between the biblical literature and other ancient literature of the same era. Critics have perceived the utilization of rhetorical forms in sections of the New Testament Gospels, in many of the Pauline writings and in the book of Revelation.

Revelation and the rhetorical-critical approach. Rhetorical literature is, in essence, persuasive literature, written for the purpose of convincing

---

[71]David A. deSilva, *Seeing Things John's Way: The Rhetoric of the Book of Revelation* (Louis-ville: Westminster John Knox, 2009), pp. 18-23.

an audience of a particular point of view. In his own peculiar way the author of the book of Revelation arranges material and includes and omits material for his intended purpose. John's goals were to persuade his listeners, influence the values affecting their lives, promote certain courses of action, and arouse a distain for evil and a desire for righteousness within their societal culture.

As a backdrop, it is helpful to review the historical, imperial setting behind the writing of the book of Revelation. At the end of the first century, thirty-five cities in Asia Minor held the title of "temple warden" (*neokoros*) that supported a site of the imperial cult. Specifically, all seven cities mentioned in Revelation 1–3 had cultic sites: six (with the exception of Thyatira) had imperial temples; five (except Philadelphia and Laodicea) had imperial altars and priests. In Pergamum the most notable building was "the great altar of Zeus," located on a mountain overlooking the city, with the appearance of a great throne (see Rev 4). Ephesus was also a center of emperor cult activity, displaying a large new Flavian temple and statue in honor of the Emperor Domitian, not far from the older temple built in honor of Julius Caesar. Moreover, the imperial cult was more than stones and statues. The cult involved numerous priests and common people who followed a calendar of feasts and celebrations that brought honor to the reigning human emperor.[72]

In Asia Minor, Roman imperialism was most visible in two ways: in the disparate economy and in the profane imperial cult. These two issues are the main themes of Revelation 4–22 and are the direct focus of Revelation 17–18.[73] First, the original readers would have quickly recognized the economic picture of the Roman Empire in these chapters. The wealth and luxury of the elite class in Rome becomes a target of John's criticism. Second, the worship by the "inhabitants of the earth" (Rev 17:8) resembles the worship of the emperor in Rome.

Powerful, vivid images in Revelation stand out in the narrative; the primary image is that of "Babylon the Great," a dramatic picture of the city of Rome and its emperors. The "fall of Babylon" is the destruction of the "kings of the earth who commit adultery with her" (Rev 18:9). While for centuries scholars have debated the identity of several Revelation images, there is no doubt that the first-century readers would have had no problem

---

[72]Ibid., pp. 41-43.
[73]Ibid., p. 48.

in making the associations and identifying the symbols as aspects of their own imperial culture.[74]

Revelation and apocalyptic literature. The literary form of Jewish apocalyptic literature blossomed after the Jewish exile in Persia and was transformed under the influence of the Hellenistic culture in the closing century BCE. This genre of literature existed in Jewish tradition well before the first century CE and was used for at least a century afterward. It appears to have been used by early Christian writers, as evidenced by a number of apocalyptic writings found in collections of noncanonical documents from the early centuries of the church. It may have been a popular form of literature in the first century CE; yet modern biblical scholarship has had difficulties arriving at a consensus concerning the origins, content and purpose of apocalyptic literature.

Apocalyptic literature may be considered protest literature, reflecting the point of view of an oppressed minority of the population. The persecution language that pervades the book of Revelation helps scholars to date the book from either the time of the Nero persecutions (the late 60s CE) or, more likely, during the reign of Domitian (late 90s CE).[75] The images and symbols of Revelation spoke plainly to the first-century Christians about their own conditions in the Empire; however, it may have been even more valuable to the Christians in the second and third centuries if the maltreatment of Christians intensified during that time.

The book of Revelation is a letter, a prophecy and an apocalyptic literary masterpiece; by disregarding any aspect of its literary genres, modern readers can be led astray in their comprehension of the messages of the book. The two most critical and most obvious literary features of apocalyptic literature are cryptic images (pictures, characters) and figurative language. Unfortunately, from the Middle Ages to the time of the Branch Davidian sect in Waco, Texas (1993), biblical apocalyptic images and symbols have been abused and misunderstood. Therefore, when modern readers concentrate too intensely on past historical events and the predictions of yet-future events, they can overlook key features of apocalyptic literature which clearly affect the way the text is interpreted.

Our current understandings of apocalyptic literature have their roots in

---

[74]Ibid., pp. 37-39.
[75]David E. Aune, *Apocalypticism, Prophecy and Magic in Early Christianity* (Grand Rapids: Baker Academic, 2006), p. 3.

the work of three noted scholars, John J. Collins; his wife, Adela Yarbro Collins; and Elisabeth Schüssler Fiorenza. John Collins clearly defines the literary genre and determines that by its very nature, apocalyptic literature is figurative and highly symbolic. This type of literature is an attempt at pulling the readers into the intents and significance of the writing. Adela Yarbro Collins features the historical aspects of the Roman Empire, especially as they affected the Jews and the early Christians living in the empire. For the recipients of the book, Revelation functioned in a manner similar to Aristotle's term *catharsis*. The medical term *catharsis* refers to the removal of a painful foreign object (or substance) from the body to promote the healing of the body. In the same way, painful human emotions, such as fear, can be alleviated. Apprehension caused by the Roman imperial system is shared by the readers and intensified by the author's use of specific symbols and conflicts. The narratives are told in such a way that the symbolism is understood to be typical of the readers' own situations. The book of Revelation, then, creates a catharsis for its readers through the use of symbolic narrative and in the structure of the book as a whole. Human emotions such as fear and resentment are intensified through the repeated cycles of persecution and the final destruction of the audience's enemies.[76]

With Collins, Elisabeth Schüssler Fiorenza suggests that imagery and language are used to intensify the readers' emotions. The positive images are used to persuade the readers to make righteous decisions about God in their present, and to live accordingly in this life to prepare for the future to come. Negative images were intended to convince the readers to turn away from erroneous loyalties and allegiances, especially those given to the Roman imperial powers. The obvious symbols of Rome (e.g., Rev 18) represent humiliation, disgrace and ugliness; yet the ultimate end of Rome is complete failure and defeat. The literary technique of using a vision (Rev 1:19) speaks to the readers in a significant manner, in an attempt to persuade the readers to choose to worship God, who is not "doomed to failure and destruction." By weaving together recognizable Jewish and the Roman Empire imagery, the author uses the apocalyptic genre of literature as a vehicle to respond to the social, political and religious situations so familiar to his audience.[77]

---

[76]Adela Yarbro Collins, *Crisis and Catharsis: The Power of the Apocalypse* (Philadelphia: Westminster Press, 1984), pp. 153-54.

[77]Elisabeth Schüssler Fiorenza, *The Book of Revelation: Justice and Judgment* (Philadelphia: Fortress Press, 1985), p. 192.

The vivid imagery in the divine throne room scene (Rev 4–5) is a depiction of the power and the authority of God in pictures that would speak to both the Jewish and the Gentile Christians. For the original readers the royal picture was a dramatic and ironic reminder of the human throne room of the Roman emperor.[78] Thus, with a creativity that is difficult to match, the author of Revelation wove together the two cultures by using descriptions that would impact a broad spectrum of early Christians.

Revelation and empire. Because of its rich subversive language and imagery, Revelation is almost in a class all by itself with respect to the study of anti-imperial rhetoric in the New Testament. Even beyond what we read in the New Testament epistles, the "gloves are off," the conflict is wide open, and Revelation clashes with the formidable military power of Rome itself.[79] Critical scholarship has reckoned Revelation as the "most uncompromising attack on the Roman Empire, and on Christian collusion with the empire."[80] Yet only recently have some Revelation scholars regarded the book in a postcolonial light. While we may note a consistent movement in scholarship from history to theory, a methodology like postcolonialism depends heavily on both the historical and the theoretical approaches, and it all becomes useful when engaging a book like Revelation.

The conflict of Revelation is between two distinctive ways of life: the "civilized and the barbaric."[81] The author of Revelation sets up this binarism specifically to disturb the acknowledged Roman order and structures. The author creates an incredible reversal of power between the two ways of life, between the elites and the nonelites, and between Rome and Christianity. Furthermore, the strict divisions of authority and status become less obvious because the author creates two empires: the earthly empire and an alternative empire of God and of "the Lamb." The boundaries of these empires become hazy, until it becomes almost impossible to separate the two.[82]

Another key postcolonial concept is hegemony, which is "domination by consent." Hegemony is the active participation of a dominated group or a colonized people (especially a socially lower class) in their own subjugation.

---

[78]Aune, *Apocalypticism*, p. 12.

[79]Westfall, "Running the Gamut," p. 251.

[80]Steven D. Moore, "Revelation," in *A Postcolonial Commentary on the New Testament Writings*, ed. Fernando F. Segovia and R. S. Sugirtharajah (New York: T & T Clark, 2007), p. 436.

[81]Ibid., p. 451.

[82]Ibid.

At the time of the writing of Revelation the people of Asia Minor were not colonized by Rome by force but by invitation. Principal cities such as Ephesus, Pergamum and Smyrna voluntarily competed for rank, reputation and imperial favor. Honors and loyalties were measured against that of the neighboring city; statues, temples and the worship of the emperor were as competitive as the Roman games.[83] However, John creatively convinces his audience that there is only one authority in the world that is worthy of human devotion and service, and it is not the Roman emperor (e.g., Rev 5:12-13). His bold rhetoric moved his work beyond the first-century society and turned it into timeless concepts about the nature of and the legitimate recipient of human worship.[84]

It is not difficult then to see how and why scholarship tends to place the book of Revelation among those texts we now consider to be empire, liberation or postcolonial documents. In addition, as an exemplar of apocalyptic literature in its finest form, Revelation appears to be the best example of anti-imperial rhetoric and anti-emperor worship in the New Testament.

CONCLUSION

Scholarly interest in early Christianity and the Roman Empire is growing steadily. Historical research is critical to our understanding of the Roman imperial context, and the historical spotlight has been shining on three very different, though intertwined, religious factions in the late-first-century CE: the imperial cult of the Roman Empire, Judaism and the early Christian church. More recent sociocultural ideologies help us to understand the thoughts and forces that influenced the ancient writers who lived, wrote (and were perhaps even martyred) within these deeply connected cultures. Literarily, familiar vehicles of communication such as apocalyptic literature carried both the historical and the ideological features that were deemed valuable and appropriate by the original authors and were recognized by the original readers of the New Testament documents. By engaging the New Testament writings historically, ideologically and literarily, we seek to better know the life and mission of Jesus Christ, to better understand the lives of the early Christians and to more fully comprehend how Christians today are to revere and follow Christ in our own culture.

---

[83]Ibid., p. 439.
[84]Ibid., p. 451.

BIBLIOGRAPHY

Aune, David E. *Apocalypticism, Prophecy and Magic in Early Christianity.* Grand Rapids: Baker Academic, 2006.

_____. *Revelation 17–22.* Word Biblical Commentary 52C. Nashville: Thomas Nelson, 1998.

Baldwin, Barry. *The Roman Emperors.* Montreal: Harvest House, 1980.

Bird, Jennifer G. "The Letter to the Ephesians." In *A Postcolonial Commentary on the NT Writings*, pp. 265-80. Edited by Fernando F. Segovia and R. S. Sugirtharajah. New York: T & T Clark, 2007.

Black, C. Clifton. "Was Mark a Roman Gospel?" *Expository Times* 105 (1993): 36-40.

Boda, Mark J. "Walking in the Light of Yahweh: Zion and the Empires in the Book of Isaiah." In *Empire in the New Testament*, pp. 54-89. Edited by Stanley E. Porter and Cynthia Long Westfall. Eugene, OR: Pickwick, 2011.

Broadbent, Ralph. "The First and Second Letters to Timothy and the Letter to Titus." In *A Postcolonial Commentary on the NT Writings*, pp. 323-28. Edited by Fernando F. Segovia and R. S. Sugirtharajah. New York: T & T Clark, 2007.

Carter, Warren. "Paul and the Roman Empire: Recent Perspectives." In *Paul Unbound: Other Perspectives on the Apostle*, pp. 7-26. Edited by Mark Given. Peabody, MA: Hendrickson, 2010.

_____. *The Roman Empire and the New Testament: An Essential Guide.* Nashville: Abingdon, 2006.

Cassidy, Richard J. *Society and Politics in the Acts of the Apostles.* Maryknoll, NY: Orbis, 1987.

Chow, John K. "Patronage in Roman Corinth." In *Paul and Empire: Religion and Power in Roman Imperial Society*, pp. 104-25. Edited by Richard Horsley. Harrisburg, PA: Trinity Press International, 1997.

Collins, Adela Yarbro. *Crisis and Catharsis: The Power of the Apocalypse.* Philadelphia: Westminster, 1984.

Collins, John J. *Apocalypse: The Morphology of a Genre.* Semeia 14. Missoula, MT: Scholars Press, 1979.

deSilva, David A. *Seeing Things John's Way: The Rhetoric of the Book of Revelation.* Louisville: Westminster John Knox, 2009.

Elliott, Neil. *The Arrogance of Nations; Reading Romans in the Shadow of Empire.* Paul in Critical Contexts Series. Minneapolis: Fortress, 2008.

_____. "The Letter to the Romans." In *A Postcolonial Commentary on the NT Writings*, pp. 194-219. Edited by Fernando F. Segovia and R. S. Sugirtharajah. New York: T & T Clark, 2007.

_____. "Romans 13:1-7 in Context of Imperial Propaganda." In *Paul and Empire: Religion and Power in Roman Imperial Society*, pp. 184-205. Edited by Richard Horsley. Harrisburg, PA: Trinity Press International, 1997.

Esler, Philip F. *The First Christians in their Social Worlds: Social-Scientific Approaches to NT Interpretation*. London: Routledge, 1994.

_____. "Rome in Apocalyptic and Rabbinic Literature." In *The Gospel of Matthew in its Roman Imperial Context*, pp. 9-33. Edited by John Riches and David Sim. New York: T & T Clark, 2005.

Fee, Gordon D. *Paul's Letter to the Philippians*. New International Commentary on the New Testament. Grand Rapids: Eerdmans, 1995.

Friesen, Steven J. "The Cult of the Roman Emperors in Ephesos." In *Ephesos, Metropolis of Asia: An Interdisciplinary Approach to its Archaeology, Religion and Culture*, pp. 229-50. Edited by Helmut Koester. Valley Forge: Trinity Press International, 1995.

_____. *Imperial Cults and the Apocalypse of John: Reading Revelation in the Ruins*. Oxford: Oxford University Press, 2001.

_____. "Paul and Economics: The Jerusalem Collection as an Alternative to Patronage." In *Paul Unbound: Other Perspectives on the Apostle*, pp. 27-54. Edited by Mark Given. Peabody, MA: Hendrickson, 2010.

_____. *Twice Neokoros: Ephesus, Asia and the Cult of the Flavian Imperial Family*. Religions in the Graeco Roman World, 116. Leiden: Brill, 1993.

Godawa, Brian. *Word Pictures: Knowing God through Story and Imagination*. Downers Grove, IL: InterVarsity Press, 2009.

Horsley, Richard A. "The First and Second Letters to the Corinthians." In *A Postcolonial Commentary on the NT Writings*, pp. 220-45. Edited by Fernando F. Segovia and R. S. Sugirtharajah. New York: T & T Clark, 2007.

_____. *Hearing the Whole Story: The Politics of Plot in Mark's Gospel*. Louisville: Westminster John Knox, 2001.

_____. *In the Shadow of the Empire: Reclaiming the Bible as a History of Faithful Resistance*. Louisville: Westminster John Knox, 2008.

_____. "Introduction." In *Paul and Empire: Religion and Power in Roman Imperial Society*, pp. 10-24. Edited by Richard A. Horsley. Harrisburg: Trinity Press International, 1997.

_____. *Paul and the Roman Imperial Order*. Harrisburg, PA: Trinity Press International, 2004.

Horsley, Richard A. and Neil Asher Silberman. *The Message and the Kingdom: How Jesus and Paul Ignited a Revolution and Transformed the Ancient World.* Minneapolis: Fortress, 1997.

Incigneri, Brian. *The Gospel to the Romans; the Setting and Rhetoric of Mark's Gospel.* Biblical Interpretation Series, edited by R. Alan Culpepper and Rolf Rendtorff. Leiden: Brill, 2003.

Kahl, Brigitte. *Galatians Re-Imagined; Reading with the Eyes of the Vanquished.* Paul in Critical Contexts Series. Minneapolis: Fortress, 2010.

Kim, Seyoon. *Christ and Caesar: The Gospel and the Roman Empire in the Writings of Paul and Luke.* Grand Rapids: Eerdmans, 2008.

Lowe, Matthew F. "'This Is Not an Ordinary Death': Empire and Atonement in the Minor Pauline Epistles." In *Empire in the New Testament*, pp. 197-229. Edited by Stanley Porter and Cynthia Long Westfall. Eugene, OR: Pickwick, 2011.

Malina, Bruce J. *The Social Gospel of Jesus; The Kingdom of God in Mediterranean Perspective.* Minneapolis: Augsburg Fortress, 2001.

Malina, Bruce J. and John J. Pilch. *Social-Science Commentary on the Book of Revelation.* Minneapolis: Augsburg Fortress, 2000.

Miller, Colin. "The Imperial Cult in the Pauline cities of Asia Minor and Greece." *Catholic Biblical Quarterly* 72 (2010): 314-32.

Moore, Stephen D. *Empire and Apocalypse: Postcolonialism and the New Testament.* Sheffield: Phoenix, 2006.

_____. "Revelation." In *A Postcolonial Commentary on the New Testament Writings*, pp. 436-54. Edited by Fernando F. Segovia and R. S. Sugirtharajah. New York: T & T Clark, 2007.

Nanos, Mark D. *The Irony of Galatians; Paul's Letter in First-Century Context.* Minneapolis: Fortress, 2002.

Oakes, Peter. *Philippians: From People to Letter.* Society for New Testament Studies Monograph Series 110. Cambridge: Cambridge University Press, 2001.

_____. "Re-Mapping the Universe: Paul and the Emperor in 1 Thessalonians and Philippians." *Journal for the Study of the New Testament* 27 (2005): 301-22.

_____. "A State of Tension: Rome in the New Testament." In *The Gospel of Matthew in its Roman Imperial Context*, pp. 75-90. Edited by John Riches and David Sim. New York: T & T Clark, 2005.

Oakes, Peter, ed. *Rome in the Bible and the Early Church.* Grand Rapids: Baker, 2002.

Porter, Stanley E. "Introduction." In *Empire in the New Testament*, pp. 1-16. New Testament Study Series, 10. Edited by Stanley E. Porter and Cynthia Long Westfall. Eugene, OR: Pickwick, 2011.

_____. "Paul Confronts Caesar with the Good News." In *Empire in the New Testament*, pp. 164-96. Edited by Stanley Porter and Cynthia Long Westfall. Eugene, OR: Pickwick, 2011.

Price, S. R. F. *Rituals and Power: The Roman Imperial Cult in Asia Minor.* Cambridge: Cambridge University Press, 1984.

Punt, Jeremy H. "The Letter to the Hebrews." In *A Postcolonial Commentary on the NT Writings*, pp. 338-68. Edited by Fernando F. Segovia and R. S. Sugirtharajah. New York: T & T Clark, 2007.

Rieger, Joerg. *Christ and Empire: From Paul to Postcolonial Times.* Minneapolis: Augsburg Fortress, 2007.

Ringe, Sharon H. "The Letter of James." In *A Postcolonial Commentary on the NT Writings*, pp. 369-80. Edited by Fernando F. Segovia and R. S. Sugirtharajah. New York: T & T Clark, 2007.

Rowe, C. Kavin. *World Upside Down; Reading Acts in the Graeco-Roman Age.* Oxford: University Press, 2009.

Sanders, E. P. *Paul.* Oxford: Oxford University Press, 1991.

_____. *Paul and Palestinian Judaism: A Comparison of Patterns of Religion.* London: SCM, 1977.

Schüssler Fiorenza, Elisabeth. *The Book of Revelation: Justice and Judgment.* Philadelphia: Fortress, 1985.

_____. *Revelation: Vision of a Just World.* Minneapolis: Fortress, 1991.

Smith, Michael G. "The Empire Theory and the Empires of History—A Review Essay." *Christian Scholar's Review* 39:3 (2010): 305-22.

Stanton, Graham N. *Jesus and Gospel.* Cambridge: Cambridge University Press, 2004.

Starr, Chester G. *Civilization and the Caesars; the Intellectual Revolution in the Roman Empire.* New York: W. W. Norton, 1965.

Stuart, Douglas K. "The Old Testament Context of David's Costly Flirtation with Empire-Building." In *Empire in the New Testament*, pp. 17-53. Edited by Stanley E. Porter and Cynthia Long Westfall. Eugene, OR: Pickwick, 2011.

Sugirtharajah, R. S. "Postcolonial Criticism and Biblical Interpretation: the Next Phase." In *A Postcolonial Commentary on the New Testament Writings*, pp. 455-66. Edited by Fernando F. Segovia and R. S. Sugirtharajah. New York: T & T Clark, 2007.

Yamazaki-Ransom, Kazuhiko. *The Roman Empire in Luke's Narrative.* Library of New Testament Studies 404. New York: T & T Clark, 2010.

Walsh, Brian J. and Sylvia C. Keesmaat. *Colossians Remixed: Subverting the Empire.* Downers Grove, IL: InterVarsity Press, 2004.

Walton, Steve. "Aristotle and Paul in 1 Thessalonians." *Tyndale Bulletin* 46.2 (1995): 229-50.

Westfall, Cynthia Long. "Running the Gamut: The Varied Responses to Empire in Jewish Christianity." In *Empire in the New Testament*, pp. 230-58. Edited by Stanley Porter and Cynthia Long Westfall. Eugene, OR: Pickwick, 2011.

Wright, N. T. *The New Testament and the People of God.* Christian Origins and the Question of God, Vol 1. London: SPCK, 1992.

_____. *Paul: In Fresh Perspective.* Minneapolis: Fortress, 2005.

_____. "Paul's Gospel and Caesar's Empire." In *Paul and Politics: Ekklesia, Israel, Imperium, Interpretation*, pp. 160-83. Edited by Richard Horsley. Harrisburg, PA: Trinity Press International, 2000.

_____. "Paul's Gospel and Caesar's Empire." *Center of Theological Inquiry*, Reflections, pp. 1-13. 2010. http://ctinquiry.org/publications/wright. Accessed 09/03/2010.

3

Matthew

Joel Willitts

Anti-Roman Matthew

As best I can tell, the idea that Matthew directly addressed the dark side of Roman imperial rule was raised first by Andrew Overman in his 1995 SBL paper, "Matthew's Parables and Roman Politics: The Imperial Setting of Matthew's Narrative with Special Reference to His Parables."[1] Christopher Bryan corroborates this approximate timetable with his autobiographical reflection about anti-Roman readings of the New Testament more generally:

> When I was at school, we read Virgil's *Aeneid* and Theodor Mommsen's *History of Rome*. Of course, we knew Rome's *imperium* ("supreme administrative power") had its limitations and from time to time, before Constantine the Great, some emperors had persecuted Christians. But still, taken all in all, we understood that the Roman Empire had been, as Sellar and Yeatman would have put it, "a good thing." Even in relation to Christianity, therefore, we tended to speak of Roman rule as "providential" . . . questions were raised (for me, at any rate) *during the last decade of the twentieth century* as a part of the

---

[1] Andrew Overman, "Matthew's Parables and Roman Politics: The Imperial Setting of Matthew's Narrative with Special Reference to His Parables," in *Society of Biblical Literature 1995 Seminar Papers*, ed. Eugene H. Lovering (Atlanta: Scholars Press, 1995).

kind of thinking and critique that we have come to call "postcolonial."[2]

Overman's efforts were followed by the underdeveloped observations of David Sim in his 1996 book, *Apocalyptic Eschatology in the Gospel of Matthew*, particularly in his interpretation of Matthew 24:27-31.[3] Along these lines Robert Mowery in 2002 published a brief but important study on the *Son of God* phrase in Matthew, concluding that some of Matthew's readers would have understood it in direct relationship to the Roman imperial claim of divine sonship of the emperor.[4]

But the approach has been most thoroughly developed by Warren Carter. Carter's work on the Roman Empire and Matthew began with his 1998 SBL paper, "Toward an Imperial-Critical Reading of Matthew's Gospel."[5] He rounded off his early phase of work on Matthew and Empire with two books in the first two years of the twenty-first century: *Matthew and Empire: Initial Investigations* and a commentary *Matthew and the Margins*.[6] Since 1998, Carter has published no less than twenty journal articles, essays and books on the topic.[7]

---

[2]Christopher Bryan, *Render to Caesar: Jesus, the Early Church, and the Roman Superpower* (Oxford: Oxford University Press, 2005), p. 5, emphasis added.

[3]David Sim, *Apocalyptic Eschatology in the Gospel of Matthew* (Cambridge: Cambridge University Press, 1996); See also Warren Carter, "Are There Imperial Texts in the Class? Intertextual Eagles and Matthean Eschatology as 'Lights Out' Time for Imperial Rome (Matthew 24:27-31)," *Journal of Biblical Literature* 122, no. 3 (2003): 486.

[4]Robert Mowery, "Son of God in Roman Imperial Titles and Matthew," *Biblica* 83, no. 1 (2002).

[5]Warren Carter, "Toward an Imperial-Critical Reading of Matthew's Gospel," in *Society of Biblical Literature 1998 Seminar Papers Part One* (Atlanta: Scholars Press, 1998).

[6]Warren Carter, *Matthew and Empire: Initial Explorations* (Harrisburg: Trinity Press International, 2001); Carter, *Matthew and the Margins: A Sociopolitical and Religious Reading* (Sheffield: Sheffield Academic Press, 2000).

[7]Warren Carter, "Imperial Texts in the Class"; Carter, "Imperial-Critical Reading"; Carter, *Empire*; Carter, *Margins*; Carter, "Contested Claims: Roman Imperial Theology and Matthew's Gospel," *Biblical Theology Bulletin* 29, no. 2 (1999); Carter, "Paying the Tax to Rome as Subversive Praxis: Matthew 17.24-27," *Journal for the Study of the New Testament* 76 (1999); Carter, "'To save his people from their sins' (Matt 1:21): Rome's Empire and Matthew's Salvation as Sovereignty," in *Society of Biblical Literature 2000 Seminar Papers* (Atlanta: Scholars Press, 2000); Carter, "Resisting and Imitating the Empire: Imperial Paradigms in Two Matthean Parables," *Interpretation* 56, no. 3 (2002); Carter, "Vulnerable Power: The Roman Empire Challenged by the Early Christians," in *Handbook of Early Christianity: Social Science Approaches*, ed. Anthony Blasi, Jean Duhaime and Paul-Andre Turcotte (Walnut Creek, CA: AltaMira, 2002); Carter, *Matthew: Storyteller, Interpreter, Evangelist* (Peabody, MA: Hendrickson, 2004); Carter, "Matthew and the Gentiles: Individual Conversion and-or Systematic Transformation," *Journal for the Study of the New Testament* 26, no. 3 (2004); Carter, "Matthean Christology in Roman Imperial Key: Matthew 1.1," in *The Gospel of Matthew in its Roman Imperial Context*, ed. John Riches and David Sim (London: T & T Clark, 2005); Carter, "Matthew and Empire," *Union Seminary Quarterly Review* 59, no. 3 (2005); Carter, "Construc-

It appears that the fascination with Matthew and empire is a distinctively North American phenomenon, however. I found no continental or British scholars who either have paid much notice to Carter's work positively or negatively, or published independently on the topic. This fact is of course interesting and perhaps even significant. As Daniel Gurtner has recently noted, "Few have since advocated an anti-imperial polemic to the extent of Carter and Sim."[8] He further notes that statements about Matthew's comprehensive anti-imperial polemic have "largely passed from scholarly discussion."[9]

Given Carter's preeminence on the topic, this chapter will deal primarily with his work and particularly focus on his very recent publication "Matthew and Empire" in the book *Empire in the New Testament*. The essay provides a suitable entry into empire studies on Matthew because of its general focus. Based on Carter's essay, I will (1) sketch the methodological foundations of Carter's anti-Roman reading of Matthew, (2) summarize four key elements of Matthew's Gospel that reveal imperial resistance and negotiation, and (3) evaluate Carter's anti-Roman reading of Matthew.

If I may tip my hand here, I am sympathetic to Carter's interpretation of Matthew. This sympathy is largely because Carter's leading represents a significant improvement over Matthean scholarship's spiritualizing interpretations of themes and the tendency to inappropriately divide religion from

---

tions of Violence and Identities in Matthew's Gospel," in *Violence in the New Testament*, ed. Shelly Matthews and E. Leigh Gibson (London: T & T Clark, 2005); Carter, "Matthew's Gospel: An Anti-Imperial-Imperial Reading," *Concordia Theological Monthly* 34, no. 6 (2007); Carter, "Matthew's Gospel, Rome's Empire, and the Parable of the Mustard Seed (Mt 13:31-32)," in *Hermeneutik der Gleichnisse Jesu: Methodische Neuansätze zum Verstehen urchristlicher Parabeltexte*, ed. Ruben Zimmermann and Gabi Kern, *Wissenschaftliche Untersuchungen zum Neuen Testament* 231 (Tübingen: Mohr Siebeck, 2008); Carter, "Matthew Negotiates the Roman Empire," in *In the Shadow of Empire: Reclaiming the Bible as a History of Faithful Resistance*, ed. Richard Horsley (Louisville: Westminster John Knox, 2008); Carter, "Love as Societal Vision and Counter-Imperial Practice in Matthew 22.34-40," in *Biblical Interpretation in Early Christian Gospels*, vol. 2, *The Gospel of Matthew*, ed. Thomas R. Hatina, Library of New Testament Studies 310 (London: T & T Clark, 2008); Carter, "Matthew and Empire," in *Empire in the New Testament*, ed. Stanley Porter and Cynthia Long Westfall, McMaster New Testament Studies Series (Eugene, OR: Pickwick, 2011); Carter, "God as 'Father' in Matthew: Imperial Intersections," in *Finding A Woman's Place: Essays in Honor of Carolyn Osiek*, ed. David L. Balch and Jason T. Lamoreaux (Eugene, OR: Pickwick, 2011).

[8]Daniel Gurtner, "The Gospel of Matthew from Stanton to Present: A Survey of some Recent Developments," in *Jesus, Matthew's Gospel, and Early Christianity: Studies in Memory of Graham N. Stanton*, ed. Daniel M. Gurtner, Joel Willitts and Richard A. Burridge, Library of New Testament Studies 435 (London: T & T Clark, 2011), p. 33.

[9]Ibid.

other elements of life such as politics, economics and culture.[10] Moreover, I can agree with Carter that Matthew is anti-Rome.[11] But where I part with him is that I believe Matthew's political vision is not reducible to a single anti-Roman interest. And Carter's nearsighted interpretive impulses lead him to overreach in his exegesis.

Matthew's genealogy with its three pivot points suggests that Matthew was *not* preoccupied with Rome, which amounted to simply the latest representation (in a long line) of satanic political powers that dominated Israel since the Babylonian captivity (Mt 1:12, 17). Matthew was interested in the much more *expansive* message of the coming of the empire of God (Mt 3:2; 4:17; 10:7). In view of this central Matthean concern, I don't think Matthew is anti-imperial at all. Matthew's problem with empire, if one can even put it that way, was *not* empire per se, but *which* empire.

Any discernible critique of empire in Matthew cannot be disconnected, then, from the fundamental claim that with Jesus, God is establishing his long-awaited kingdom, the kingdom of Israel, a kingdom, once established, that will exhibit the justice, mercy and faithfulness one would have expected of a fully Torah-observant realm. Thus, far from an empireless "alternative" society, as Carter labels it, Matthew envisioned the renewed and perfected kingdom of Israel, the coming of the society that finally expressed the fullness of Israel's potential shaped by Torah. Thus if Matthew is perceived as anti-imperial, it is because any alternative empire is *not* the Messiah's, not because it is an empire.

METHODOLOGICAL FOUNDATIONS

In the first paragraph of his chapter on Matthew and empire, Carter states clearly his conviction that the Roman Empire is *central* to the story of Jesus Matthew tells:

> My argument is that the Roman Empire comprises not the New Testament background but its foreground. Matthew and Mark are works of imperial negotiation. They tell the story of Jesus crucified by the Empire because he challenges its power, yet he is raised by God thereby revealing the limits of Roman power and the sovereign power of God. They negotiate Rome's power through a self-protective yet contestive approach that

[10]See Bryan's comment, "The attempt to suggest a division here between 'religious' and the 'political' is entirely unhistorical" (Bryan, *Render to Caesar*, p. 27).
[11]See ibid., p. 9, for a similar take on Jesus and early Christianity's view of Rome.

offers a (largely) alternative (though in part also imitative) worldview and social experience lived out in the practices of the community of Jesus' followers (ecclesiology).[12]

How did he come to this conviction? Contemporary cultural shifts and the new methods that take shape as a result go a long way in explaining the genesis of new departures in biblical interpretation. Carter has used a method referred to as "cultural intertextuality" that combines new methodologies with older approaches. The employment of this approach exposed the imperial interests of Matthew. Carter defines cultural intertextuality, drawing on the work of other scholars, as the task of "locating [a] text within (the text of) society and history."[13] It is the task of the reader of Matthew to place the text "within the general text (culture) of which [they are] a part and which is in turn part of [them]."[14] Thus, abstract ideas such as society and history are viewed figuratively as "texts" that must be considered in the interpretation of Matthew.

While background studies in the history and culture of a biblical text have been the fabric of biblical interpretation, cultural intertextuality, at least the way Carter employs it, represents an integrated, multidisciplinary approach consisting of (1) historical studies, (2) classical and archaeological studies, (3) social-scientific models of empire, (4) cultural anthropological models of power negotiation by nonelites in a society like Rome's, (5) postcolonial criticism and (6) literary criticism. One can see that the approaches of 3-6 have only come into their own in recent decades. This fact underscores the recent emergence of anti-empire interpretations of Matthew.

So how does this cultural intertextuality work?

First, the historical, classical and archaeological evidence is culled for information. Yet often this data is fragmentary at best. Material evidence from archaeology is very limited and the ancient literary evidence is one-sided, tilted toward an elite minority in society. Still, Carter notes the evidence from these sources overwhelmingly reveals the pervasive presence of the Roman Empire in the provinces of Judea and Syria from where Matthew's Gospel likely emerged.

Supporting and complementing this evidence, Carter has applied social-scientific models to the Roman Empire. Where evidence is scarce, such

---

[12]Carter, "Matthew and Empire," p. 90.
[13]Ibid., p. 92.
[14]Ibid.

models help the interpreter to envision life in societies where there are vast sociocultural distances between the elites and the peasants. Based on these models it is estimated that only 1-3 percent of the population controlled the power and wealth and status, leaving 97 percent of the population relatively powerless and impoverished.[15] The models also show that the empire was hierarchically structured with little to no opportunity for economic advancement. Rome exercised its control through political, economic, social, military and religious power.

In addition, cultural anthropology reveals that subjected peoples resist oppressive regimes in a variety of ways. Most prevalent is not open and violent resistance, but rather covert, self-protective political protest. The latter represents disguised forms of resistance to domination. Carter points out that these "hidden transcripts" of resistance "expose the inadequacies of the view that since Jesus did not advocate open revolt, the gospel story is 'apolitical' or 'pre-political' or 'politically indifferent' or 'spiritual.'"[16] Instead, by exposing the limits of Roman power through the story of a crucified but raised-by-God central character, Matthew's Gospel "is a hidden transcript that contests the public transcript or elite, 'official,' normalizing view of reality."[17]

> Jesus exemplifies the politics of disguise and anonymity, notably through his proclamation and demonstration of the rumor of God's imminent removal of Rome's world and establishment of God's empire.[18]

Finally, to this conglomeration of methods Carter adds the approach of postcolonial criticism. This approach has become fashionable in the last decade of the twentieth- and early-twenty-first centuries. According to R. S. Sugirtharajah, one of the leading lights of the approach, postcolonial criticism concentrates on the "politics, culture, and economics of the colonial milieu out of which the texts emerged"; it is about "unveiling biblical and modern empires and their impact."[19] Thus, in Carter's words, "postcolonial studies unmask the complex experiences, dynamics, strategies, impact, and legacy of imperial power—political, economic, societal, cultural, religious, military—on the minds, bodies,

---

[15]Ibid., p. 94.
[16]Ibid., p. 99.
[17]Ibid.
[18]Ibid.
[19]Sugirtharajah, *Exploring Postcolonial Biblical Criticism: History, Method, Practice* (Malden, MA: Wiley-Blackwell, 2012), pp. 2-3.

resources, societal interactions, cultural expressions, institutions, media, the past and the future, etc."

For Carter, the pay dirt of a postcolonial approach is the framing of Matthew's Gospel as a "resistant discourse that contests dominant scholarly views of Rome's empire."[20]

These methods, it should be noted, relate to elements of the interpretation of Matthew that are *outside* the text of Matthew. It is only with the final method of literary criticism that the text of Matthew is placed in relation to the evidence garnered from these other methods. This of course is the most important step where the multifaceted reading strategy delivers its results in the interpretation of the Matthean text.

Let's pause here to make two observations about methodology. First, not all the evidence gleaned in this interdisciplinary approach carries the same weight. While archaeological and literary evidence from ancient sources can be dated with relative accuracy, there are clearly problems in the application to ancient empires, such as Rome, of recently invented comparative methods from the social sciences, cultural anthropology and postcolonial criticism.[21]

Second, even if evidence from these methods stands up under critical scrutiny, it cannot be automatically assumed that the information is applicable for interpreting Matthew's Gospel. Carter does not seem to be critical enough of his employment of the information drawn from his interdisciplinary methods. Carter's interpretation of Matthew as anti-Roman, to a great degree, is the result of a very simple assumption that can be put skeptically: *Because Rome was big and bad, Matthew certainly addressed it.* And Sim approvingly summarizes just this view in his comment:

> According to Carter, Roman imperialism was such a dominant reality in the daily lives of all those who lived within the empire that *it must have made some impression on the evangelist and his intended readers. . . .* Carter argues that since Roman power and authority were an everyday reality in the lives of the evangelist and his community, we would expect that their views about Rome would be given expression in the Gospel.[22]

---

[20]Carter, "Matthew and Empire," p. 101.

[21]See, e.g., the criticism of Bryan, *Render to Caesar*, pp. 112-23.

[22]David Sim, "Rome in Matthew's Eschatology," in *The Gospel of Matthew in Its Roman Imperial Context*, ed. John Riches and David Sim (New York: T & T Clark International, 2005), p. 92, emphasis added.

While it seems beyond doubt that Rome's power was pervasive in Matthew's cultural world, that Matthew's story about Jesus was concerned *primarily* with Roman imperial power certainly is not. The Gospel must be read if such an assumption is to be adjudicated. It is this that Carter's next section of the chapter "Matthew and Empire" is concerned to show.

KEY INTERPRETIVE ELEMENTS

Carter uses four elements of Matthew's Gospel to show its anti-Roman emphasis: plot, Christology, eschatology and ecclesiology. I will briefly sketch his interpretation of each of these topics as examples of Matthew's negotiation of the Roman Empire.

Matthew's plot. Carter's construal of Matthew's plot as a "means of imperial negotiation" begins with the end. He writes, "I will be guided by Aristotle's focus on the end as a consequence of the sequence of events. The plot ends with the resurrection of the crucified Jesus; its central dynamic comprises conflict between Jesus and the Rome-allied Jerusalem leaders."[23]

Notice should be taken of two important aspects of his statement as it relates to how he understands Matthew's plot. First, Carter construes the point of the resurrection, the so-called "end" of the Gospel, to be a revelation of the limits of Rome's power: "Jesus' resurrection is the plot's final scene in which God's sovereignty and Rome's limited power are revealed."[24] With the resurrection of Jesus, Matthew creates a "hidden transcript" (here Carter is employing cultural anthropology) that shows the ultimate end of Roman imperial power.

Notice too that for Carter the central issue is *not* Judaism's leaders but the Roman power *behind* them, which is propping up these puppets. For Carter every one of Jesus' enemies in the story Matthew tells, Herod the Great and his sons, Archelaus and Antipas; scribes; high priests; Pharisees; Sadducees; and of course Pilate, are *Rome incarnate*. Carter's view is informed by the Roman practice of ruling provinces through alliances with local elites (here he is using history and archaeology, social-scientific models). So the mere mention of Herod or Pharisees, for Carter, is actually a reference indirectly to Rome. For example, consider these statements:

---

[23]Carter, "Matthew and Empire," pp. 102-3.
[24]Ibid., p. 112.

- "Herod is the face of imperial power."[25]

- "Like Mark, Matthew presents these leaders as constituting an alliance of chief priests, scribes, Pharisees, and Sadducees who are primarily Jerusalem-based allies of Rome."[26]

Matthew's sustained criticism throughout the Gospel of the inadequacies and exploitative authority of Israel's leaders is *not* really a statement about Israel's leaders, as it turns out, but of Roman imperial order. Carter states, "the Jerusalem leaders allied with Rome enforce a society contrary to God's purposes. Their rule is illegitimate; their days are numbered."[27] In an earlier essay, Carter sums up the theme of Matthew's plot as "The Roman Empire under God's judgment." According to Carter, through the unfolding narrative Matthew asserts that Rome's rule is violent, exploitative, pervasively present in every sphere of the world, satanic, an instrument of judgment on Israel that will itself be judged, and ultimately limited.[28]

From start to finish, then, the story Matthew tells of Jesus' life, death and resurrection is the story of how God through his Messiah is overthrowing the imperial world of Rome. The story of the coming of the empire of God is *intentionally* told to subvert the story of Roman imperial propaganda.

Christology. Following literary-critical approaches to the study of Matthew's understanding of Jesus, Carter believes that Matthew presents his Christology through the characterization of Jesus exhibited in the unfolding plot. So one can see Jesus' character by observing his actions, words, attitudes and interactions. From this commonplace approach, Carter concludes that Matthew presents Jesus as God's agent "who manifests God's sovereignty, presence, will, and blessing among human beings."[29]

These points are widely recognized by Matthean scholars even if they would not list them exactly in this way. However, what Carter does with these literary observations is unique. Employing his cultural intertextuality approach, Carter asserts that these are central claims of imperial theology presented in the Roman propaganda of Matthew's day. Carter suggests that in presenting Jesus in this way, Matthew is mimicking Rome's claims, thereby contesting their validity.[30]

---

[25]Ibid., p. 103.
[26]Ibid.
[27]Ibid., p. 105.
[28]Carter, "Matthew Negotiates," pp. 118-27.
[29]Carter, "Matthew and Empire," p. 109.
[30]Ibid.

Matthew is making a counter assertion that it's not the Roman emperor who manifests God's true sovereignty, presence and will for the well-being of humanity, but Jesus.

Jesus, not Caesar, is acclaimed in Matthew to be the one alone who is God's agent of divine purposes. Jesus is the anointed one, the Christ, who is sent to save and usher in God's kingdom. Jesus, not Caesar, is the one who "manifests God's sovereignty over this world and its attendant blessings."[31] Jesus, not Caesar, is the manifestation of God's presence; he's Emmanuel, God with us. Jesus, not Caesar, manifests God's will and purposes in the world.

Conversely, the power animating Rome's sovereignty is the very opposite of God's; it, in fact, is Satan. Finally, Jesus, not Caesar, brings shalom to the earth: "Matthew presents Jesus as God's agent in manifesting God's blessing, and societal well-being" looks very different in God's empire than it does in Caesar's.[32]

In sum, imperial theology and Matthew's Christology, according to Carter, collide as the Gospel both protests and imitates imperial claims.

Eschatology. Matthew's eschatological vision is most clearly seen in his discourse in Matthew 24. Particularly clear is his presentation of the end-time battle at Jesus' return in verses 27-31. I quote the text here:

"For as lightning that comes from the east is visible even in the west, so will be the coming of the Son of Man. Wherever there is a carcass, there the vultures will gather.

"Immediately after the distress of those days

'the sun will be darkened,
and the moon will not give its light;
the stars will fall from the sky,
and the heavenly bodies will be shaken.'

"Then will appear the sign of the Son of Man in heaven. And then all the peoples of the earth will mourn when they see the Son of Man coming on the clouds of heaven, with power and great glory. And he will send his angels with a loud trumpet call, and they will gather his elect from the four winds, from one end of the heavens to the other." (Mt 24:27-31 NIV)

In contrast to *all* other interpreters and English translations, Carter translates the Greek term *aetoi* (vultures) of verse 28 as "eagles"; "eagle" is an al-

[31]Ibid., p. 110.
[32]Ibid., p. 112.

ternative translation for the Greek term. He then concludes that with the image of an eagle, Matthew is making a figurative connection to the Roman army whose legions carried the image of an eagle into battle. At the end-time battle Rome's army will be destroyed. "Matthew presents Jesus' return as the end of all empires, especially Rome's," while at the same time envisioning the establishment of God's everlasting dominion and kingship in their place.[33]

Ecclesiology. Carter believes that the Gospel's story of God's rule coming in and through Jesus established a "counter-cultural community" whose existence reflected an alternative worldview and set of societal practices. The alternative community, which was "embedded in and subordinate to the empire," was to embody God's reign as a protest against Rome's societal reality.[34] To this end, Carter contends, the "Gospel offers strategies, both self-protective and contestive, in which Matthew's people can negotiate imperial demands while maintaining allegiance to God's purposes manifested in Jesus."[35] Carter refers to these strategies as "in the meantime" practices. Among these practices are:

- nonviolent resistance (Mt 5:38-48)
- paying taxes as subversive protest (Mt 17.24-27, 22:15-22)
- humble leadership (Mt 20:25)
- egalitarian structure that challenges conventional, androcentric, patriarchal, patterns (Mt 19–20)
- embracing marginality and the place of the lowliest among the empire (Mt 20:26-28)
- avoiding the dangers of wealth and economic exploitation (Mt 6:24, 33-34; 13:19-22; 19:23, 24)
- contradicting the practices of the elite by advocating for the poor (Mt 19:21)
- doing mercy, justice, faithfulness (Mt 23:23)
- performing prayer, almsgiving and fasting (Mt 6:1-18)
- preaching, healing, raising the dead, cleansing lepers and casting out demons (Mt 10:7-8)

---

[33]Ibid., p. 113.
[34]Ibid., p. 114.
[35]Ibid.

- freedom from the anxiety of material goods (Mt 6:19-34)[36]

Carter summarizes, "Jesus' (counter)cultural formation involves a changed identity, societal orientation and economic activity. Acts of restitution and justice set right inequalities and transform unjust structures, relationships, and practices."[37] To put it simply, "this lifestyle focuses on love for neighbor as for oneself (22:39) and love for enemy in imitation of God's ways (5:45-48)."[38]

EVALUATION

So what do we make of this interpretive approach? As I hinted at the beginning of the chapter, the results are mixed. Carter and others have made a contribution, and a significant one at that. Focusing on Rome's imperial power places the focus of Matthew's message much more appropriately on the concrete and everyday-ish existence of life. The kingdom of God is not a purely spiritual reality—a reign of God in one's heart. The coming of the kingdom of God in the world has political implications. In addition, it is surely helpful to emphasize the pervasive presence of Roman imperial power, much of it domineering and oppressive, in the world of Jesus and the writer of the first Gospel several decades later.

But on the whole, and these contributions notwithstanding, this approach appears over a decade later not to be leaving much of a footprint on Matthean studies. I think this is for several reasons. One reason is postcolonial interpretation, for all its contemporary appeal, has not proven to be a very reliable method for interpreting ancient texts. Bryan for example rightly questions its application to the Roman Empire:

> How far can techniques of analysis that were developed in connection with the post-Enlightenment colonial—to be precise, *post*colonial—experience of cultures formerly subject to nineteenth- and twentieth-century Western domination be applied *at all* to the ancient, largely Mediterranean world of the Roman Empire?[39]

Bryan's answer is skeptical. While parallels do exist between the experience under Western colonialism and ancient imperialism, the results from the application of postcolonial criticism are of very limited usefulness for the

---

[36]This list is drawn from ibid., pp. 114-16. See also Carter, "Matthew Negotiates," pp. 128-36.
[37]Carter, "Matthew and Empire," p. 115.
[38]Ibid., p. 116.
[39]Bryan, *Render to Caesar*, p. 114.

interpretation of life under Roman imperialism because of the significant differences between the two.

Related to the first point is a second. Recent studies have shown the apparently deep ambivalence among Jewish and Christian writers about Rome. Peter Oakes has presented the spectrum of responses that ranged from awe to an expectation of its overthrow. What he notes concerning Mark is as true for Matthew:

> So many elements could be read in relation to Rome but the prominence of other issues makes one wonder whether many of these elements point another way. . . . Any book that can say "Give to Caesar the things that are Caesar's" cannot be wholly on the negative side of the equation in relation to Rome.[40]

Another reason for the lack of traction of anti-Roman imperial readings of Matthew is the quite apparent overreaching by advocates in their Rome-focused interpretations. While there are places in Matthew where a robust understanding of Roman presence is instructive—I think of the opening stories of Herod and Jesus—there are many places, where upon careful reflection, Carter's Rome-focused interpretations appear unconvincing. Here I'll reference two cases. First, very few Matthean scholars have been convinced by Carter's Rome-focused interpretation of *aetoi* mentioned earlier.[41] Second, both Carter and Sim are guilty of far too narrowly reducing the reference to "kingdoms of the world" in Matthew 4:8 to Rome.[42] The satanic temptation in Matthew 4:8-10, in which Satan offers Jesus all the "kingdoms of the world" if he'll only bow and worship him, obviously *includes* Rome. But the word is plural: "all the kingdoms" of the earth. This reference would no doubt have had to also include the kingdoms of the East such as Parthia.[43] What's more, there's almost a sense of timelessness to Satan's invitation in its apocalyptic flavor that gives it a transcendent feel.

---

[40]Peter Oakes, "A State of Tension: Rome in the New Testament," in *The Gospel of Matthew in Its Roman Imperial Context*, ed. John Riches and David Sim, Library of New Testament Studies 276 (London: T & T Clark, 2005), p. 85.

[41]See Sim, "Rome," p. 96, who has adopted Carter's interpretation.

[42]Ibid., p. 93.

[43]In this regard, one should note here the recent piece by J. Andrew Overman, "Between Rome and Parthia: Galilee and the Implications of Empire," in *A Wandering Galilean: Essays in Honour of Seán Freyne*, ed. Zuleika Rogers, Margaret Daly-Denton, and Anne Fitzpatrick-McKinley, *Journal for the Study of Judaism in the Persian, Hellenistic and Roman Periods* Supplement 132 (Leiden: Brill, 2009).

This fistful of considerations is significant, but in my view Carter's interpretation of Matthew as a piece of anti-Roman propaganda falls foul *primarily* in its lack of appreciation of Matthew's thoroughgoing Davidic messianism, that is, the belief that God's end-time purposes for Israel's kingdom would be realized through a new Davidic king who sits on God's throne ruling over the nations.

This weakness is best captured in these two lengthy passages from Carter's book *Matthew and Empire*. I include them because they are revealing:

> The bold vision of the completion of God's salvation and overthrow of Roman imperial power *co-opts and imitates* the very imperial worldview that it resists! For Rome and God, the goal is the supreme sovereignty of the most powerful. For both, the scope or extent of their sovereignty is the cosmos. Both appeal to the divine will for legitimation. Both understand the establishment of their sovereignty to be through a chosen agent and by means of the violent overthrow of all resistance. Both offer totalizing perspectives. Both demand compliance. Both destroy enemies without room for the different or the noncompliant. . . . The Gospel depicts God's salvation, the triumph of God's empire over all things including Rome, *with the language and symbols of imperial rule. . . . In the end, it seems, the Gospel cannot imagine a world without imperial power.* It cannot find an alternative to this sovereignty model of power. . . . *The imperial worldview is so pervasive that even this story of protest against imperial rule cannot escape its own cultural world.* It has no other language to use. As much as it resists and exposes injustice of Rome's rule, as much as it points to God's alternative community and order . . . *it cannot, finally, escape the imperial mindset.*[44]

• • •

> The alternative to Rome's rule is framed in imperial terms. Salvation comprises membership in a people that embodies, anticipates, and celebrates the violent and forcible establishment of God's loving sovereignty, God's empire, over all, including the destruction of oppressive governing powers like imperial Rome. The Gospel depicts God's salvation, the triumph of God's empire over all things including Rome, with the language and symbols of imperial rule. . . . We cannot be blind to the irony in Matthew's presentation of this eschatological hope. *It seems clear that*

---

[44]Carter, *Matthew and Empire*, pp. 89-90, emphasis added.

*in depicting the future violent and forceful imposition of God's empire
(13:41-42; 24:27-31), the Gospel has not lived up to its own critique.* The
Gospel has presented God's empire at work in the present world in terms
of mercy not violence (4:23-25), service not domination (20:25-28). In the
present, God's authority is exercised on behalf of the weak (chapters 8-9),
by servants (Jesus and disciples, 20:24-28) who seek the good of others.
Yet in presenting the final triumph of God's reign, the Gospel *resorts* to
the age-old imperial methods of domination and violence.[45]

In these passages Carter's assumption is that had Matthew known *better*
he would not have wanted to present God's kingdom in imperial terms. *For
Carter, Matthew couldn't get out of his own way.* But is it really true? Would
Matthew have wanted to present his story of God's kingdom differently *if* he
had only known better? Given Matthew's claim of Jesus' identity as the son
of David, Israel's Messiah, I think not.

While there is not space to pursue this criticism in any detail, the Jewish
Scriptures provided the *larger story* in which Matthew's story of Jesus fits. In
that Story the pagan superpowers who subjugated Israel (Assyria, Babylonia, Persia, Greece), were given such power by God himself *for the sake of
Israel.* The Story, a story that now from Matthew's perspective included
Rome, was pointing forward to God's vindication of his universal kingship
by the restoration of Israel's Davidic kingdom. And this time David's
kingdom, which is one and the same Israel's and God's kingdom, would be
worldwide (Amos 9:11-12; Zech 9:9-10; Ps 72).

Perhaps D. Michael Cox said it best:

According to Carter, the vision of God's kingdom remains derivative, presenting, at best, a reactionary critique of empire. The problem with this
perspective is that it presumes that the empire is the only constellation of
imaginative resources upon which the Gospel writer draws. As the more
conventional reading of Matthew reminds us, however, the Gospel clearly
stands in the Jewish tradition. Therefore, when Jesus announces the
kingdom of God, it cannot simply be heard as the inverse or the negative
image of the Roman empire. Far from being wholly parasitic on Rome,
the Gospel draws on the Jewish tradition of understanding Israel as the
basileia tou theou, undermining Carter's thesis that the kingdom was defined solely in terms of reactive counterviolence to Rome. Instead, the

---

[45]Ibid., pp. 171-76, emphasis added.

Gospel's conception of the kingdom is informed by the story of Israel.[46]

In sum, it may be the case that if a Roman political leader had taken the time to read and study the text of Matthew he would have perceived that its message and vision of the society of God's kingdom stood opposed to his own. He may have perceived, had he carefully reflected on the story, the Roman Empire was not on the right side of the God of Israel. He may have heard, perhaps for the first time, that his empire was under the dominion not ultimately of a god but of *the* God's (the God of Israel) adversary, who was destined for judgment in eternal fire (Mt 25:46).

This hypothetical Roman imperial official may have come to see that the Gospel of Matthew asserted that Rome's days were numbered (Mt 24:29-31). That the time of Israel's exile (Mt 1:17) had come to its end, and they, like Greece, Persia, Babylonia and Assyria before them, would face God's judgment, and this in spite of being a tool in God's hands for the sake of his people. This Roman imperial official, had he made the effort to read the Gospel and understand it, had he taken it seriously, may have had a similar reaction to this news as Herod's to the news of the birth of Jesus. *He may have perceived the threat of God's Messiah.*

While this seems quite possible to me, it is entirely another thing to say, as Carter and other advocates of this approach do, that Matthew's *purpose* in his gospeling, in his writing down the story of Jesus, was to oppose Rome. Matthew was hailing the coming of Israel's Davidic Messiah and announcing the concomitant restoration of the kingdom of Israel. To the extent that Israel's restoration would have been a frontal assault on *any* earthly kingdom, Matthew's Gospel opposed Rome. But, and this is the significant point, Matthew was neither critiquing "empire" per se nor singling out Rome uniquely. To take this view would be to inappropriately diminish Matthew's message. Jesus is not *only* or *primarily* God's answer to Rome. *Jesus is God's answer to Israel's unfulfilled story.* A story, as it turns out, not only about Israel. It is a story that encompasses *all* the kingdoms and nations of the world (Mt 4:8; 28:19-20).

BIBLIOGRAPHY

Bryan, Christopher. *Render to Caesar: Jesus, the Early Church, and the Roman Superpower.* Oxford: Oxford University Press, 2005.

Carter, Warren. "Are There Imperial Texts in the Class? Intertextual Eagles

---

[46]D. Michael Cox, "The Gospel of Matthew and Resisting Imperial Theology," *Perspectives in Religious Studies* 36, no. 1 (2009): 47.

and Matthean Eschatology as 'Lights Out' Time for Imperial Rome
(Matthew 24:27-31)." *Journal of Biblical Literature* 122, no. 3 (2003): 467-87.

_____. "Constructions of Violence and Identities in Matthew's Gospel."
In *Violence in the New Testament*, 81-108. Edited by Shelly Matthews and E.
Leigh Gibson. London: T & T Clark, 2005.

_____. "Contested Claims: Roman Imperial Theology and Matthew's
Gospel." *Biblical Theology Bulletin* 29, no. 2 (1999): 56-67.

_____. "God as 'Father' in Matthew: Imperial Intersections." In *Finding
A Woman's Place: Essays in Honor of Carolyn Osiek*, 81-102. Edited by David
L. Balch and Jason T. Lamoreaux. Eugene, OR: Pickwick, 2011.

_____. "Love as Societal Vision and Counter-Imperial Practice in
Matthew 22.34-40." In *Biblical Interpretation in Early Christian Gospels*.
Vol. 2, *The Gospel of Matthew*, 30-44. Edited by Thomas R. Hatina. Library
of New Testament Studies 310. London: T & T Clark, 2008.

_____. "Matthean Christology in Roman Imperial Key: Matthew 1.1." In
The Gospel of Matthew in its Roman Imperial Context, 143-65. Edited by
John Riches and David C. Sim. London; New York: T & T Clark, 2005.

_____. "Matthew and Empire." *Union Seminary Quarterly Review* 59,
no. 3 (2005): 85-91.

_____. "Matthew and Empire." In *Empire in the New Testament*, 90-119.
Edited by Stanley Porter and Cynthia Long Westfall. McMaster New Testament Studies Series. Eugene, OR: Pickwick, 2011.

_____. *Matthew and Empire: Initial Explorations*. Harrisburg: Trinity
Press International, 2001.

_____. "Matthew and the Gentiles: Individual Conversion and-or Sys-
tematic Transformation." *Journal for the Study of the New Testament* 26, no.
3 (2004): 259-82.

_____. *Matthew and the Margins: A Sociopolitical and Religious Reading*.
Sheffield: Sheffield Academic Press, 2000.

_____. "Matthew Negotiates the Roman Empire." In *In the Shadow of
Empire: Reclaiming the Bible as a History of Faithful Resistance*, 117-36.
Edited by Richard A. Horsley. Louisville: Westminster John Knox, 2008.

_____. "Matthew's Gospel: An Anti-imperial–Imperial Reading." *Con-
cordia Theological Monthly* 34, no. 6 (2007): 424-33.

_____. "Matthew's Gospel, Rome's Empire, and the Parable of the
Mustard Seed (Mt 13:31-32)." In *Hermeneutik der Gleichnisse Jesu: Methodische Neuansätze zum Verstehen urchristlicher Parabeltexte*, 181-201.

Edited by Ruben Zimmermann and Gabi Kern. Wissenschaftliche Untersuchungen zum Neuen Testament 231. Tübingen: Mohr Siebeck, 2008.

_____. *Matthew: Storyteller, Interpreter, Evangelist.* Rev. ed. Peabody, MA: Hendrickson, 2004.

_____. "Paying the Tax to Rome as Subversive Praxis: Matthew 17.24-27." *Journal for the Study of the New Testament* 76 (1999): 3-31.

_____. "Resisting and Imitating the Empire: Imperial Paradigms in Two Matthean Parables." *Interpretation* 56, no. 3 (2002): 260-72.

_____. "'To save his people from their sins' (Matt 1:21): Rome's Empire and Matthew's Salvation as Sovereignty." In *Society of Biblical Literature 2000 Seminar Papers*, 379-401. Atlanta: Scholars Press, 2000.

_____. "Toward an Imperial-Critical Reading of Matthew's Gospel." In *Society of Biblical Literature 1998 Seminar Papers Part One*, 296-324. Atlanta: Scholars Press, 1998.

_____. "Vulnerable Power: The Roman Empire Challenged by the Early Christians." In *Handbook of Early Christianity: Social Science Approaches*, 453-88. Edited by Anthony J. Blasi, Jean Duhaime and Paul-Andre Turcotte. Walnut Creek, CA: AltaMira, 2002.

Cox, D. Michael. "The Gospel of Matthew and Resisting Imperial Theology." *Perspectives in Religious Studies* 36, no. 1 (2009): 25-48.

Gurtner, Daniel M. "The Gospel of Matthew from Stanton to Present: A Survey of Some Recent Developments." In *Jesus, Matthew's Gospel, and Early Christianity: Studies in Memory of Graham N. Stanton*, 23-38. Edited by Daniel M. Gurtner, Joel Willitts and Richard A. Burridge. Library of New Testament Studies 435. London: T & T Clark, 2011.

Mowery, Robert L. "Son of God in Roman Imperial Titles and Matthew." *Biblica* 83, no. 1 (2002): 100-110.

Oakes, Peter. "A State of Tension: Rome in the New Testament." In *The Gospel of Matthew in its Roman Imperial Context*, 75-90. Edited by John Riches and David C. Sim. Library of New Testament Studies 276. London: T & T Clark, 2005.

Overman, J. Andrew. "Between Rome and Parthia; Galilee and the Implications of Empire." In *A Wandering Galilean: Essays in Honour of Seán Freyne*, 279-99. Edited by Zuleika Rogers, Margaret Daly-Denton and Anne Fitzpatrick McKinley. *Journal for the Study of Judaism in the Persian, Hellenistic and Roman Periods Supplement* 132. Leiden: Brill, 2009.

_____. "Matthew's Parables and Roman Politics: The Imperial Setting of Matthew's Narrative with Special Reference to His Parables." In *Society of Biblical Literature 1995 Seminar Papers*, 425-39. Edited by Eugene H. Lovering Jr. Atlanta: Scholars Press, 1995.

Sim, David C. *Apocalyptic Eschatology in the Gospel of Matthew*. Society for New Testament Studies Monograph Series. Cambridge: Cambridge University Press, 1996.

_____. "Rome in Matthew's Eschatology." In *The Gospel of Matthew in its Roman Imperial Context*, 91-106. Edited by John Riches and David C. Sim. New York: T & T Clark International, 2005.

Sugirtharajah, R. S. *Exploring Postcolonial Biblical Criticism: History, Method, Practice*. Malden, MA: Wiley-Blackwell, 2012.

4

The Gospel of Luke
and the Roman Empire

Dean Pinter

My youngest son, Carl, wants to be a Roman archaeologist. It was no surprise that when he finished his chemotherapy for leukemia in 2010 and was granted a "wish" by a charitable foundation, his choice was to visit the ancient sites of Rome and Ostia Antica. He was not disappointed; Rome is impressive! Even after centuries of decay, the power projections of the Roman Empire continue to be visually stunning. The architecture was meant to impress upon all who visited that the Romans were the "lords of the earth." They believed that their legions were braver, their emperors smarter and their gods more powerful than any other known nation. Two of the most iconic structures in Rome are specifically aimed at portraying victory over the Jewish people and their God: the Arch of Titus and the great Flavian Amphitheater, the Coliseum. Titus's Arch commemorates the victory over the Jews in AD 70 by depicting their defeated citizens and sacred articles from their temple in triumphal procession. But the real visual spectacle is the Coliseum, funded by the spoils of the Jewish War, which can be viewed, intentionally, through the triumphal arch.

Of course, one did not have to be in Rome to view imperial projections of power or to be exposed to the worship offered by the imperial cult to the emperor. There is hardly a location mentioned in the narrative of Luke or

Acts that would not bear the marks of divine exaltation of the emperor. In short, it would be virtually impossible for those living in the first-century Roman Empire to avoid the projections and pretentions of that empire. S. R. F. Price notes that "Travellers in the empire would not have been surprised to meet the cult wherever they went: they would have found the cult located both in local communities and in the associations formed of these communities in particular Roman provinces."[1] This chapter is concerned with addressing how the Gospel of Luke perceives and negotiates the reality of the Roman Empire. Two questions will preoccupy us. First, does the Gospel of Luke employ language or themes that evoke imperial authorities? Second, does this invocation indicate an antagonism or rivalry toward the Roman Empire in general or Caesar in particular?

It is worth recognizing the difficulty that comes with this kind of historical investigation. Consider the Gospel's named addressee: "most excellent Theophilus" (Lk 1:3; cf. Acts 1:1). In spite of the tradition that Luke, an associate of the apostle Paul, is the author of the Gospel, modern scholarship cannot agree on *who* wrote it.[2] The same story is almost true concerning the recipient(s). Though addressed to "most excellent Theophilus," we have no firm indication *when* it was written, *where* Theophilus was residing or *what* community (if any!) he was associated with. These are important details, especially with respect to the imperial cult, because circumstances varied under the reigns of different emperors and even in different locations throughout the empire. One helpful way of placing the Gospel of Luke meaningfully within the discussion of empire relations would be to draw in another first-century writer who is culturally engaged with the Roman world as a comparative foil. The need for this kind of comparison is plain. To assess the possible ways in which people in the Jewish tradition express religious differences with the imperial cult we should know how they could talk about the Roman Empire and emperor. Did they have to set God and the emperor in antithesis? Did historical events color their views, and if so, how? Without points of comparison, we risk misreading or overreading the evidence in Luke.

Thankfully an excellent candidate for comparing with Luke is available in the Jewish historian T. Flavius Josephus. We know much more about Jo-

---

[1] S. R. F. Price, *Rituals and Power: The Roman Imperial Cult in Asia Minor* (Cambridge: Cambridge University Press, 1984), pp. 2-3.

[2] For the purposes of this chapter, I will simply refer to the unnamed author of the Gospel as "Luke."

sephus than about the author of the Gospel. He is commonly known as the Jewish general who betrayed his own people shortly after the onset of the Jewish War in AD 66. At the conclusion of the war he settled into emperor Vespasian's former private residence in Rome, where he set out to write about the Jewish War. Sometime between AD 75-79 Josephus completed his first work, the *Jewish War*, before going on to write three more works (*Jewish Antiquities*, *Life*, and *Against Apion*).

There are several good reasons for employing Josephus as a foil of comparison with Luke. First, there are a number of similarities between the two authors, both in the narrative form of their writings and the content of their work. Both wrote what can broadly be described as Hellenistic histories, adopting the forms of this genre (e.g., a structured prologue, historical date markers, set speeches for leading characters), they both wrote sequels to their first volumes (the *Antiquities* and Acts respectively), and they both mention a remarkable number of similar events (e.g., the importance of the census under Quirinius in *War* 2.117-118, *Antiquities* 18.1-5 and Lk 2:1-3; the specific discussion of the Jewish rebels: Theudas [*Antiquities* 20.97 and Acts 5:36], Judas the Galilean [*Antiquities* 20.102 and Acts 5:37], and the Egyptian Prophet [*War* 2.261-3 and Acts 21:38]).

More importantly, both Josephus and Luke wrote from the margins of society to help shape the identity of the communities to which they wrote. In Josephus's case, even though he enjoyed some benefits of patronage from the emperors Vespasian and Titus, he still believed he was a committed Jew. As a Jew, he was desperate to set the record straight about the Jewish War in the face of inaccurate accounts and to reinforce the shape of a Jewish identity in postwar Rome. In the mid-70s, the new Flavian dynasty used the Jewish War in their propaganda machine to validate and promote their imperial claims. Most Romans, like the well-known historian Tacitus, regarded the Jews and their unique practices as quaint and "sanctioned by their antiquity" at best, or "sinister and revolting" at worst (*The Histories* 5.5). After the war, with their beloved temple destroyed and Jewish spoils used to construct the Coliseum, every Jew in the empire was required to pay a special tax for the building of Roman shrines. The deep humility of this tax is that it was deliberately established to replace the annual half-shekel tax paid by adult Jewish men for the maintenance of the Jewish temple. Josephus wrote in part to legitimate his faith and sustain his people in the midst of these difficult days. Luke's community faced similar difficulties and in some ways even worse circumstances. While the Romans disdained the Jews for their "barbaric superstition" (Cicero, *Pro Flacco* 67), the Christians in the late first century were doubly disdained. They not only reflected many of the peculiar characteristics and "antisocial" behavior of Judaism, they also were *new* and lacked even the "sanction of antiquity." For Luke the challenge was not simply one of maintaining an identity in the face of imperial pretensions but of forming a Christian identity for Theophilus and those who would be transformed by the story of the crucified Lord Jesus.

In short, both Josephus and Luke knew that the military might of Rome had been meted against subjects at the center of their respective theological worlds: Roman armies devastated Jerusalem and destroyed Josephus's temple; Roman soldiers tortured and crucified Luke's Christ. There are strong grounds here to compare their views of the relationship between God and imperial authorities. The more we can set Luke in context with comparable writers of his day the more we can see where his distinctive view protrudes. Josephus, like Luke, rooted in Jewish tradition and speaking from the margins of Roman society, is a perfect foil.

DOES THE GOSPEL OF LUKE EVOKE IMPERIAL AUTHORITIES?

How, if at all, does the Gospel of Luke evoke imperial authorities in his language and narrative themes? Noticeably absent is any direct mention of the imperial cult, but there is frequent mention of Roman officials—especially so if one takes into account Luke's second volume in Acts. But limiting our focus to the Gospel, it is apparent that Luke's portrait of these officials is mixed. There are positive encounters with imperial agents: tax collectors and soldiers respond to John the Baptist's call to repentance (Lk 3:1-10); a centurion from Capernaum expresses "great faith" in Jesus (Lk 7:1-10); and Zacchaeus, "the chief tax collector" in Jericho, exhibits actions befitting a son of Abraham (Lk 19:1-9). There are also negative encounters: Herod Antipas ("that fox"), the client-tetrarch for the Romans, imprisons (Lk 3:19-20) and beheads (Lk 9:7-9) John the Baptist; Jesus predicts that Jerusalem will be destroyed by Roman armies (Lk 21:20, 24); and Governor Pilate is ambiguously portrayed as brutal toward the Galileans (Lk 13:1), clement toward Jesus (exonerating him three times, see Lk 23:3, 14, 22), and easily manipulated by Jewish chief priests and rulers (Lk 23:24-25).

Strikingly, Luke is the only writer to mention a Caesar by name. In Luke 2:1 and Luke 3:1 he specifically mentions "Caesar Augustus" and "Tiberius

Caesar" along with other Roman officials. Some scholars (e.g., Paul Walaskay and Raymond Brown) view this as evidence that Luke has a positive view of the empire, while Allen Brent argues in the opposite direction. He concludes that Luke "wished to parallel the birth of Jesus with that of Augustus not simply as Emperor but as founder of the Imperial Cult, and thus to compare the religious claims made by the latter with his claims for the former."[3] We cannot be sure what Luke intends. On one level this may be simply the Evangelist's way of grounding the story of Jesus in history; yet Luke names these emperors and officials after a detailed birth narrative that emphasizes God bringing to fulfillment (Lk 1:1, 45) that which he has promised (Lk 1:45, 55, 73) and prepared in advance to do (Lk 1:17, 76). Augustus may issue his decrees, but God is providential and orchestrates history.

Providence or fate is a common theme in first-century imperial ideology, and by the time of the Flavians it was common to portray Roman rule of the world as the testament to the divine favor of the gods. This Roman opinion was vigorously promoted publicly in Roman poetry and prose as well as on Roman victory coins and columns. Josephus draws extensively on this motif of divine providence and it punctuates his narrative of the *War* at key junctures (e.g., *War* 4.622-29; 6.398-99, 411; 7.360). One of the clearest examples derives from a speech, with the author Josephus as the speaker addressing the besieged inhabitants of Jerusalem. He implores them to recognize that "it is evident from all sides that fortune has gone over to [the Romans], and God who went the round of the nations *now* rests sovereign power upon Italy. . . . God [is] on the Roman side" (*War* 5.367-8). Likening himself to the prophet Jeremiah, Josephus begs the Jewish people to acknowledge that God, their God, is using the Romans as his instruments to purge and punish the Jewish nation for their impiety (*War* 4.323; 6.109-10). Luke does not go nearly as far as Josephus in describing how God providentially works his purposes through Rome. Yet in light of the earlier affirmation of Mary ("He has brought down rulers from their thrones" [Lk 1:52 NIV]; cf. Acts 4:25-29), Luke would agree with Josephus that Roman power is dependent on and derivative from the sovereign Lord who directs history and distributes power.

---

[3]Allen Brent, "Luke-Acts and the Imperial Cult in Asia Minor," *Journal of Theological Studies* 48, no. 2 (1997): 431; compare with Paul W. Walaskay, *And So We Came to Rome: The Political Perspective of St. Luke*, Society for New Testament Studies Monograph Series 49 (Cambridge: Cambridge University Press, 1983), pp. 25-28, and Raymond Brown, *The Birth of the Messiah* (London: Geoffrey Chapman, 1993), pp. 415-16.

The mention of "sovereign Lord" alerts us to two further categories that Luke stresses about Jesus: Jesus is King, and Jesus is Lord. In the opening chapters the angel of the Lord announces, "the Lord God will give [Jesus] the *throne of his father David* . . . and . . . his *kingdom* will never end" (Lk 1:32-33, emphasis added) and "today in the town of David a Savior has been born to you; he is the *Messiah*, the *Lord*" (Lk 2:11, emphasis added). That early Christians confessed Jesus as their King and Lord is evident throughout the New Testament. However, as Kavin Rowe points out, "what has not been seen until recently is the degree to which Luke in particular systematically and with narrative artistry develops this confession in his Gospel."[4] Walton points out that "Jesus is referred to as 'king' by Luke more frequently than the other evangelists, not least in the birth narratives in reference to him 'reigning' (Lk 1:33) and the insertion of 'king' into the acclamation at the 'triumphal entry' (Lk 19:38)."[5] Further, in the trial of Jesus the charge leveled against him is that he "claims to be Messiah, a king" (Lk 23:2)—a charge that he does not deny. With respect to Luke's stress that Jesus is the "Lord" (Greek *kyrios*; for example, see Lk 2:10-11; 7:13; 10:39; 22:61; 24:34), Rowe is correct that

> it would be virtually impossible to overemphasize the importance κύριος [*kyrios*] has for Luke. . . . Luke uses κύριος roughly two hundred times in Luke-Acts, about one hundred in each book. . . . Luke is the only one of the (canonical) Gospel authors to use the absolute ὁ κύριος [*ho kyrios*/the Lord] consistently and expansively for Jesus in his earthly career (7.13, etc).[6]

Luke applies titles appropriately used of the God of Israel to Jesus, and important for the focus of this study the titles "king" and "lord" are also epithets for Caesar, as archaeological and inscriptional evidence makes clear. In the Roman world, sovereignty also implied (some connection to) divinity and the emperor was "worshiped" (as a god) alongside the Roman gods. Luke's emphasis of these titles for Jesus leads many to conclude that this would have led to a collision with the Roman Empire for the vast majority of Christians. Rowe insists that this clash was inevitable: "the Chris-

---

[4]C. Kavin Rowe, *World Upside Down: Reading Acts in the Graeco-Roman Age* (Oxford: Oxford University Press, 2009), p. 103.

[5]Steve Walton, "The State They Were In: Luke's View of the Roman Empire," in *Rome in the Bible and the Early Church*, ed. Peter Oakes (Grand Rapids: Baker, 2002), pp. 26-27.

[6]C. Kavin Rowe, "Luke-Acts and the Imperial Cult: A Way Through the Conundrum?" *Journal for the Study of the New Testament* 27, no. 3 (2005): 294-95.

tians have to deny what the Roman emperor has to be."[7] Craig Evans agrees: "from the accusations leveled against Jesus himself . . . it is clear that Jesus was perceived as king and rival to Caesar himself."[8] These assertions lead us to our next question: does the invocation of imperial authorities and the confession that Jesus is Lord and King indicate an antagonism or rivalry toward the Roman Empire in general or Caesar in particular?

DOES LUKE INDICATE ANTAGONISM OR RIVALRY TOWARD THE ROMAN EMPIRE?

If authors such as Luke and Josephus can openly write about the empire and the emperor, then this generates our second area of inquiry. Did they have to set God and the emperor in antithesis? Did the climactic event of the crucifixion of Jesus generate an antagonism or rivalry toward the empire from Luke? Again, Josephus provides assistance in contextualizing these questions. Josephus wrote *The Jewish War* in the mid-70s, while living under the roof and the patronage of the new emperor, Vespasian. When he completed the work, he presented a copy of the seven-book history to the emperor and his son Titus (*Life* 361-63; *Apion* 1.50-51). Throughout this time Vespasian and Titus used their military victories over the Jewish nation as propaganda to validate their dynasty. They had returned peace and stability to the empire and were rejuvenating the capital city with public buildings funded by the spoils of the war. Deploying the Jewish War in propaganda, the Flavians ensured that the Jewish people, their soldiers and their deity were represented as inferior, if not depraved in comparison to the superiority of Roman arms, military virtue and divine favor. The Jewish defeat served to solidify typical Roman perceptions that they were a nation that had conquered the world and that the greatest of all cities was Rome. Indeed, it was by the favor of the gods that the empire was sustained and enlarged. Needless to say, Josephus was required to write shrewdly in the face of these claims.

Yet for all the care Josephus took in writing his narrative of the Jewish War, he also "snarls sweetly" in the face of Roman propaganda.[9] He does so by

---

[7]Rowe, *World Upside Down*, p. 111.
[8]Craig A. Evans, "King Jesus and His Ambassadors: Empire and Luke-Acts," in *Empire in the New Testament*, ed. Stanley E. Porter and Cynthia Long Westfall (Eugene, OR: Pickwick, 2011), p. 125.
[9]A phrase borrowed from John M. G. Barclay, "Snarling Sweetly: Josephus on Images and Idolatry," in *Idolatry: False Worship in the Bible, Early Judaism and Christianity*, ed. S. C. Barton (London: T & T Clark), pp. 73-87.

carefully framing his narrative so as to show his Roman readers that not all Jews are seditious. He makes special mention of the Jews offering daily prayers and sacrifices in the temple for (not to) the emperor (*War* 2.197; cf. *Apion* 2.76-77) even in the face of poor Roman governance. He boldly names Roman officials, such as the procurators Pontius Pilate (*War* 2.169-175; *Antiquities* 18.55-87) and Gessius Florus (*War* 2.277; *Antiquities* 18.25; 20.253), who provided turbulent and sometimes disastrous oversight of Judea for years.

Josephus snarls further. He also demonstrates that although the Jews are under Roman dominion and were defeated, they are not cowed and vanquished. They are still an ancient and noble people whom God will one day restore. In short, his narrative critically pushes back against the dominant portrayal of the war and the Jews in Rome. He does this in a number of deliberate ways, but I will highlight only two. First, in the face of the claim that the "gods" (plural) favor Rome, he consistently speaks of the providence of "God" in the singular—even when Vespasian and Titus refer to divine favor. In so doing he makes the emperors appear to be good Jewish monotheists—the modern equivalent of putting a capital "G" on the word *God* in place of *gods*. Further, in a move that is most provocative, he portrays the emperor Titus as poor general in the war. While he does repeatedly underscore Titus's bravery on the battlefield, the picture he paints of him, as a *Roman* general and set against recognized standards of Roman generalship, is less than flattering. He describes Titus as repeatedly losing control of his men, regularly outwitted by Jewish stratagems and, worst of all, often recklessly leading the charge into battle himself. These points illustrate how one Jewish historian, even in the midst of considerable constraints, could and *did* "snarl sweetly" under the very noses of the Roman emperors.

Can Josephus help us to assess Luke's disposition toward the ideological claims of Caesar? Until recently the dominant view of scholars (e.g., Henry J. Cadbury, Hans Conzelmann and F. F. Bruce) is that Luke (and its sequel, Acts) offered an apology from the church to persuade Roman authorities that they were not a political threat. Of course, as Judith Diehl has sketched in the second chapter of this book, other views of Luke's political relationship to Rome have been offered more recently. Some explain that the Gospel of Luke offers guidance for Jesus' disciples living under Roman rule,[10] or that Luke "perhaps more than the other Gospel writers" declares

[10]See Richard J. Cassidy, *Society and Politics in the Acts of the Apostles* (Maryknoll, NY: Orbis, 1987), pp. 145-70.

Jesus as king in contrast to the emperor,[11] or that Luke is "singing in the reign" of the emperor and writing a carefully constructed "hidden transcript" countering the claims of Caesar.[12]

With Josephus's work helping frame the discussion, does Luke's frequent mention of Roman authorities imply an antagonism to the empire? To begin with, I think it is a mistake to envision conditions anywhere close to those experienced by Josephus that would demand Luke to write in coded language. The Roman Empire was not a police state with secret agents ready to intercept written communications of voluntary associations, religious communities or personal correspondence. Nonetheless, there is a recent surge among scholars to find coded language in the documents of the New Testament. In particular, a number of recent scholars appeal to the notion of "hidden transcripts," a phrase coined by James Scott in his work *Domination and the Arts of Resistance: Hidden Transcripts*. Scott's interesting book explores the way those who are socially or politically dominated form patterns of resistance by using "hidden transcripts." According to Scott, this hidden language refers to the offstage, inside and honest discourse of the weak when they are "beyond direct observation by powerholders."[13] This notion of insider, hidden transcripts has then been applied to various New Testament texts, including Luke, to illustrate that biblical writers also use coded language as a form of resistance to the Roman Empire. In my judgment this seems unlikely. The application of Scott's approach requires the documents to be *public* documents containing these hidden messages. Although we know very little about Luke's named recipient, "most excellent Theophilus," the Gospel is written as a *private* document and to an "insider" who is likely favorably disposed to the message of Jesus and his followers. If this is the case, there is no need for Luke to disguise his true intentions about the empire and Caesar. Yet even if the Gospel is not written for an insider audience, the sheer brazenness of Luke's assertion that Jesus is Lord and King uncovers the author as a rather poor code writer.

Second, if indeed Luke is free to write as he chooses, then it is surprising that he does not use this freedom to make any direct comments *against* the

---

[11]Evans, "King Jesus and His Ambassadors," p. 125.

[12]Warren Carter, "Singing in the Reign: Performing Luke's Songs and Negotiating the Roman Empire (Luke 1-2)," in *Luke-Acts and Empire: Essays in Honor of Robert L. Brawley*, ed. David Rhoads, David Esterline and Jae Won Lee (Eugene: Pickwick, 2011), p. 35.

[13]J. C. Scott, *Domination and the Arts of Resistance: Hidden Transcripts* (New Haven, CT: Yale University Press, 1990), pp. 4-5, 18, 25, 27.

empire. Luke does not even mention the imperial cult. While modern readers are often fixated on the role of the imperial cult, and some Jews were certainly concerned by it at various times and in various respects, Luke depicts no confrontation with it, and no Roman practicing it. Devoid of that, for Luke, the emperors can be vassals of the one true God. They can inadvertently bring about the Bethlehem birth of Jesus and, through their procurators, the fulfillment of the will of God in the death of Jesus. Either Luke is naive about the imperial cult and the pretensions of the emperor, or he can imagine that relationships with Rome can be developed by working around them.

Third, for all his numerous references to Jesus as Lord and King, Luke never creates a direct antithesis between Jesus and Caesar. These titles may have implied a challenge to Caesar but it is inappropriate to suggest that common vocabulary—even common political language like these terms can carry—signals a competitive relationship between those holding the same titles. Before Luke ever wrote his Gospel this was the case described in the Jewish writer Philo's *Embassy to Gaius*. In this document, as Philo leads Jewish opposition to Emperor Gaius's (a.k.a. Caligula) maniacal self-deification, he can simultaneously refer to God as the "benefactor of all" (*Embassy* 118), the "savior of Israel" (196), "the father and king of all" (3) as well as referring to individual emperors as "master" (271, 276, 290), "lord" (286, 356), "benefactor" (148-9) and "savior" (22). In other words, the relationship between two holders of the same title need not be antagonistic. It may simply be that one holder is subordinate to the other. In other words, overlap in terminology—even between divine and human possessors of the same title—need not signal a competitive relationship.

Finally, Luke seems capable of imagining, as Josephus largely does not, different kinds of power relationships at work in the life and ministry of Jesus than simply portraying the emperor and his agents as the "enemy." For example, Luke clearly portrays Jesus as the agent of liberation for his people. After Jesus' triumph over Satan in the wilderness, he returns to Galilee "in the power of the Spirit" to inaugurate his ministry, defined by the hopeful words of Isaiah describing Israel's restoration from exile (Lk 4:18-19; cf. Is 61:1-2; 58:6). His ministry is characterized by delivering those oppressed by demonic possession (Lk 4:31-37, 41; cf. Acts 10:38), healing the sick (Lk 4:38-44; 6:18-19), and restoring outcasts (e.g., the leprous [Lk 5:12-15]; "tax collectors and sinners" [Lk 15:1]). Luke distinctively highlights that Jesus does all this as the Lord. He is "Lord of the Sabbath" (Lk 6:5); Lord of demonic powers (Lk 10:17; cf. Lk 9:1); Lord over death (Lk 24:34); indeed, in the words of Peter in Acts 10:36, Jesus is "Lord of all."

While some may construe this lordship language as narrowly targeting the Caesars who did indeed assert that they were "Lord of all," Luke never explicitly draws this parallel or gives rhetorical clues that he creates a necessary antagonism between Jesus and Caesar. If anything, as Rowe rightly concludes,

> Jesus does not challenge Caesar's status as Lord, as if Jesus were somehow originally subordinate to Caesar in the order of being. The thought—at least in its Lukan form—is rather much more radical and striking: because of the nature of his claims, it is Caesar who is the rival; and what he rivals is the Lordship of God in the person of Jesus Christ.[14]

It appears that for Luke, Jesus' lordship and Caesar's lordship are categorically different. In particular, the lordship of Jesus is marked by humble service and sacrificial death. When he invites his disciples to follow his example, he reminds them that they are not to be like the "kings of the nations"—including Caesar, but certainly not limited to him—who "lord it over them" and exercise authority over them by calling themselves "benefactors." "Instead, the greatest among you should be like the youngest, and the one who rules like the one who serves. For who is greater, the one who is at the table or the one who serves? Is it not the one who is at the table? But I am among you as one who serves" (Lk 22:25-27). The antithesis is certainly mapped in contrast to an alternative "lordship" in terms of how it is exercised, but there is nothing to indicate that the alternative to Jesus is narrowly Caesar and the power he wields.

Luke, of all the Gospel writers, appears interested in developing themes of salvation that cover a broad social critique of power. Luke is interested in social inequalities and justice as demonstrated in his interest in portraying God as the advocate of the economically poor (Lk 1:51-53; 4:18; 6:20; 7:22; 14:12-14; 16:19-31); the marginalized (e.g., women like Elizabeth, Mary and Anna [cf. Lk 7:11-17; 7:36-50; 8:2-3; 10:38-42; 21:1-4; 23:27-31]; common laborers, like the shepherds around Bethlehem [Lk 2:10]; Samaritans [Lk 10:25-37; 17:11-19]); and "sinners" (a term used seventeen times in Luke in contrast with six occurrences in Mark and five in Matthew). Luke is interested in authority and how power is wielded as indicated in the opening

---

[14]Rowe, *World Upside Down*, p. 112.

songs of Mary (Lk 1:46-55; especially vv. 51-53) and Zechariah (Lk 1:67-79).

Luke is also interested in the complexities of politics, and his social critique can include the ways political power is wielded. Sometimes, like the Capernaum centurion (Lk 7:5) or chief tax collector Zacchaeus (Lk 19:8-9), the agents of imperial power are good and useful servants of God; at other times, they play a more ambiguous role. For example, while Luke refers to the destruction of Jerusalem more obviously with reference to armies than any other Gospel (compare Lk 21:20ff. with Mk 13:14 and Mt 24:15), he has no criticism of Rome for this cataclysmic event which he regards as the divine will. His categorizing Jerusalem's destruction as divine judgment is parallel to Josephus, but for very different reasons.

Roman political power comes to a particular focus in the governor Pontius Pilate amid the trial of Jesus. Luke seems to be at pains to make several points about Pilate. First, Pilate did not instigate the trial, he did not want Jesus' death and did not see anything in Jesus deserving of death—a point explicitly stated in Luke 23:22 (see also Lk 23:3, 14). Second, Pilate dismisses the political charges introduced by others (Lk 23:24). Finally, Pilate did not construe the question about Jesus being the "king of the *Jews*" as a threat to King Caesar; it was the Jewish leaders who did this. For Pilate the proclamation directed to Jesus is one of "King of the *Jews*" and not "King of the *Empire.*" The title "King of the Jews" may signal an upstart pretender to the local throne, but this is nothing like saying "here is another one claiming to be the emperor." Whatever else, Luke appears keen to show that Pilate is not guilty at the trial of Jesus, but as one who still plays a role in God's salvation purposes (cf. Acts 13:27-28). In the end, the climactic event of Jesus' trial, and ultimate crucifixion, does not necessarily induce a straightforward hostility to Rome.

Concluding Comments

The recent interest in the New Testament and empire studies raises a number of important questions and has helped us think of Luke beyond the simple longstanding category of "pro-empire." On the other hand, what this chapter has tried to indicate is that questions of empire should not set the primary agenda for reading the Gospel of Luke either. In particular, attempts at narrowly construing Luke as subversively anti-imperial do not account for the varied ways he portrays the relationship between imperial authorities and the Lord Jesus. The reality is more complex and more interesting than that. In the end, I think the implication that Luke draws an antagonistic, antithetical relationship between Lord Jesus and Lord Caesar seems to narrow the target too much against his broader interests of redemption, liberation and social critique of power. Further, it avoids the multiple kinds of hierarchies that he sees existing in the world, not least demonic powers. This is not to say that Luke is simply interested in a "spiritual" enemy: Luke is a political thinker, but the question is whether his primary polarity is between Jesus as Lord and Caesar as Lord. A more appropriate polarity could be construed this way: Luke is interested in social inequalities and how they are intertwined with demonic powers and their challenge against God's sovereignty in the larger cosmic battles. In the Gospel of Luke it is hard to demonstrate that the Roman Empire simply equals an "Evil Empire." As we have seen, despite being easily manipulated Pilate does not gleefully crucify Jesus, and even Roman centurions are open to Jesus. A similarly diverse picture emerges in Luke's companion volume, Acts. In Acts 10 the Roman centurion is open to the apostle Peter. Some Roman officials, like Gallio (Acts 18:17) and Felix (Acts 24:24-27), exhibit disdain or indifference toward the gospel, while Asiarchs can be friendly to Paul (Acts 19:31), and even a proconsul like Sergius Paulus can believe in the gospel (Acts 13:12).

All in all, Luke seems interested in demonstrating that even though Roman political agents often misunderstand them, neither Jesus nor his followers are dangerous or seditious, an opinion also held by the Roman historian Tacitus (*Annals* 15.44-45). Luke does not envision followers of Jesus in acute tension with the empire, as does the Apocalypse of John (Rev 18) or the Essene community (e.g., 1QM). Of course, Luke insists on the lordship of Jesus. But it is quite possible to say both that Caesar is "lord" and Jesus is "Lord of all"—the two for Luke, it seems, are not categorically on the same field of play. As long as the former does not impinge on the latter, one may honor and pray for the emperor (e.g., in Acts 10, Peter does not tell Cornelius that he can no longer serve as a Roman soldier—just that his allegiances are clear and his loves are ordered). Other Jews in the first century did this without whitewashing Rome and denying its regular abuses and ruthlessness. As we have seen from Josephus's own example (and Philo too), it is possible to affirm a certain loyalty to Rome, as his comments on the daily temple sacrifices for the emperor suggest, while simultaneously criticizing, albeit carefully, Roman propaganda about the Jewish War and the role of their gods, their legions and their general in this war. It is a complex relationship, but not impossible.

In the end, a clash between Roman authority and Christian confession of Jesus as Lord and King may always be a possibility, but it is striking that for much of early Christian history and for the vast majority of Christians in the Roman Empire this collision did not occur. Rather, Christians, as the Jews did before them, found ways of making a distinction between *honoring* and *praying* for the emperor and *worshiping* him beneath their ultimate commitment to their Lord. As this chapter has tried to demonstrate, the Roman emperor and his empire are impressive, and Jewish and Christian writers in the late first century could not—and did not—avoid reflecting on imperial dynamics of power. Josephus was almost overinterested in trying to comprehend and communicate how God could use pagan rulers to punish and purge his chosen people. As a near contemporary of Luke, he could write a history of the Jewish War from the residence of the emperor—and offer it to the emperor—that attempted to maintain a credible and noble identity for God's ancient people while also "snarling sweetly" in the face of the victorious Roman generals/emperors Vespasian and Titus. As for Luke, it should be clear that he is in some respects a political thinker, but the question is whether he understood the primary power polarity as existing between Jesus and Caesar. In my judgment, I think not. Next to Jesus "the Lord of all," Caesar is, at best, demoted to a subordinate role. Caesar is lord and king, *and* Jesus is "Lord of lords" and "King of kings."

BIBLIOGRAPHY

Brent, Allen. "Luke-Acts and the Imperial Cult in Asia Minor." In *Journal of Theological Studies* 48, no. 2 (1997).

Carter, Warren. "Singing in the Reign: Performing Luke's Songs and Negotiating the Roman Empire (Luke 1-2)." In *Luke-Acts and Empire: Essays in Honor of Robert L. Brawley.* Edited by David Rhoads, David Esterline and Jae Won Lee. Eugene, OR: Pickwick, 2011.

Cassidy, Richard J. *Jesus, Politics and Society: A Study of Luke's Gospel.* Maryknoll, NY: Orbis, 1983.

Evans, Craig A. "King Jesus and His Ambassadors: Empire and Luke-Acts." In *Empire in the New Testament.* Edited by Stanley E. Porter and Cynthia Long Westfall. Eugene, OR: Pickwick, 2011.

Kim, Seyoon. *Christ and Caesar: The Gospel and the Roman Empire in the Writings of Paul and Luke*. Grand Rapids: Eerdmans, 2008.

Lee, Jae Won. "Pilate and the Crucifixion of Jesus in Luke-Acts." In *Luke-Acts and Empire: Essays in Honor of Robert L. Brawley*. Edited by David Rhoads, David Esterline and Jae Won Lee. Eugene, OR: Pickwick, 2011.

Mason, Steve. *Josephus and the New Testament*. Peabody, MA: Hendrickson, 2003.

Rowe, C. Kavin. "Luke-Acts and the Imperial Cult: A Way Through the Conundrum?" *Journal for the Study of the New Testament* 27, no. 3 (2005).

_____. *World Upside Down: Reading Acts in the Graeco-Roman Age*. Oxford: Oxford University Press, 2009.

Walaskay, Paul W. *And So We Came to Rome: The Political Perspective of St. Luke*. Society for New Testament Studies Monograph Series 49. Cambridge: Cambridge University Press, 1983.

Walton, Steve. "The State They Were in: Luke's View of the Roman Empire." In *Rome in the Bible and the Early Church*. Edited by Peter Oakes. Grand Rapids: Baker, 2002.

5

John's Gospel and the Roman Imperial Context

An Evaluation of Recent Proposals

Christopher W. Skinner

Today, travelers at airports throughout the United States are subjected to a number of security measures that were not in place just over a decade ago. For example, only those with boarding passes are permitted beyond security checkpoints. Everyone passing through security must remove their shoes and put them on a conveyor belt to send through screening. Occasionally a passenger will be selected randomly for extra screening and pulled aside for questioning. In previous years these measures would have been considered strange requirements for air travel, though today they are commonplace. In addition to these changes in air transport, the federal government has created an entire agency that oversees the safety of American citizens. It is known as the Department of Homeland Security (DHS). The stated mission of the DHS is to secure the nation from the many threats it faces. In the so-called "age of terror," there is an ever-present awareness of the potential harm that could come to American citizens and institutions. This awareness and all of the aforementioned precautions can be traced back to the catastrophic events of September 11, 2001—a day that has arguably shaped the contemporary American psyche more than any other event in recent memory. Though the events of 9/11 have faded from the day-to-day consciousness of most Americans, there remains a ripple effect that continues to inform the daily American experience. Simply stated, it is impossible to live in America without feeling the impact of that fateful day in 2001. The threat of future terrorism and the memory of 9/11 together lie under the surface of everyday life in the United States.

While this is not a perfect illustration, it can be quite useful for helping us understand the Roman imperial context of the New Testament. Just as the United States in the twenty-first century cannot be separated from its experience on September 11, 2001, neither can first-century Palestine be extracted from its Roman context in particular, or from its experience of foreign subjugation in general.[1] The experience of Roman occupation was a lived reality from which those in the New Testament era could not escape. This does not mean that every element of Jewish and Christian expression, especially their sacred literature, was intended as a response to Roman imperialism, only that the specter of the Roman Empire cast its shadow over daily life in first-century Palestine in a way that cannot and should not be ignored.

While much of the New Testament has been subjected to the anti-imperial current of scholarship (notably the Gospels of Mathew and Luke, Paul's letters and Revelation), relatively little has been written about John's response to Rome until very recently. In recent years scholars have suggested that John, while clearly presenting a high Christology and a conflict with a group known as "the Jews," is also interested in Rome. This essay will examine some of the current scholarly proposals on the Johannine response to the Roman Empire. Before moving into our consideration of those proposals it will prove helpful to begin with a series of objections that have been offered against anti-imperial readings of the Fourth Gospel.

OBJECTIONS TO CONSIDER

Objection 1: By comparison, the Gospel of John is less interested in Rome than the Synoptic Gospels. While it is true that the Fourth Gospel is less concerned with Rome than the Synoptics, this objection actually reveals

---

[1]Almost continuously from 605 BCE to 192 CE, Israel was under the rule of one of the following foreign empires: Babylonian (605 BCE-539 BCE), Persian (539 BCE-331 BCE), Greek (331 BCE-143 BCE), or Roman (63 BCE-192 CE). The only period in which the Jews had both religious and political autonomy was during the Hasmonean era (143 BCE-63 BCE). This series of foreign subjugations no doubt played an important part in Jewish self-identity during the first century CE.

very little about the Johannine view of Rome. Each Gospel is an autonomous narrative and should be treated as such before an attempt is made to compare the Gospels to one another. This means that we must read John's Gospel on its own terms without imposing emphases or categories from other New Testament texts. Thus, if we are going to evaluate John's view of Rome, we must look at the Fourth Gospel independently of its canonical counterparts.

Objection 2: Specific references to Rome and Roman political terms are largely absent from the Fourth Gospel. This objection also contains some truth, though it requires qualification. I like to remind my students that it is possible for a concept to be present even when the terms that denote that concept are absent. Take for example, the following statement: The Colts are going to the Super Bowl to face the Redskins in a battle of epic proportions.

For those "in the know," it would certainly be ridiculous to read this statement as if it were describing a literal battle between horses and red-skinned people inside a large open container. Instead, anyone remotely familiar with the context and cultural scripts would immediately recognize that the statement refers to a major event in professional American football. Serious fans will know instinctively that it refers to the National Football League's championship game between the Indianapolis Colts and the Washington Redskins. However, the basic terms, *football, game, team, championship* and *NFL*, as well as the names of both cities, are absent from the sentence. Despite the omission of these terms, the statement is filled with enough culturally scripted information to allow the concept to be grasped by those familiar with the background. In the same way, those familiar with the setting of first-century Palestine would have possessed sensitivities to cultural scripts that contemporary readers may miss. This includes subtexts related to the Roman Empire. What makes this observation more important is that some scholars build their case for John's anti-imperial reading on the very omission of explicit references to Rome. Warren Carter refers to this, in part, as John's "rhetoric of distance."[2]

Objection 3: John's Gospel is inherently theological and is not interested in politics or in promoting a political ideology. The modern, mainly Western insistence on separating politics and religion would have been foreign in the context of first-century Palestinian culture. One's view of

---

[2]This phrase is found in Warren Carter's volume, *John and Empire: Initial Explorations* (New York: T & T Clark, 2008). More will be said about this subject in the discussion that follows.

God (or the gods) had immediate implications and practical relevance for the development of one's political views and vice versa. Thus, terms such as *king, kingdom, son of God, Lord* and so forth often had important political implications in light of the Roman occupation, as well as religious implications for Jews and Jewish followers of Jesus. Therefore, we must be careful to avoid hastily dismissing the potential political significance behind explicitly theological terms in John.

Having considered and offered some necessary qualifications to these objections, we are now in a position to look at John in light of recent proposals that suggest a focus on Rome. The next portion of this essay will examine and critique core elements of contemporary anti-imperial readings of John's Gospel. Because of space limitations we will focus on the three recent book-length studies on the subject: Tom Thatcher's *Greater Than Caesar*, Warren Carter's *John and Empire* and Lance Byron Richey's *Roman Imperial Ideology and the Gospel of John*. Our discussion will examine important elements of each work and will proceed thematically rather than chronologically. This brief essay will not be able to provide a comprehensive interaction with each book. Instead, what follows is a broad-strokes analysis and should not be regarded as a substitute for reading the works themselves.

Negative Christology and Anti-Roman Rhetoric

One of the universally recognized and theologically significant elements of the Gospel of John is its high Christology. The narrative begins with an in-your-face flourish that openly declares the equality shared by God and the Logos ("the Word was God" [Jn 1:1]). The remaining verses of John's prologue (Jn 1:2-18) go on to provide a detailed description of the incarnate Logos (i.e., Jesus, cf. Jn 1:17): he is the agent of all creation (v. 3), the light of humanity which enlightens those in the world (vv. 4, 9), the purveyor of authority to appoint God's children (v. 12), the possessor of God's glory (v. 14), and, most important, the one who reveals the Father to humanity (v. 18). This comprehensive Christological presentation prepares the reader of John's Gospel for all that will follow in the narrative. It sets the stage by providing the audience with enough information to evaluate every character's response to Jesus, and thereby becomes the interpretive grid through which the audience can understand the Gospel's main purpose—to engender belief in those who hear the story (cf. Jn 20:31).

Whereas in previous decades there was much speculation about the supposed Hellenistic or Gnostic backgrounds of John, most scholars today are convinced that the Fourth Gospel is rooted in a thoroughly Jewish way of thinking. The Gospel's Jewish character is clear from the outset of the narrative, which harkens back to the opening lines of Genesis with the intertextual echo, "In the beginning . . ." (Gen 1:1; Jn 1:1). There is also the interplay between God speaking and creating light and life (Gen 1:3, 6, 9, 11, 14, 20, 24, 26, 29) with the activity of God's "Word" (Jn 1:1, 14), particularly in relationship to life (Jn 1:4) and light (Jn 1:5, 9). Further, as the story progresses the audience learns that great Jewish feasts (e.g., Passover) and memorialized events (e.g., God's provision of manna in the wilderness) find their ultimate significance in the life and ministry of the Johannine Jesus. A close reading of the narrative reveals that the Fourth Evangelist has carefully constructed a complex Christology that is rooted in Jewish monotheism but which also moves beyond prominent Jewish figures and established messianic categories. To put it plainly, John's Christology presents a detailed portrait of a figure that both lies within and transcends Jewish expectation.

In his book *Greater Than Caesar*, Tom Thatcher argues that John's Christology, while comprehensive in its scope, is largely negative and is presented in comparative rather than absolute terms. This, he argues, is a key component to John's anti-Roman rhetoric. He writes:

> John's Christology is "negative" in that it tells us less about who Christ *is* than about who he *is not* or what he is *greater than*. . . . John's response to Roman power is so wrapped up in his Christology, and vice versa, that the two cannot be separated. I do not believe, in other words, that John held an abstract set of beliefs about Christ that he pulled out of his mind and packaged in imperial terms to illustrate what he was talking about. I believe, rather, that imperial terms and images were foundational to John's Christology, and that his thinking about Christ was always informed by the premise that Jesus is greater than Caesar.[3]

We have already established that the New Testament writings are intertwined with the cultural realities of Roman imperial rule. However, it is an overstatement to assert that Roman terms and images are "foundational" to the Christology of the Fourth Gospel. There can be little doubt though that John presents Jesus in comparative terms. For instance, the audience learns

---

[3]Tom Thatcher, *Greater Than Caesar: Christology and Empire in the Fourth Gospel* (Minneapolis: Fortress, 2008), p. 11.

very early in the narrative that the revelatory work of Jesus is superior to that of Moses (Jn 1:17). In another scene replete with Christological significance, Jesus comments, "Before Abraham was, I am" (Jn 8:58 NRSV). John's Jesus also exemplifies the very best of the personified wisdom tradition of the Hebrew Bible. The list could go on. It would not be a stretch to argue, along with Thatcher, that Jesus is "greater than Caesar." According to the Fourth Evangelist Jesus is greater than Caesar, but he is also greater than all other symbols of human power—religious, political or otherwise.

For Thatcher, it is not problematic that John's Jesus is so connected with Jewish religious culture, mainly because he regards the Jewish authorities as a central symbol of Roman power. He writes, "In the Gospel of John the Jewish authorities essentially act like Roman prefects, or at least like a puppet aristocracy that serves as an interface between the procurator and the masses and thereby attempts to maintain the imperial status quo."[4] Thus, Thatcher ultimately regards the Jewishness of John's Gospel as a handmaiden to its Roman focus. Thatcher's novel thesis is creative and well articulated, but I believe it goes too far in identifying the Jewish leaders as a symbol of Roman power. Yes, the Jewish authorities collude with Roman officials to bring about the death of Jesus (cf. Jn 18:1-11), but by and large they represent their own interests quite well throughout the rest of the Gospel (cf. e.g., Jn 1:19-28; 2:18-20; 5:9-18; 7:32-52; 8:12-58). In fact, many Johannine characters approach Jesus on the basis of their own interests, and their sectarian concerns, both religious and ethnic, are consistently identified by the Evangelist. Jewish characters discuss Jesus in terms that reflect their personal beliefs (e.g., "Behold the Lamb of God" [Jn 1:29, 36]; "We have found the Messiah" [Jn 1:41]; "We have found the one about whom Moses wrote in the Law, and the prophets also" [Jn 1:45]; "You are the son of God, the King of Israel" [Jn 1:49]); the Samaritan woman struggles to come to terms with Jesus on the basis of her own preconditioned cultural and religious understandings (Jn 4:4-30); Pontius Pilate, the key Roman figure in John, lords his authority over Jesus and eventually responds to him with the question "What is truth?" (Jn 18:33-40); there are even Greeks who come looking for Jesus (Jn 12:20-21), though the substance and significance of their encounter with him is never elaborated.

The depth and complexity of John's presentation of various characters are significantly flattened out by viewing the narrative through the grid of

---

[4]Ibid., p. 52.

anti-Roman rhetoric. Further, it seems inadvisable to downplay the significance of Jewish elements in John, while placing pronounced emphasis on
the Roman context. As stated earlier, readers should assume that Rome is
lurking in the background of the narrative. To give Rome too much attention, though, is to major on a minor issue. It is too reductionistic to
focus on John's meager presentation of Rome, while neglecting more explicit and seemingly more important points of emphasis. Apart from Jesus'
trial and interaction with Pilate, Rome is present mostly in signs and
shadows, not on a neon billboard. Even as a subtext Rome should not be
accorded the narrative or theological significance Thatcher proposes. At
the end of the day, Thatcher's discussion of John's "negative" and "comparative" Christology provides insights that make Rome necessarily visible
within the story. However, he overreaches both in his assertion that Roman
images are foundational to John's Christology and in his attempt to establish
"the Jews" as symbols of Roman power.

John's Historical Context and Rhetoric of Distance

Since the publication of J. L. Martyn's groundbreaking work *History and
Theology in the Fourth Gospel* (1968), Johannine scholars have relied heavily
on the thesis that John's Gospel provides a two-level story concerned with
Jesus and with the struggles of the Johannine community.[5] In other words,
the conflicts and concerns of John's community have been read back into
the life of Jesus with the result that the two stories have become intertwined. There is not space here to critique Martyn's proposal or rehearse
the history of its reception among scholars. Suffice it to say that, while
some of his original thesis has been qualified or discarded, many scholars
still operate under the basic assumption that the Fourth Gospel tells the
interrelated stories of Jesus and the Johannine community. Scholars commonly agree that the Gospel's three references to believers being expelled
from the synagogue (Jn 9:22; 12:42; 16:2) represent evidence of a conflict
within the Johannine community. Since Christ followers were not being
expelled from the synagogue during Jesus' lifetime, this appears to represent a concern for John's religious community. Among scholars this element of the narrative remains one key to locating the struggles of John's
community in the Gospel story.

---

[5]See the recently revised and expanded edition: J. Louis Martyn, *History and Theology in the
Fourth Gospel*, New Testament Library (Louisville: Westminster John Knox, 2003).

In his book *John and Empire*, Warren Carter challenges this dominant scholarly opinion, referring to it as the "sectarian-synagogal reading." He finds it to be an inadequate interpretive framework that ignores the Gospel's historical context and renders Rome invisible in the process. His basic argument is that those in the Jewish world had learned how to live within the confines of Roman rule while finding ways to resume their life, including their way of worship. The Fourth Evangelist regarded this way of life as too accommodating toward Rome and sought to address this lifestyle by demonstrating how the crucified and resurrected Jesus necessarily challenges Rome's power and theopolitical claims. John accomplishes the challenge to Rome not overtly, but through subtle subtexts as part of a larger "rhetoric of distance." Carter writes:

> With its rhetoric of distance and differentiation, the Gospel seeks to disturb cozy interactions and ready participation in Rome's world by emphasizing Jesus' challenge to and conflict with the Roman world, by delineating an either/or dualistic worldview, and by emphasizing the alternative world created by God's life-giving purposes manifested in Jesus. The Gospel's rhetoric of distance should not, though, mislead us into thinking that such a differentiated way of life already exists. The Gospel works so hard to create it precisely because levels of accommodation are so high.[6]

In addition, Carter states that the major problem for the sectarian-synagogal reading is that there is little historical evidence outside the Gospel to support it. He examines the historical context—primarily that of Ephesus—to provide a plausible scenario for the use of the Gospel and asserts that "John's rhetoric of distance seeks in part to disturb the Jesus-believers' general sense of at-homeness in late first-century Ephesus and impose greater distance."[7]

Carter's historical reconstruction includes discussions of Revelation, 1 Peter and Acts 19, after which he concludes that

> *The synagogue community in Ephesus in which John's Jesus-believers participated* was in all likelihood reasonably at home in and accommodated to Roman power. . . . The Gospel presents claims about Jesus as troubling for the synagogue's accommodation, thereby attempting not only to separate Jesus-believers from the synagogue, but also to create a more antithetical relationship between Jesus-believers and the empire.[8]

---

[6]Carter, *John and Empire*, p. 14.
[7]Ibid., p. 43.
[8]Ibid., p. 45, emphasis added.

From there, Carter engages in a lengthy and complex argument in which he attempts to demonstrate Rome's importance to an effective reading of the Gospel.

Students and scholars of the Fourth Gospel should feel indebted to Carter for making Rome visible in the narrative in a way that reflects the realities of life under Roman rule. He is correct in his assertion that Johannine scholars have long overlooked Rome's presence in the narrative. Further, his argument is immersed in a strong awareness of Roman political and societal issues as well as a breadth of secondary literature, and these strengths will surely open new vistas for those interested in Rome as it relates to New Testament studies. Nevertheless, despite the valuable contributions that can be mined from the margins of his work, Carter's main thesis is problematic for several reasons.

First, I do not believe Carter has provided sufficient reasons to justify a wholesale abandonment of the sectarian-synagogal reading of John. He superficially addresses concerns about synagogue expulsion and intra-community conflict, and seemingly only as a means to dismissing it to provide his own interpretive grid. In every generation the majority opinions of scholarship need to be reexamined, if only to remind scholars why those opinions have been so influential. Carter is to be applauded for his attempt to question the consensus, though his alternative to the two-level reading is not convincing.

Second, Carter's use of Ephesus as the basis for his historical context is also problematic and is one reason why his alternative to the sectarian-synagogal reading is so difficult to accept. His reconstruction focuses solely on the role his reading of John would have played in Roman Ephesus, irrespective of where and under what circumstances the Fourth Gospel actually emerged. As a historical reconstruction his argument coheres, but it is not self-evident that John's Gospel arose out of an Ephesian context. Carter uses as a foundation for his argument, evidence that cannot be demonstrated clearly within or outside the Fourth Gospel. Much historical scholarship is speculative, and if the Ephesian context was part of an ancillary point supported by other, more secure historical evidence, Carter's overall thesis might prove to be more convincing. As it stands, Carter tries to do too much history with too little evidence.

Third, like Thatcher, Carter places heavy emphasis on less prominent features of the narrative in order to draw out a political reading while paying insufficient attention to the wider Jewish context of the narrative. This raises a much larger hermeneutical question: Should we pay attention primarily (or only) to the subtleties of a given text while glossing over repeated literary and theological motifs? Perhaps I am opening myself up to the charge of being an unsophisticated reader of the narrative, but my answer to that question is "surely not." Subtexts are an important means of textual communication and they should not be overlooked. However, neither should we abandon clear points of emphasis for elements that, frankly, may not even be present in the text. Warren Carter has been one of the leading figures in moving New Testament research into the field of empire studies. In particular, his work on Matthew has been influential for showing that Gospel's interest in Roman issues. However, as is the case with anyone doing research in the related fields of biblical and early Christian studies, there is a strong temptation to see our own interests in the texts we examine. Because of his research interests, Carter is conditioned to look for Roman images and themes, and in some of his other published works he has proven particularly adept at it. It seems to me that in the case of John's Gospel—at least as it relates to his main thesis—Carter has found what he was looking for rather than what is actually in (or behind) the text.

AUGUSTAN IDEOLOGY, THE SON OF GOD AND JOHN'S PROLOGUE

Unlike Warren Carter, Lance Byron Richey begins his book *Roman Imperial Ideology and the Gospel of John* by affirming the validity of the two-level reading of John's Gospel; this affirmation subsequently becomes a foundational element of his reconstruction. Richey explains that the "Augustan Ideology" established under Caesar Augustus was a way of legitimating and perpetuating the emperor's supremacy within and over his government.[9] Once this ideology was firmly in place throughout the Roman Empire, all sectors of society would have been affected. This, argues Richey, would have included the Johannine community of believers.

If indeed the Johannine believers were expelled from the synagogue, that event would have rendered them vulnerable to external social and religious pressures. Under Roman law, Jews were exempt from participation in the imperial cult. Following their break with Judaism the Johannine Christians would have been exposed, resulting in an increasingly intensified pressure

---

[9]This is the ideology that would have lauded both the greatness of Caesar and his power over all of Rome.

to participate in the imperial cult. Against this backdrop, Richey argues that the Fourth Gospel, presumably in its final redactional layer, includes a polemic against the Augustan ideology. Specifically, the Johannine polemic is communicated through special vocabulary such as "the Savior of the world" (*ho sōtēr tou kosmou* [Jn 4:42]), and "the Son of God" (*ho huios tou theou* [Jn 1:34, 49; 5:25; 10:36; 11:4, 27; 19:7; 20:31]). The attentive audience would have been aware that the use of each phrase affirmed something about Jesus while also making strong counterimperial assertions. In Rome, the power and titles belonged to Caesar; in John's Gospel they belong to Jesus.

For the most part Richey presents a compelling case for how readers should understand Rome's function in the Fourth Gospel. He highlights Rome's presence in the narrative and helpfully posits John's polemic against the Augustan ideology as a relatively late development in the Gospel's formation, thereby providing a plausible case for Roman themes in John without suggesting that these were in view during the substantial periods of the Gospel's composition and redactional development. However, in the fourth chapter of the book, Richey's argument runs into a huge problem. There he attempts to read the Johannine prologue as an explicit polemic against Rome. Richey acknowledges that any interpretation of John must plausibly attend to the Gospel's Christology, especially as it is expressed in the prologue. To his credit, Richey admits that his reading of the prologue is new inasmuch as it breaks from any dominant strand of scholarly interpretation.[10] He also admits that references to the preexistent Logos have no parallel in Roman imperial thought. On the other hand, he finds it possible to contrast the witness of John the Baptist (Jn 1:6-8) with the testimonies of pagan prophets who supported the imperial cult. Richey also reads the material related to the children of God (Jn 1:9-13) in contrast to clients of the imperial cult. Finally, the Johannine doxology (Jn 1:14-18), which exalts Jesus as the unique Son of God, is thought to offer a counterpart to claims of divine ancestry made by Julius Caesar and subsequent emperors.

It is widely recognized that the prologue sets the literary and theological agendas for the remainder of the Gospel, and while Richey's reading is not

---

[10]He writes, "In this chapter *I will offer a new reading of the Prologue* as the evangelist's attempt to respond to the Augustan ideology and the figure of emperor that it presented to Roman society" (Lance Byron Richey, *Roman Imperial Ideology and the Gospel of John*, Catholic Biblical Quarterly—Monograph Series 43 [Washington, DC: Catholic Biblical Association of America, 2007], p. 107, emphasis added).

without its merits, it is difficult to accept that the Evangelist intended the prologue to be read *primarily* as a response to Roman imperial ideology. Had the anti-imperial polemic been a primary thrust of the prologue, one would expect Roman themes and images to appear more explicitly throughout the remainder of the story. Such is the case with theological themes such as life (*zōē* [Jn 1:4]),[11] light (*phōs* [Jn 1:4, 5, 7, 8, 9]),[12] witness (*martyria* [Jn 1:7, 8, 15]),[13] the world (*kosmos* [Jn 1:9, 10]),[14] truth (*alētheia* [Jn 1:9, 14, 17]),[15] and glory (*doxa* [Jn 1:14]).[16] While these specific Johannine themes appear in the prologue and reappear throughout the narrative, Richey does not successfully connect the appearance of his proposed Roman themes in the wider Gospel story to their supposed appearance in the prologue. That, coupled with his failure to address the presence of explicitly Jewish ideas in the Gospel's opening verses, makes his reading of the prologue unconvincing.

Apart from his exegesis of the prologue, Richey's argument is balanced and makes a plausible case for John's response to Rome while still situating the Gospel in a Jewish context that includes a break with the synagogue. He has provided the groundwork for future discussions of John's response to Rome without having to jettison some of the foundational starting points in Johannine scholarship.

CONCLUSION

Is Rome anywhere in view in John's Gospel? In light of the foregoing discussion, the answer to this question must necessarily be yes. There is no doubt that the Gospel was written in a Roman context and contains some Roman images and characters. In that light, perhaps the more important question is, To what degree is Rome in view in John's Gospel? There are places in John that show contact with the Roman world. For example, the title Savior of the world is not a distinctly Jewish or Samaritan phrase and therefore is likely meant to serve as a vehicle for

---

[11]The term also occurs in Jn 3:15-16, 36; 4:14, 36; 5:24, 26, 29, 39, 40; 6:27, 33, 35, 40, 47, 48, 51, 53, 54, 63; 8:12; 10:10, 28; 11:25; 12:25, 50; 14:6; 17:2, 3; 20:31.

[12]See also Jn 5:35; 8:12; 9:5; 12:35, 36, 46.

[13]See also Jn 1:19; 3:11, 32, 33; 5:31, 32, 34, 36; 8:13, 14, 17; 19:35; 21:24.

[14]See also Jn 1:29; 3:16, 17, 19; 4:42; 6:14, 33, 51; 7:4, 7; 8:12, 23, 26; 9:5, 39; 10:36; 11:9, 27; 12:19, 25, 31, 46, 47; 13:1; 14:17, 19, 22, 27, 30, 31; 15:18, 19; 16:8, 11, 20, 21, 28, 33; 17:5, 6, 9, 11, 13, 14, 15, 16, 18, 21, 23, 24, 25; 18:20, 36, 37; 21:25.

[15]See also Jn 3:21; 4:23, 24; 5:33; 8:32, 40, 44, 45, 46; 14:6, 17; 15:26; 16:7, 13; 17:17, 19; 18:37, 38.

[16]See also Jn 2:11; 5:41, 44; 7:18; 8:50, 54; 9:24; 11:4, 40; 12:41, 43; 17:5, 22, 24.

some kind of counterimperial sentiment. That example is debatable, but there are a few places where Rome is clearly visible. The audience learns that Rome is complicit in the death of Jesus (Jn 18:1-11). Also Jesus has a lengthy interaction with Pilate (Jn 18:28–19:16) in a scene which provides this essay's conversation partners with an unassailable example of Rome's place in the narrative. In short, Rome is not completely absent from the Fourth Gospel, and we are indebted to Thatcher, Carter and Richey for pointing out some of the ways John intends Rome to be visible to the literary audience. Even in the face of evidence that John's Gospel contains some interest in Rome, interpreters must proceed with hermeneutical and exegetical caution.

In all types of literature, secular and sacred, ancillary features of a narrative are often used to make a point loosely related to the main thrust(s) of the story. The presence of secondary or tertiary themes need not detain the exegete to the same degree as the story's plotline, character development and recurring motifs. No one familiar with James Joyce's *Ulysses* would assume that bar patrons in the town of Dublin constitute a major area of interest for the story. The bar patrons, along with the other residents of Dublin, help to create a realistic picture of the physical setting in which the story takes place. To spend too much time focusing on these ancillary elements of the story would be to badly misread Joyce's intent. Joyce is concerned to a much greater degree with issues like sexual desire, anti-Semitism and death. The authenticity of the Dublin scenery merely serves as a backdrop to the story.

In the same way, the Fourth Gospel is largely concerned with the incarnate Logos who has come down from above. The Johannine Jesus steps down into a specifically Jewish context which is admittedly within a wider Roman context, but his conversations, discourses and signs are all related to distinctly Jewish concerns. Jesus has come to fulfill and transcend Jewish expectations. The Roman scenery serves as the realistic backdrop to the wider story, but it is not the story and should not be confused with the story. The studies of Thatcher, Carter and Richey insist that we pay attention to Roman concerns and remain open to the fruit of future research in this area. While we must ultimately recognize that Rome is present in John, specific points of contact with Roman characters and images are minimal and do not constitute a major emphasis for the Fourth Gospel.

BIBLIOGRAPHY

Carter, Warren. *John and Empire: Initial Explorations.* New York: T & T Clark, 2008.

Cassidy, Richard J. *Christians and Roman Rule in the New Testament: New Perspectives.* New York: Crossroad, 2001. Especially chapter four.

_____. *John's Gospel in New Perspective: Christology and the Realities of Roman Power.* Maryknoll, NY: Orbis, 1992.

Rensberger, David. "The Politics of John: The Trial of Jesus in the Fourth Gospel." *Journal of Biblical Literature* 103, no. 3 (1984).

Richey, Lance Byron. *Roman Imperial Ideology and the Gospel of John.* Catholic Biblical Quarterly—Monograph Series 43. Washington, DC: Catholic Biblical Association of America, 2007.

Thatcher, Tom. *Greater Than Caesar: Christology and Empire in the Fourth Gospel.* Minneapolis: Fortress, 2008.

_____. "'I Have Conquered the World': The Death of Jesus and the End of the Empire in the Gospel of John." In *Empire in the New Testament.* Edited by Stanley E. Porter and Cynthia Long Westfall. McMaster Divinity College New Testament Study Series 10. Eugene, OR: Wipf & Stock, 2011.

6

Proclaiming Another King Named Jesus?

The Acts of the Apostles and the Roman Imperial Cult(s)

Drew J. Strait

Recent events in the Middle East have inspired a new level of sophistication for critiquing political tyrants. Before the eyes of the watching world, the peoples of Tunisia and Egypt organized resistance movements not through violence but through Internet networking sites such as Twitter and Facebook. In a world far removed from the Internet, the early Christians too lived under the shadow of a regime—the Roman Empire. At the heart of the Roman Empire stood the towering figure of Caesar, whose unprecedented control of power and bestowal of peace and material benefits to his subjects inspired him to be "worshiped as a god." Before and contemporaneous with the early Christian movement, the worship of Caesar evolved into a widespread political and religious institution called the Roman imperial cult. The significance of the imperial cult is evident in the many temples, statues, coins, inscriptions and other media that have been uncovered by archaeologists in many of the cities that dot the missionary itineraries of Paul in the book of Acts. In the city of Myra, where Paul changed ships on his way to Rome (Acts 27:5), an inscription honoring the emperor Tiberius after his death reads: "The people of Myra [honor] the emperor Tiberius, the exalted god, son of exalted gods, lord of land and sea, the benefactor and savior of the entire world."[1] One has to wonder if Luke's emphasis on Jesus as the Son of God, Lord and Savior is in response to inscriptions like this, making clear that such titles belong to Jesus and not to Caesar. Indeed, over the past twenty years it has become increasingly popular among scholars to argue that the New Testament is embedded with so-to-speak anti-imperial "Tweets" that communicate that Jesus is Lord and Caesar is not. What follows is an evaluation of Luke's attitude toward Caesar in the book of Acts or, better yet, a journey through the Roman roads and open seas of Acts, with the aim of interpreting whether or not Luke intentionally presented Jesus as Lord against Caesar.

As the only author in the New Testament to acknowledge Roman emperors by name (e.g., Augustus [Lk 2:1], Tiberius [Lk 3:1] and Claudius [Acts 11:28; 18:2]), one would think that, if Luke is anti-imperial, he would explicitly critique Caesar. Ironically, when one travels down the Roman roads and open seas of Acts, the presence of Jewish Diaspora synagogues and Greek pagan cults take center stage rather than Roman imperial temples and statues of Caesar. The lack of interaction with Caesar in Luke-Acts has led to a scholarly consensus for the past three centuries that Luke is the most pro-Roman author in the New Testament. Luke's purportedly positive portrayal of Roman officials and characterization of Paul's innocence in Roman custody inspired numerous scholars to argue, in one way or another, that Luke wrote a political apology on behalf of the church to show Roman officials that Christianity is politically harmless (*apologia pro ecclesia*).[2] In the wake of recent anti-imperial scholarship, Luke's positive attitude toward Caesar has been reevaluated by several scholars—namely, Steve Walton, Gary Gilbert, Kavin Rowe, Brigitte Kahl and Kazuhiko Yamazaki-Ransom—who have paved a new way forward by acknowledging anti-imperial motifs in Acts and, therefore, the highly complex theological tension that exists in Luke's narrative. In dialogue with this newer scholarship, I will critically evaluate an anti-imperial reading of Acts through a

---

[1]See Hans-Josef Klauck, *The Religious Context of Early Christianity* (Minneapolis: Fortress, 2003), p. 302.

[2]For an overview of political apology approaches to Luke-Acts see Alexandru Neagoe, *The Trial of the Gospel: An Apologetic Reading of Luke's Trial Narratives*, Society for New Testament Studies 116 (Cambridge: Cambridge University Press, 2002), pp. 4-22.

consideration of three layers of Acts: (1) the impact of Jesus' ascent to heaven on the narrative of Acts, (2) the missionary preaching of Peter and Paul, and (3) Luke's presentation of Roman rulers and officials.

Setting the Stage: Acts and the Roman Imperial Cult(s)

Much like the intellectuals of Athens debating on the Areopagus in Acts 17, New Testament scholars love to "spend their time in nothing but telling or hearing something new" (Acts 17:21 NRSV). With the arrival of postcolonial theory in the 1990s, scholars began to rethink how the Roman Empire and the imperial cult, in particular, influenced the political perspectives of the New Testament authors. Interpreting the imperial cult's impact on the New Testament, however, is an exercise in hermeneutical discipline. Three points of caution are worth reflecting on here.

First, Luke's attitude toward Caesar is profoundly shaped by the story of Israel. For centuries the Jewish people had to navigate how to faithfully worship the one God of Israel amid the empires around and often in control of them, whose worship of multiple gods contradicted Israel's allegiance to Yahweh alone. After the Roman general Pompey brought Israel under Roman power in 63 BCE, some Jews resisted Rome with banditry, while others employed terrorist tactics through kidnappings and spontaneous stabbings with concealed daggers; still others, according to the Jewish historian Josephus, created a "fourth philosophy," which urged Jews to affirm that Yahweh is Lord rather than Caesar (*Antiquities* 18.23-24; Acts 5:36-37). Israel's long history with imperial domination cast a long shadow under which Luke narrates how early disciples followed Jesus as the fulfillment of God's promises to Israel. A viable anti-imperial interpretation of Acts cannot neglect Luke's rootedness in the story of Israel and its history of accommodation and resistance to imperial domination.

Second, for many years emperor worship was caricatured as a strictly political phenomenon. Simon Price's groundbreaking study in 1985, called *Rituals and Power*, set a new scholarly course by arguing that Caesar had political *and* religious significance for the Greco-Roman world, along with an impact on public space and power dynamics between ruler and subject.[3] Numerous studies in recent years have piggybacked on the work of Price, now showing that the worship of Caesar extended into the private world of

---

[3]Simon Price, *Rituals and Power: The Roman Imperial Cult in Asia Minor* (Cambridge: Cambridge University Press, 1984).

households.[4] There is a tendency among anti-imperial interpreters to take this new scholarship and embellish the imperial cult as if it were a coherent system of thought. It is no longer fashionable among scholars of the Greco-Roman world, however, to speak of *the* imperial cult but rather of imperial cults. This distinction indicates the diversity of imperial cults, extending from the Latin West to the Greek East, from one emperor to the next, and from one city to another. In the case of Acts, the diversity of imperial cults presents a major obstacle for interpreters, since we do not know with any certitude what city or cities in the Roman Empire Acts was written to.

A third caution counters the trend among anti-imperial interpreters who treat imperial cults as if they were *the* singular dominant cult in the Roman Empire. N. T. Wright succumbs to such oversimplification in writing that "already by Paul's time it [the imperial cult] had become the dominant cult in a large part of the Empire."[5] In Acts, the missionary travels of Paul, for example, cut through several cities that housed Roman imperial cults, yet Luke is more concerned to highlight the presence of other pagan cults (e.g., Zeus and Hermes [Acts 14:12], Python [Acts 16:16], Artemis of Ephesus [Acts 19:28], and Castor and Pollux [Acts 28:11]). As Luke sees it, the early Christians were in more danger of persecution from Jewish synagogues and the Ephesian silversmiths than from imperial powers. Aside from the sporadic persecutions of Nero and Domitian in the first century, it is not until the second century under the emperor Hadrian that Christians faced loyalty tests before the Roman magistrates. Even then, as Fergus Millar has noted, when Roman provincial magistrates questioned the Christians who were brought before them, they "applied the test of the recognition of the imperial cult, but along with that of the cults of the other gods."[6] Millar's observation should caution us against embellishing Roman imperial cults as if they were the only pagan cult early Christians had to negotiate.

The tension here is clear: although we are aware of the presence of Roman imperial cults in Luke's world, Luke does not openly acknowledge their existence in the various cities through which he narrates the spread of the gospel. Either Luke intentionally avoids Roman imperial cults for safety

---

[4]See Ittai Gradel, *Emperor Worship and Roman Religion* (Oxford: Clarendon Press, 2002), pp. 198-212.

[5]N. T. Wright, "Paul's Gospel and Caesar's Empire," in *Paul and Politics* (Harrisburg, PA: Trinity Press International, 2000), p. 160.

[6]Fergus Millar, "The Imperial Cults and Persecutions," in *Le Culte des Souverains dans L'Empire Romain* (Genève: Fondation Hart, 1973), p. 164.

reasons or his polemical concerns lie elsewhere—leaving anti-imperial interpreters in the seemingly awkward position of having embellished the significance of Caesar as a target of Christian anti-imperial polemic. Still, at different points in the narrative of Acts, Luke subtly reminds his audience that Jesus is Lord and Caesar is not. With careful attention to the historical and literary culture of Luke's world, we can cautiously commence our journey from Jerusalem to Rome with an eye toward unlocking the anti-imperial language and theological motifs employed by Luke's anti-imperial Twitter feed.

THE ASCENT OF JESUS AND IMPERIAL APOTHEOSIS

At the beginning of Acts, the disciples ask Jesus a religious and political question before Jesus ascends into heaven: "Lord, is this the time when you will restore the kingdom to Israel?" (Acts 1:6). Still confused by the aims of Jesus, the disciples are prepared for Jesus to initiate the overthrow of Rome and the restoration of Israel to political independence. Jesus quickly corrects the disciples and commissions them not to violent resistance in an apocalyptic scenario but rather to missional witness in "Jerusalem, . . . Judea and Samaria, and to the ends of the earth" (Acts 1:8). The disciples' commission is immediately followed by Jesus' ascent to heaven. Until recently, the heavenly dimension of Acts has been largely neglected by scholars.[7] The geographical arc of Acts as it extends from Jerusalem to Rome is well noted, but heaven is an equally important geographical point for Luke, where Jesus sits at the right hand of the Father and empowers the disciples' witness "with power from on high" (Lk 24:49). Although Jesus' ascent to heaven is traditionally interpreted through a Jewish lens (2 Kings 2:11; 1 Enoch 39:3), which will be discussed later, it can also be evaluated in light of Roman imperial apotheosis—that is, in light of Caesar's ascent to heaven, where he purportedly becomes a god.

A description of Jesus' ascent only occurs in the New Testament at the end of Luke's Gospel (Lk 24:50-53) and the beginning of Acts (Acts 1:9-11). In the Greco-Roman world, ascension into heaven traditionally accompanied the process of becoming a god, which in Greek was called *apotheosis* and in Latin *consecratio*. Caesar Augustus in particular took advantage of the political ramifications of heavenly ascent when he put on

---

[7]See Matthew Sleeman, *Geography and the Ascension Narrative in Acts*, Society for New Testament Studies 146 (Cambridge: Cambridge University, 2009).

games to honor his stepfather, Julius Caesar, for his military victories. At the games a comet appeared which, according to Augustus, was a sign that Julius Caesar had ascended into heaven. Thereafter, Augustus was able to push the senate to confirm Julius's heavenly ascent and exploit his new-found status as the adopted son of a god. According to Simon Price, thirty-six of the sixty emperors in the period between 14 BCE and 337 CE ascended to heaven and received the title *divus*.[8] One of the more creative anti-imperial interpreters of Acts, Gary Gilbert, argues that by construing Jesus' ascent in the language of Roman imperial propaganda, Luke is able to make a profound theological claim: that Jesus is the true ascended Lord of the empire and Caesar is not.[9]

For Luke's audience to affiliate Jesus' ascent with Caesar is plausible—as the church father Justin Martyr did—but Jesus' ascent cannot be divorced from its Judaic roots.[10] Still, Gilbert rightly acknowledges key parallels between Caesar's and Jesus' ascents, such as the presence of an eyewitness. In the case of Caesar this witness was usually a member of the senate; in a similar way, the apostles witness Jesus' ascent. A key difference, however, and one that Gilbert does not adequately address, is that beyond this witness, Caesar's ascent had to be approved by senatorial vote based on a given emperor's behavior. The importance of an emperor's behavior for achieving imperial ascent is evident in the Roman politician Seneca's parody of the tyrannical emperor Claudius, humorously titled *The Pumpkin-ification of the Divine Claudius*. Seneca critiques Claudius by portraying his banishment from heaven to the underworld because of his tyrannical behavior. This parody illustrates that an emperor's behavior had significant implications for convincing the senate that he deserved apotheosis. For the senate, heavenly ascension, then, was a powerful political ritual, for it gave the senate political power over the emperor while simultaneously encouraging emperors to act with virtue.[11] What Gilbert fails to note is that before Jesus ascends to heaven, there is no apostolic vote to decide if Jesus is deemed worthy to ascend into the abode of the gods. It is not Jesus' band of

---

[8]See Simon Price, "From Noble Funerals to Divine Cult: The Consecration of Roman Emperors," in *Rituals of Royalty*, ed. D. Canadine and S. Price (Cambridge: Cambridge University Press, 1987), p. 57.

[9]Gary Gilbert, "Roman Propaganda and Christian Identity in the Worldview of Luke-Acts," in *Contextualizing Acts: Lukan Narrative and Greco-Roman Discourse* (Atlanta: Society of Biblical Literature, 2003), pp. 233-56.

[10]Justin Martyr, *Apology I* 21.

[11]Price, "From Noble Funerals to Divine Cult," p. 91.

misfit disciples who hold authority to sanction Jesus' ascent but rather the God of Israel who raised Jesus from the dead (Lk 24:44; Acts 3:15). That Jesus' ascent is determined by the God of Israel is further illustrated in Peter's sermon to the people of Jerusalem in Acts 2. Peter preaches about Jesus' ascension to the right hand of God in tandem with Psalm 110:1 (Acts 2:34-35) and attributes Jesus' ascension to "God [who] made him [Jesus] both Lord and Messiah" (Acts 2:36).

A Jewish framework for interpreting Jesus' ascent is further evident when Stephen experiences a postascension vision of the ascended Jesus. Before his Jewish persecutors—including Paul!—Stephen looks up to the ascended Jesus and says, "Look, I see the heavens opened and the son of Man standing at the right hand of God" (Acts 7:56). Stephen's reference to the Son of Man evokes Jewish apocalyptic traditions from Daniel 7:13, where the Son of Man will come on the clouds of heaven. Consistent with Stephen's vision of the Danielic Son of Man, Jesus ascends to heaven on a cloud (Acts 1:9), distinguishing his ascent from the emperors who were said to have ascended on the back of an eagle. Moreover, unlike Caesar, Jesus continues to rule as the absent-yet-present King who empowers disciples' witness with power from heaven and will one day return on a cloud (Acts 1:11). Stephen's vision of the ascended Jesus cautions us from embellishing parallels with Caesar. For Luke, Jesus' ascent is the fulfillment of God's promises to Israel and functions to call both worshipers of Yahweh and Caesar to change their posture heavenward—toward the Messiah, King Jesus in heaven.

THE MISSIONARY PREACHING OF PETER AND PAUL

The missionary sermons in Acts give us a unique opportunity to assess whether Luke understood the gospel anti-imperially. Of the nine missionary sermons Luke records, Peter preaches five times to Jews in Jerusalem (Acts 2:14-36, 38-39; 3:12-26; 4:8-12, 19-20; 5:29-32) and once to a Roman centurion's household (Acts 10:34-43). Paul, on the other hand, preaches once to a Jewish audience (Acts 13:16-41) and twice to pagan audiences (Acts 14:15-17; 17:22-31). The content of Peter's preaching in the first five chapters of Acts repeatedly appeals to Jewish themes—the Old Testament prophets (Acts 2:16), Davidic kingship (Acts 2:34) and God's promises to Abraham (Acts 3:25). Most of these Jewish concepts, including resurrection (Acts 3:15), have no counterpart in Roman imperial theology.

A Roman reader of Peter's sermons would likely have felt like the Ethiopian eunuch reading the prophet Isaiah in Acts 8: "How can I [understand it], unless someone guides me?" (Acts 8:31). A. D. Nock appropriately comments, "If it [Luke-Acts] had come into the hands of a pagan, would he have understood it unless he was already half-converted?"[12] Though a pagan may have had a hard time making sense of Luke's Jewish theological jargon, we cannot preclude the possibility that Luke's intent was for believers, rather than unbelievers, to sense an anti-imperial motif.

It is possible that believers could sense an anti-imperial motif when Peter and Paul apply the imperial title Savior to Jesus in three sermons to Jewish audiences. Just as Augustus and other emperors were hailed as Savior in several imperial inscriptions, Peter too calls Jesus Savior before the Jewish high council in Jerusalem (Acts 5:31) and boldly preaches that, "There is salvation in no one else, for there is no other name under heaven given among mortals by which we must be saved" (Acts 4:12). In a synagogue at Pisidian Antioch, where Roman imperial architecture rivaled that of Rome—including a massive temple to Augustus connected to the colonnaded Augusta Platea—Paul boldly claims that through David God has brought to Israel a Savior (Acts 13:23). What is curious is that Luke only employs *Savior* before Jewish audiences and, even then, embeds it within Jewish salvation history, which should caution us against reading too far into these titles.

As it becomes increasingly fashionable to read imperial titles like "Savior" anti-imperially—as Steve Walton, Gary Gilbert and Brigitte Kahl do—it will be important to better identify whether Luke is evoking the Jewish or Greco-Roman meaning of *Savior*. Luke's use of *Savior* may have stemmed from either Greek pagan cults or the Old Testament. In Greek culture, for example, *Savior* had been applied to Zeus Soter, Artemis Soter and the Ptolemaic kings in Egypt well before the rise of Roman imperial cults. Furthermore, *Savior* has a rich history in the Greek translation of the Old Testament. Foreseeing the problem with proof-texting words like *Savior* anti-imperially, Adolf Deissmann aptly commented in 1908: "I am sure that in certain cases a polemical intention against the cult of the emperor cannot be proved; but mere chance coincidences might later awaken a powerful

---

[12]Arthur D. Nock, "Acts," in *Essays on Religion and the Ancient World* (Cambridge, MA: Harvard University Press, 1972), p. 825.

sense of contrast in the mind of the people."[13] Still, whether by happenstance or intention, Luke's use of *Savior* could have evoked a powerful sense of allegiance to Jesus as *the* Savior.

As the gospel moves away from the heart of the Jewish world, Peter makes a provocative theological claim that Jesus is Lord of all in an imperial context—a Roman centurion's household. The story takes place in Caesarea, where we know Herod built a colossal statue of and temple for Caesar Augustus, which, according to Josephus, could be seen by sailors from miles away (*Antiquities* 15.339). Cornelius's status as a Roman Gentile is evident when he falls down to worship Peter as a god (Acts 10:25). After commanding Cornelius to stand up—because followers of the ascended Jesus don't receive pagan apotheosis!—Peter gives the most important sermon in Acts. One verse of Peter's sermon, in particular, deserves our attention: "You know the message he sent to the people of Israel, preaching peace by Jesus Christ—this one is Lord [*kyrios*] of all" (Acts 10:36). Kavin Rowe draws attention to this verse as a point of entry for understanding Luke's attitude toward Caesar. Drawing on inscriptional evidence that Caesar was understood as "Lord of all," Rowe argues that Peter's phrase "this one is Lord of all" is not a parenthetical remark but a profound theological claim: namely, that "this one," being Jesus of Nazareth, is Lord of all rather than Caesar.[14]

Justin Howell takes Rowe's thesis further, making three critical points about Roman centurions: (1) centurions functioned as benefactors and judges for their local communities; (2) they were often active participants in Roman imperial cults; and (3) they were notorious for using unjust means to acquire wealth (Lk 3:14).[15] Howell argues that Luke's polemic is not aimed at Caesar alone but also at Caesar's subordinate authorities—that is to say, both Caesar and centurions are under the authority of Jesus Christ, who is the true Lord and Judge of all. Rowe and Howell focus so much on the latter half of Acts 10:36, however, that they fail to highlight Luke's equally important message of "peace by Jesus Christ" (v. 36a). Caesar, of course, was famous for initiating peace (*pax Romana*) through military

---

[13]Adolf Deissmann, *Light from the Ancient East: The New Testament Illustrated by Recently Discovered Texts of the Graeco-Roman World*, trans. Lionel Strachan (New York: George H. Doran, 1927), pp. 342-43.

[14]Kavin Rowe, "Luke-Acts and the Imperial Cult: A Way Through the Conundrum?" *Journal for the Study of the New Testament* 27, no. 3 (2005): 279-33.

[15]Justin Howell, "The Imperial Authority and Benefaction of Centurions and Acts 10:34-43: A Response to C. Kavin Rowe," *Journal for the Study of the New Testament* 31, no. 1 (2008): 39.

might. For Luke, however, Jesus is the true initiator of a gospel of peace.[16]

After the extension of salvation to the Gentiles in Cornelius's household, Paul takes center stage for the remainder of Acts as he preaches his way into the Gentile world. Given the popularity of anti-imperial readings of Paul's letters, it is surprising that Luke never depicts Paul taking an open swipe at Caesar. Paul's lack of explicit critique of Caesar in Acts has been a source of frustration—what Brigitte Kahl labels "a stumbling block"—for those who wish to read Paul's letters anti-imperially. In response to this stumbling block, Kahl argues that Luke "concealed and blurred the original subversive message of Paul."[17] By supposedly partaking in a historical revision of the Paul of history, Kahl credits Luke with creating the reading framework that "made the inclusion of Paul's Letters in the canon appear 'safe.'"[18] Kahl is correct in her judgment that the Paul of Acts is not overtly anti-imperial, but her agenda to justify an anti-imperial reading of Paul's letters misreads Paul as a "safe" character in Acts. As Kavin Rowe recently argued, Paul's "collision" with pagan culture in Acts was "culturally destabilizing" for paganism in the cities of Lystra (Acts 14), Philippi (Acts 16), Athens (Acts 17) and Ephesus (Acts 19).[19] To take one example, the Ephesian silversmiths start a massive riot because they experience an economic loss from people turning away from their silver idols in response to Paul's preaching (Acts 19:23). Notably, it is in Ephesus that we have a good example of Roman imperial cults assimilating with a regional god—for example, the basilica at Ephesus was dedicated to Artemis; to Emperor Caesar Augustus, son of god; to Tiberius Caesar, son of Augustus; and to the people of Ephesus.[20] Given Caesar's insistence on maintaining peace in the Roman Empire and his own embeddedness in the cult of Artemis, Paul's culturally and economically destabilizing preaching would hardly appear safe.

Paul's two missionary sermons to pagan audiences at Lystra (Acts 14:15-18) and Athens contain forthright criticism of pagan idolatry, but it is not openly

---

[16]See also Seyoon Kim, *Christ and Caesar* (Grand Rapids: Eerdmans, 2008), p. 84.

[17]Brigitte Kahl, "Acts of the Apostles: Pro(to)-Imperial Script and Hidden Transcript," in *In the Shadow of the Empire: Reclaiming the Bible as a History of Faithful Resistance*, ed. Richard A. Horsley (Louisville: Westminster John Knox, 2008), p. 156.

[18]Ibid.

[19]Kavin Rowe, *World Upside Down: Reading Acts in the Graeco-Roman Age* (Oxford: Oxford University Press, 2009), pp. 17-49.

[20]Simon Price, *Rituals and Power*, pp. 254-57; Paul Trebilco, *The Early Christians in Ephesus From Paul to Ignatius* (Tübingen: Mohr Siebeck, 2004), p. 35; Steven Friesen, *Imperial Cults and the Apocalypse of John* (Oxford: Oxford University Press, 2001), p. 95.

directed at Caesar. At Lystra the crowds attempt to divinize and worship
Barnabas as the Greek god Zeus and Paul as the Greek god Hermes. In response, Paul summons the people to turn from these worthless things—presumably, Hermes and Zeus—to the living God (Acts 14:15-18). Luke continues
to critique pagan idolatry through Paul's famous speech on the Areopagus at
Athens. It would be a breath of fresh air if Paul critiqued the Roma-Augustus
temple near the Parthenon in Athens, but Luke records Paul focusing his
criticism elsewhere—toward an altar to an unknown god (Acts 17:23). Paul's
speech comes close to a universal critique of pagan idolatry when Paul says,
"Since we are God's offspring, we ought not to think that the deity is like gold,
or silver, or stone, an image formed by the art and imagination of mortals"
(Acts 17:29). This verse is a bold denunciation of pagan idolatry that, for a
Roman audience, could translate into a critique of Caesar's transformation of
public space through imperial temples and statues. What eventually sets the
Athenian crowd off is not Paul's denunciation of pagan statues and altars, but
Paul's appeal to Jesus' resurrection (Acts 17:31-32). Paul's preaching is hardly
innocuous in that it destabilizes pagan culture and reorients it heavenward—
away from pagan temple and images—toward the God of Israel. That Luke
watered down Paul's anti-imperial message of the letters is a misguided
scholarly pursuit; it is a better use of our time to ask if the anti-imperial Paul
coalition embellished Paul's subversive gospel and consequently misread the
Paul of Luke. After all, as Luke sees it, Paul's preaching landed him in custody
in Rome, where Luke says Paul preached "the kingdom of God . . . with all
boldness and without hindrance" (Acts 28:31).[21]

LUKE'S PRESENTATION OF ROMAN RULERS AND OFFICIALS

The book of Acts displays an extraordinary tension between two dimensions: namely, the kingdom of God and the kingdoms of Satan. If a Lukan
cosmology of the world exists, one statement from Luke's Gospel should
capture our imaginations. During Jesus' temptation with Satan, Luke writes:
"Then the devil led him [Jesus] up and showed him in an instant all the
kingdoms of the world. And the devil said to him, 'To you I will give their
glory and all this authority; for it has been given over to me, and I give it to
anyone I please'" (Lk 4:6).

---

[21]On the ending of Acts, see Richard Cassidy, "Paul's Proclamation of *Lord* Jesus as a Chained
   Prisoner in Rome: Luke's Ending Is in His Beginning," in *Luke-Acts and Empire* (Eugene,
   OR: Pickwick, 2011), pp. 142-53.

According to Luke, the kingdoms of this world, which include the Roman Empire, lay under the authority of Satan. The implications of this audacious claim defy our expectations in Luke's second volume: though Luke claims that the Roman Empire is under the authority of Satan, Luke portrays *some* Roman officials positively and several pronounce Paul innocent (*dikaios*). According to previous generations of scholars, Luke intentionally paints the Roman Empire as the church's friend to show Roman officials that Christianity is politically harmless. In the past three years scholars have painted a much more complex picture of Luke's portrayal of Roman rulers and officials.

The Gospel of Luke anticipates the apostles' testimony before Roman rulers and officials. Jesus warns the disciples prior to his death: "they will arrest you and persecute you; they will hand you over to synagogues and prisons, and you will be brought before kings and governors because of my name. This will give you an opportunity to testify" (Lk 21:12-13). The dangers of preaching Jesus become apparent in an oft-noted event at Thessalonica in Acts 17. Incited by jealous Jews, a lynch mob drags Jason and some other believers before the Roman city authorities, saying: "These people who have been turning the world upside down have come here also, and Jason has entertained them as guests. *They are all acting contrary to the decrees of the emperor, saying that there is another king named Jesus*" (Acts 17:6-7, emphasis added). On the surface, this passage implies that Paul was preaching an anti-imperial gospel. It often goes unacknowledged, however, that the accusations come from Jews, not Romans, and the Roman authorities, though disturbed, dismiss the charges after receiving bail. The pattern here is typical of Acts: accusations against Christians come from Jews, not Romans, and Roman officials step in as mediators. Luke shows a remarkable concern to highlight the intra-Jewish conflicts that took place between churches and synagogues. As Loveday Alexander argues, if Luke is writing a political defense of the church, his primary focus is toward Judaism rather than Rome.[22]

Still, the conflicts between church and synagogue do not take place "in a corner" (Acts 26:26). Luke spends more verses in Acts narrating Paul in Roman custody because of "accusation from the Jews" than he does on Paul's missionary travels. As Robert Maddox points out, "it is Paul the prisoner even more than Paul the missionary whom we are meant to

[22]Loveday Alexander, "The Acts of the Apostles as an Apologetic Text," in *Apologetics in the Roman Empire* (Oxford: Oxford University Press, 1999), pp. 42-44.

remember."[23] How we remember Paul's experience in Roman custody is a critical component of how we interpret Luke's attitude toward Caesar. As Paul is passed through three layers of Caesar's agents—Lysias, Festus and Agrippa II—all three pronounce that Paul "has done nothing deserving death" (Acts 23:29; 25:25; 26:31-32). Are we to think, then, that Caesar and his agents are friends of the church or that their authority is under Satan?

It cannot be denied that Luke portrays some of Caesar's agents positively. The proconsul Sergius Paulus (Acts 13:12), for example, becomes a believer, and though we know centurions were not known for their character in the ancient world, Luke consistently portrays them positively (Acts 10:1–11:18; 27:42-43). Moreover, Claudius Lysias (Acts 21:31-34) and the centurion Julius protect Paul from being murdered (Acts 27:43). In a mysterious way, God is able to use Caesar's agents to protect Paul. Appeal to these passages in favor of a pro-empire reading of Acts, however, without acknowledgment of Luke's less favorable characterizations of Roman officials lacks hermeneutical discipline. Steve Walton points out that Gallio acts with anti-Semitic motives and turns a blind eye to the beating of Sosthenes (Acts 18:17); Lysias transfers Paul to Caesarea in spite of Paul's innocence (Acts 23:27); Felix hopes for a bribe from Paul and keeps Paul in prison for two years despite his innocence (Acts 24:26-27); and Festus appears more concerned about the Jews than Paul's justice (Acts 25:25), which forces Paul to appeal to Caesar for justice (Acts 25:11).[24] These negative features of Roman rulers are hardly flattering and, as Kazuhiko Yamazaki-Ransom has shown, Luke redefines the people of God as those who follow Jesus as Lord. Based on Luke's redefinition of the people of God and aside from the conversion of Sergius Paulus, the Roman rulers in Acts continue to operate under the realm of Satan.[25] Indeed, Paul even appeals to Agrippa to convert (Acts 26:28), but Agrippa's silent response proves that his citizenship remains in the kingdoms of the world.

One final passage in Acts is worthy of our attention. In Acts 12:1 the Jewish client king of Rome, Herod Agrippa I, martyrs the apostle James

---

[23]Robert Maddox, *The Purpose of Luke-Acts* (Göttingen: Vandenhoeck & Ruprecht, 1982), pp. 66-67.

[24]Steve Walton, "The State They Were in," p. 27; Walton, "Trying Paul or Trying Rome? Judges and the Accused in the Roman Trials of Paul in Acts," in *Luke-Acts and Empire* (Eugene, OR: Pickwick, 2011), pp. 122-41.

[25]Kazuhiko Yamazaki-Ransom, *The Roman Empire in Luke's Narrative*, Library of New Testament Studies 404 (New York: T & T Clark, 2010), pp. 201-2.

with the sword and shuts Peter in prison (Acts 12:2-3). After Peter escapes from prison by an angel of God, Luke records the death of Herod while giving a speech to the people of Tyre and Sidon:

> On an appointed day Herod put on his royal robes, took his seat on the platform, and delivered a public address to them. *The people kept shouting, "The voice of a god, and not of a mortal!" And immediately, because he had not given the glory to God, an angel of the Lord struck him down, and he was eaten by worms and died.* (Acts 12:21-23, emphasis added)

The death of Herod is typically interpreted as God's vengeance on a ruthless persecutor of the church (cf. 2 Macc 9:4-10).[26] The envoy from Tyre and Sidon, however, sense the qualities of a god in Herod Agrippa because of his benefaction of food and royal presence. In response to Herod's rhetorical performance and benefaction, the crowd begins to shout, "the voice of a god, and not a mortal!" Hans Josef-Klauck interprets Luke's peculiar emphasis on Herod's voice as an implicit critique of the egocentric emperor Nero, who was infatuated with the beauty of his voice.[27] A popular legend circulated during Luke's day that Nero would return to life (i.e., Nero Redivivus). Given these popular traditions about Nero, Klauck argues that Luke employs the ancient rhetorical device called *schema*, which Quintillian calls a form of "verbal burglary," where a person can critique a tyrant by saying one thing (e.g., Herod's voice was like a god) when in reality saying something else (e.g., Herod's voice was like Nero!).[28] Whatever one makes of Klauck's thesis, Herod's gruesome death evokes a critique of ruler worship. For Luke the line between rulers and the divine can never be blurred—Jesus Christ is the only apotheosized, ascended Lord of all.

Luke's presentation of Roman rulers and officials leaves the community of God in profound tension with imperial powers. In the end, God can use imperial powers to restrain evil in such a way as to make space for the

---

[26]See Kazuhiko Yamazaki-Ransom, "Paul, Agrippa I, and Antiochus IV: Two Persecutors in Acts in Light of 2 Maccabees 9," in *Luke-Acts and Empire* (Eugene, OR: Pickwick, 2011), pp. 107-21.

[27]On Nero's voice see Cassius Dio, *Roman History* 62.20.5; Tacitus, *Annales ab Excessu Divi Augusti* 14.15, 16.22; Philostratus, *Life of Apollonius* 4.39, 5.7.

[28]See Quintillian, *Institutio Oratoria* 9.2.67; Hans-Josef Klauck, *Magic and Paganism in Earliest Christianity* (London: T & T Clark, 2003), pp. 38-44; "Des Kaisers schöne Stimme. Herrscherkritik in Apg 12, 20-23," in *Religion und Gesellschaft im frühen Christentum: Neutestamentliche Studien*, Wissenschaftliche Untersuchungen zum Neuen Testament 152 (Tübingen: Mohr Siebeck, 2003), pp. 251-67.

growth of the church, but on the other hand, Caesar and his agents lie under the authority of Satan. The empire Luke portrays is reoriented around Jesus, not Caesar, and the apostles are prepared to "obey God rather than any human authority" (Acts 5:29) when political powers—Jewish or pagan—obstruct the mission of God. The strategy of witness here is key: the apostles' obedience to God is not a call to violent sedition but to faithful witness to God's ways in Jesus. As Kavin Rowe memorably asserts: "new culture, yes—coup, no."[29] Given the Jewish precedent for violent revolt against imperial powers, Luke's emphasis on nonviolent witness is a striking feature of Acts. Though the apostles do not teach on nonviolence in Acts, they lead by example, facing persecution in ways that uphold Jesus' teaching in Luke's Gospel. Still, embellishing imperial powers as the primary obstacle to Jesus' mission is misguided; it is more accurate to recognize with Luke that, "both Herod and Pontius Pilate, with the Gentiles and the peoples of Israel, gathered together against your holy servant Jesus . . . to do whatever your hand and your plan had predestined to take place" (Acts 4:27-28). Luke understands the enemies of God more holistically than is often acknowledged. Caesar and his agents are one piece in a much larger puzzle of human rebellion against God. Even so, God transcends the "powers that be" and carries out his divine plan of redemption for the world.

JESUS IS LORD, CAESAR IS NOT?

Does Luke openly critique Caesar? No. Does Luke subtly critique Caesar? Sure, but this is hardly Luke's main purpose in writing Acts. Luke's Twitter feed is used for theological rather than revolutionary purposes. For Luke, Jesus is *the* Lord of all, a theological claim that has implications for Jews and Gentiles—the wealthy and the poor—and, yes, Caesar and his agents too. The Roman Empire has been reoriented around the ascended Jesus, but at this point in Christian history it is the Jews rather than Caesar who are most offended by this theological claim. Where Luke does record interaction with Caesar's agents, the apostles are never portrayed as attempting to take over imperial positions of power as a vehicle for advancing God's kingdom. The primary context for Christian action and witness in Acts is not the political arena or military machinery, but the assembly of Jesus' followers that we now call the church. This point speaks

---

[29]Rowe, *World Upside Down*, p. 91.

loudly to the church of today, where we often find the church's witness woven into the ethnocentric and profoundly violent agendas of the kingdoms of the world. The book of Acts calls disciples into a new world order where, in the very midst of the kingdoms of the world, God is able to bear witness to another King through the gathering and continued mission of Jesus' followers.

BIBLIOGRAPHY

Gilbert, Gary. "Roman Propaganda and Christian Identity in the Worldview of Luke-Acts." In *Contextualizing Acts: Lukan Narrative and Greco-Roman Discourse*, 233-56. Edited by Todd C. Penner and Carline Vander Stichele. Atlanta: Scholars Press, 2003.

Howell, Justin. "The Imperial Authority and Benefaction of Centurions and Acts 10:34-43: A Response to C. Kavin Rowe." *Journal for the Study of the New Testament* 31, no. 1 (2008): 25-51.

Kahl, Brigitte. "Acts of the Apostles: Pro(to)-Imperial Script and Hidden Transcript." In *In the Shadow of the Empire: Reclaiming the Bible as a History of Faithful Resistance*, 137-56. Edited by Richard A. Horsley. Louisville: Westminster John Knox, 2008.

Klauck, Hans-Josef. *The Religious Context of Early Christianity.* Translated by Brian McNeil. Minneapolis: Fortress, 2003.

Rhoades, David, David Esterline and Jae Won Lee, eds. *Luke-Acts and Empire: Essays in Honor of Robert L. Brawley.* Eugene, OR: Pickwick, 2011.

Rowe, Kavin. "Luke-Acts and the Imperial Cult: A Way Through the Conundrum?" *Journal for the Study of the New Testament* 27, no. 3 (2005): 279-33.

_____. *World Upside Down: Reading Acts in the Graeco-Roman Age.* Oxford: Oxford University Press, 2009.

Walton, Steve. "The State They Were In: Luke's View of the Roman Empire." In *Rome in the Bible and the Early Church*, 1-41. Edited by Peter Oakes. Grand Rapids: Baker, 2002.

Yamazaki-Ransom, Kazuhiko. *The Roman Empire in Luke's Narrative.* Library of New Testament Studies 404. New York: T & T Clark, 2011.

7

"One Who Will Arise to Rule Over the Nations"

Paul's Letter to the Romans and the Roman Empire

Michael F. Bird

I t is widely recognized that words like *gospel, Lord* and *Savior* were not technical Christian religious terms but shared a linguistic background in the politics, propaganda and pantheon of the Roman Empire. For Adolf Deissmann these parallels amounted to little more than a "silent protest" against Roman power.[1] For other researchers, however, these parallels suggest a deliberate challenge to Roman imperial power, especially that associated with the imperial cult and its worship of the emperor. For many scholars, Paul's gospel has a clear sociopolitical texture and a counterimperial posture by parodying the imperial rhetoric in his "gospel" announcement.[2] It is alleged that on the surface Paul writes about matters pertaining to the pastoral situation in several churches, but he also includes

---

[1]Adolf Deissmann, *Light from the Ancient East: The New Testament Illustrated by Recently Discovered Texts of the Graeco-Roman World* (London: Hodder & Stoughton, 1927), p. 355.
[2]For surveys of empire and Paul, see Warren Carter, "Paul and the Roman Empire: Recent Perspectives," in *Paul Unbound: Other Perspectives on the Apostle*, ed. M. D. Given (Peabody, MA: Hendrickson, 2010), pp. 7-26.

a veiled critique of the political power holders and their clientele. This sets the claims of Christ and the claims of Caesar on a collision course. For N. T. Wright, "At every point, therefore, we should expect what we in fact find: that for Paul, Jesus is Lord and Caesar is not."[3] Similarly John Dominic Crossan and Jonathan L. Reed state, "to proclaim Jesus as Son of God was deliberately denying Caesar his highest title."[4]

There is good reason to be positively disposed toward the thesis that Paul possessed an anti-imperial disposition. First, by the early second century the confession that "Jesus is Lord" carried with it the impossibility of ascribing the same title to Caesar, even on the threat of death.[5] Tertullian wrote that Christians faced "the accusation of treason most of all against Roman religion," most probably because they refused to offer sacrifices to local deities.[6] The exclusive Christ devotion of the early church was perceived to cut the cords that held politics, pantheon and people together as the fabric of social cohesion. Neglect of the local deities and civic religious duties, especially those sponsored by imperial patronage, was regarded as both impious and disloyal. Christians neglected what some thought necessary (worship of the gods) and abhorred precisely what many adored (Roman power). Paul was transparently impious and intensely disloyal to the ideological web that connected empire and religion if Romans 1–8 and 1 Corinthians 8–10 are anything to go by. Second, we can note how in Acts, during Paul's time in Thessalonica, the local Jews stirred up violent opposition against Paul's converts by claiming that, "These men who have caused trouble all over the world have now come here, and Jason has welcomed them into his house. They are all defying Caesar's decrees, *saying that there is another king, one called Jesus*" (Act 17:6-7 NIV).[7] The Christian declaration that Jesus was "king" stood in apparent defiance against the kingship of Caesar.[8] Third, in terms of reception history, we might note the clear anti-imperial perspective in the *Acts of Paul*. In this fictitious narrative, the Em-

---

[3]N. T. Wright, *Paul in Fresh Perspective* (Minneapolis: Fortress, 2009), p. 69.

[4]John Dominic Crossan and Jonathan L. Reed, *In Search of Paul: How Jesus's Apostle Opposed Rome's Empire with God's Kingdom* (San Francisco: Harper San Francisco, 2004), p. 11.

[5]*Martyrdom of Polycarp* 8.1–12.2.

[6]Tertullian, *Apologeticus* 24.1; cf. Pliny, *Epistles* 10.96-97.

[7]Cf. C. Kavin Rowe, *World Upside Down: Reading Acts in the Graeco-Roman Age* (Oxford: Oxford University Press, 2009), pp. 92-116.

[8]Suetonius reports about Caligula's unwillingness to concede the idea of there being other kings: "Upon hearing some kings, who came to the city to pay him court, conversing together at supper, about their illustrious descent, he exclaimed, *eis koiranos eto, eis basileus*, 'Let there be but one prince, one king'" (*Caligula* 22).

peror Nero finds out that his servant Patroclus has been resuscitated from the dead by Paul. Nero warmly greets his servant but becomes enraged at Patroclus's new faith that has even spread to his advisers:

> But when he came in and saw Patroclus he cried out, "Patroclus, are you alive?" he answered, "I am alive, Caesar." But he said, "Who is he who made you alive?" And the boy, uplifted by the confidence of faith, said, "Christ Jesus, the king of the ages." The emperor asked in dismay, "Is he to be king of ages and destroy all kingdoms?" Patroclus said to him, "Yes, he destroys all kingdoms under heaven, and he alone shall remain in all eternity, and there will be no kingdom which escapes him." And he struck his face and cried out, "Patroclus, are you also fighting for that king?" He answered, "Yes, my lord and Caesar, for he has raised me from the dead." And Barsabas Justus the flat-footed and Urion the Cappadocian and Festus of Galatia, the chief men of Nero, said, "And we, too, fight for him, the king of the ages." After having tortured those men whom he used to love he imprisoned them and ordered that the soldiers of the great king be sought, and he issued an edict that all Christians and soldiers of Christ that were found should be executed. (*Acts of Paul* 11.2)

This document, from the late second century, seems to indicate that faith in Christ and allegiance to Caesar were mutual exclusives, and that Christians were rightly recognized as a threat to the power of the Roman emperor.

There are, however, a few problems with reading anti-imperial rhetoric into Paul's letters.[9] First, Paul's letters indicate that he was hardly consumed with political activism, and his focus pertained to establishing churches with harmonious relations between Jewish and Gentile believers. That does not necessarily make him apolitical, but he was hardly a political change agent. That should be unsurprising because in the New Testament the ratio of *Theos* to *Kaesar* is 30:1.[10] Second, a further problem is that many of these so-called anti-imperial readings come at a time when anti-American sen-

---

[9]Cf. Christopher Bryan, *Render to Caesar: Jesus, the Early Church, and the Roman Superpower* (New York: Oxford University Press, 2005), pp. 9-10, 91-93; Denny Burk, "Is Paul's Gospel Counterimperial? Evaluating the Prospects of the 'Fresh Perspective' for Evangelical Theology," *Journal of the Evangelical Theological Society* 51 (2008): 309-37; Seyoon Kim, *The Gospel and the Roman Empire in the Writings of Paul and Luke* (Grand Rapids: Eerdmans, 2008); Joel White, "Anti-Imperial Subtexts in Paul: An Attempt at Building a Firmer Foundation," *Biblica* 90 (2009): 305-33; John Barclay, *Pauline Churches and Diaspora Jews*, Wissenschaftliche Untersuchungen zum Neuen Testament 1.275 (Tübingen: Mohr/Siebeck, 2011), chaps. 18-19.
[10]Dale C. Allison, *Resurrecting Jesus* (London: T & T Clark, 2005), p. 23.

timent (and anti-conservative American politics) is experiencing a cultural spike in the academy. One is left wondering then if Paul's apparent critique of Roman power is really a veiled critique of American foreign policy by left-leaning academics. Third, it need also be noted that the experience and expression of "empire" varied around the Mediterranean according to local circumstances. The visibility of the Roman Empire varied in rural Judea, Greek cities in Asia Minor, Romanized cities in Greece and in Rome itself. Even members of the Pauline churches might have variegated experiences, good and bad, of Roman power.[11] Fourth, much of Paul's language of salvation and Jesus' lordship is inherited from Septuagintal vocabulary and not imported from Roman socioreligious language. Fifth, however one spins the details, Romans 13:1-7 gives a clear affirmation of Paul's belief in the submission of Christians to state authorities. What Paul says here looks like political quietism, an affirmation of the status quo, not a script for sociopolitical resistance.

Therefore, in light of the seeming complexity of Paul's posture vis-à-vis Roman power, it is the aim of this study to determine to what extent, if any, that Paul's theology was anti-imperial. To that end, we will briefly examine Paul's letter to the Romans since Romans is the best letter for tracing the political dimensions in Paul's thought given that Paul was writing to a cluster of churches living in the very seat of Roman power.

ROMANS AND EMPIRE IN RECENT SCHOLARSHIP

Paul's engagement with Roman imperial ideology has been mapped onto Romans in several ways.

Richard A. Horsley has perhaps done more than anyone else in the last decade to bring political readings of Paul to the surface.[12] His concern has been to recapture the biblical legitimacy of resistance and to demonstrate how Jesus and Paul both represent models of resistance to imperial power.

---

[11]Cf. Simon R. F. Price, "Response," in *Paul and the Roman Imperial Order*, ed. R. A. Horsley (Harrisburg, PA: Trinity Press International, 2004), pp. 175-83.

[12]Richard A. Horsley and Neil Asher Silberman, *The Message and the Kingdom: How Jesus and Paul Ignited a Revolution and Transformed the Ancient World* (New York: Penguin Putnam, 1997); Horsley, ed., *Paul and Empire: Religion and Power in Roman Imperial Society* (Harrisburg, PA: Trinity Press International, 1997); Horsley, ed., *Paul and Politics: Ekklesia, Imperium, Interpretation* (Harrisburg, PA: Trinity Press International, 2000); Horsley, *Paul and the Roman Imperial Order* (Harrisburg, PA: Trinity Press, 2004); Horsley, ed., *In the Shadow of Empire: Reclaiming the Bible as a History of Faithful Resistance* (Louisville: Westminster John Knox, 2008).

Horsley detects in Romans Paul's attempt to convince the Roman Christians that at the heart of their apocalyptic battle was their struggle against patronage, power and privilege as it was symbolically manifested in the rites of idolatry practiced in Rome. Horsley's Paul is asking the Romans to financially support an underground movement with subversive anti-imperial beliefs.[13]

N. T. Wright sees Paul identifying "King Jesus" with the revelation of God's redemptive *iustitia* in a way that laid down a direct challenge to Roman claims that its empire was the divine harbinger of *iustitia* through its punitive military campaigns.[14] In Wright's reading of Paul, Rome is one of the malevolent powers that needs to be dealt with. Wright suggests that Paul was not

> a traveling evangelist offering people a new religious experience, but of an ambassador for a king-in-waiting, establishing cells of people loyal to this new king, and ordering their lives according to his story, his symbols, and his praxis, and their minds according to his truth. This could only be construed as deeply counter-imperial, as subversive to the whole edifice of the Roman Empire; and there is in fact plenty of evidence that Paul intended it to be so construed, and that when he ended up in prison as a result of his work he took it as a sign that he had been doing his job properly.[15]

Ekkehard W. Stegemann maintains that while Paul's gospel is *euangelion* for believers, it is *dysangelion* for Rome, because Paul looks forward to the removal of all authorities at the return of Christ. In addition, the boundary marker of imperial *fides*, namely, the trustworthiness of the emperor that is reciprocated with loyalty to him, is replaced by Paul with the faithfulness of God that is reciprocated with human faithfulness to Jesus Christ.[16]

---

[13]Horsley and Silberman, *Message and the Kingdom*, pp. 189-90.

[14]N. T. Wright, "Paul's Gospel and Caesar's Empire," in *Paul and Politics: Ekklesia, Israel, Imperium, Interpretation*, ed. R. A. Horsley (Harrisburg, PA: Trinity Press International, 2000), pp. 160-83; Wright, "A Fresh Perspective on Paul?" *Bulletin of the John Rylands Library* 83 (2001): 21-39; Wright, "Paul and Caesar: A New Reading of Romans," in *A Royal Priesthood: The Use of the Bible Ethically and Politically*, ed. C. Bartholemew, J. Chaplin, R. Song and A. Walters (Carlisle, UK: Paternoster, 2002), pp. 173-93; Wright, "Romans," in *New Interpreter's Bible*, ed. L. E. Keck (Nashville: Abingdon, 2002), 10:404-5; Wright, *Paul: Fresh Perspectives* (London: SPCK, 2005), pp. 59-79.

[15]Wright, "Paul's Gospel and Caesar's Empire," pp. 161-62.

[16]Ekkehard Stegemann, "Coexistence and Transformation: Reading the Politics of Identity in Romans in an Imperial Context," in *Reading Paul in Context: Explorations in Identity Formation*, eds. K. Ehrensperger and J. B. Tucker, Library of New Testament Studies 428 (London: T & T Clark, 2010), pp. 2-23.

For Ian Rock, Paul offers in Romans a subcultural response to the Aeneidian mythology by reference to the kingship of David, the universal covenant with Abraham, the cosmic character of the law of Moses, the history of Israel as God's chosen people, and the articulation of Jesus as Messiah and Lord. Paul inscribes this letter with the Song of Moses (Deut 32), where nations like Rome are to be objects of God's vengeance. Consequently, Paul's Romans letter was critiquing Gentile Christians who attempted to shame and exclude the returning Jewish Christians from their exile after Claudius died (54 CE).[17]

Stanley E. Porter describes the significance of the various public inscriptions around the Roman Empire, which venerated the emperors and their achievements, for forming the background to Paul's gospel ministry. Porter sees Paul styling himself as the erector of a new inscription to the true Lord, Jesus Christ. Porter comments, "Thus, from start to nearly finish, the book of Romans is Paul's attempt to indicate in the face of Roman imperialism the nature of the true Lord, Jesus Christ, and what the good news of his lordship might indicate for those who wish to follow him in the obedience of faith."[18]

One of the most concerted advocates of a political reading of Romans has come from Neil Elliott.[19] Elliott argues that Romans is "Paul's attempt to counteract the effects of imperial ideology within the Roman congregation" due partly to anti-Jewish tendencies among the Roman cultural elites that have been imbibed into the Roman congregations.[20] The heart of Paul's mission is to create a new society, one that diametrically opposed the

---

[17]Ian E. Rock, "Another Reason for Romans—A Pastoral Response to Augustan Imperial Theology: Paul's Use of the Song of Moses in Romans 9–11 and 14–15," in *Reading Paul in Context: Explorations in Identity Formation*, eds. K. Ehrensperger and J. B. Tucker, Library of New Testament Studies 428 (London: T & T Clark, 2010), pp. 74-89.

[18]Stanley E. Porter, "Paul Confronts Caesar with the Good News," in *Empire in the New Testament*, ed. Stanley E. Porter and Cynthia Long Westfall (Eugene, OR: Cascade, 2011), p. 189.

[19]Neil Elliott, "The Letter to the Romans," *A Postcolonial Commentary on the New Testament Writings*, ed. F. F. Segovia and R. S. Sugirtharajah (New York: T & T Clark, 2007), pp. 194-219; Elliott, *The Arrogance of Nations: Reading Romans in the Shadow of Empire* (Minneapolis: Fortress, 2008); Elliott, "'Blasphemed Among the Nations': Pursuing an Anti-Imperial 'Intertextuality' in Romans," in *As It Is Written: Studying Paul's Use of Scripture*, ed. Stanley E. Porter and C. D. Stanley, Society of Biblical Literature Symposium Series 50 (Leiden: Brill, 2008), pp. 213-33; Elliott, "Paul's Political Christology: Samples from Romans," in *Reading Paul in Context: Explorations in Identity Formation*, ed. K. Ehrensperger and J. B. Tucker, Library of New Testament Studies 428 (London: T & T Clark, 2010), pp. 39-51.

[20]Elliott, *Arrogance of the Nations*, p. 158.

Roman vision for its colonies.[21] He even calls Romans an "ideological intifada" against imperial thought.[22]

Robert Jewett argues that Romans is an "anti-imperialist letter" that "comprises the antithesis of official propaganda about Rome's superior piety, justice, and honor." Paul presents himself in this letter as the "king's official," who works for the gospel of his king, and this gospel has a program for "global pacification and unification."[23]

Daniel Wallace asserts that Paul's gospel explicated in Romans counteracts significant themes from Virgil's *Aeneid*, a prophetic-poetic work heavily embedded with religious themes complete with a political eschatology and a "messianic" Augustus. Wallace sees Paul as following a similar pattern to the *Aeneid* so that Romans can be read as Paul countervailing many of the socioreligious themes in Virgil's *Aeneid*.[24]

PAULUS CONTRA ROMA: PAUL AND IMPERIAL ROME IN THE LETTER TO THE ROMANS

Not everything in Romans is directly relatable to Paul and empire. After all, Romans is chiefly a letter essay concerned with gaining support for the Pauline mission to Spain, healing fractious divisions in the Roman house churches and seeking to win over the Romans to Paul's gospel as he prepares to travel to Jerusalem.[25] In what follows, I will attempt to briefly exposit those parts of Romans that, when read against the backdrop of Roman imperialism, illustrate something of Paul's stance toward the Roman Empire.

Yahweh versus the "gods" as background to Romans. We should note that in Israel's sacred traditions there was always an explicit contest between Yahweh and the pagan gods. The people of Israel and Israel's king relied on Israel's God to deliver them from the peril of the pagan kings, who looked to their gods for victory. The exodus is the story of God rescuing the Israelites from Pharaoh and from Egypt's gods (Ex 7–12). The *Shema*—the bedrock confession of Israel's faith—contained a forthright denunciation of paganism and called for steadfast devotion in the one true God of Israel (Deut 6:4-6). There is the confrontation story about Elijah the prophet

---

[21]Elliott, "Apostle Paul and Empire," pp. 108-9.
[22]Neil Elliott, *Liberating Paul* (Minneapolis: Fortress, 2006), p. 215.
[23]Robert Jewett, *Romans*, Hermeneia (Minneapolis: Fortress, 2007), pp. 2, 49, 100-101.
[24]Daniel R. Wallace, *The Gospel of God: Romans as Paul's Aeneid* (Eugene, OR: Pickwick, 2008).
[25]Cf. Michael F. Bird, "Letter to the Romans," in *All Things to All Cultures: Paul Among Jews, Greeks and Romans*, ed. M. Harding and A. Knobbs (Grand Rapids: Eerdmans, forthcoming).

versus the Baal prophets on Mount Carmel, where Yahweh proved over-whelmingly superior (1 Kings 18). In Isaiah, there is a prophecy concerning the destruction of the nations with their pantheon along with a mocking treatment of idol worship (e.g., Is 13–24; 44). In addition, in Jewish apocalyptic literature there is a strong focus on the "kingdom of God" eclipsing the Babylonian, Persian, Greek and Roman kingdoms (e.g., Dan 2; 4; 7).[26] Some Jewish authors could even identify Rome as the ultimate enemy of God's people (e.g., 1QpHab 2.10-13; *4 Ezra* 11.1-14). We should not be surprised, then, if Jewish Christian authors like Paul—invested with a strong theocentric, apocalyptic and messianic theology—looked for the eventual downfall of pagan power and the victory of God through his Messiah.

Romans 1:1-4. Jewish sociologist of religion Jacob Taubes saw in Romans 1:3-4 a subversive and anti-Caesar gambit by Paul in his opening words. Taubes declares,

> I want to stress that this is a political declaration of war, when a letter introduced using these words, and not others, is sent to the congregation in Rome to be read aloud. One doesn't know into whose hands it will fall, and the censors weren't idiots. One could, after all, have introduced it pietistically, quietistically, neutrally, or however else; but there is none of that here. That is why my thesis is that in this sense the Epistle to the Romans is a political theology, a *political* declaration of war on the Caesar.[27]

I think Taubes is correct; Romans 1:3-4 has political teeth as long as the Messiah is envisioned as the ruler of the world.

Paul opens his letter to the Romans by weaving together a standard epistolary greeting with some traditional material about the "gospel of God" and "Messiah Jesus." The gospel of God is the good news *from* God and also *about* God. The background of this "gospel" (*euangelion*) lies on the one hand in the Jewish world with the promise of the coming reign of Yahweh to bring an end to Israel's exile (Is 52:7; *Psalms of Solomon* 11.1). Yet it also

---

[26]Cf. Norman K. Gottwald, "Early Israel as an Anti-Imperial Community," in *Paul and Empire: Religion and Power in Roman Imperial Society*, ed. R. A. Horsley (Harrisburg, PA: Trinity Press International, 1997), pp. 9-24; Bryan, *Render to Caesar*, pp. 11-37; White, "Anti-Imperial Subtexts in Paul," pp. 316-26; Mark J. Boda, "Walking in the Light of Yahweh: Zion and the Empire," in *Empire in the New Testament*, ed. Stanley E. Porter and Cynthia Long Westfall (Eugene, OR: Cascade, 2011), pp. 54-89; Anathea E. Portier-Young, *Apocalypse Against Empire: Theologies of Resistance in Early Judaism* (Grand Rapids: Eerdmans, 2011).
[27]Jacob Taubes, *The Political Theology of Paul*, trans. D. Hollander (Stanford, CA: Stanford University Press, 2004), p. 16.

fits within the Greco-Roman context about news of political victory. For
instance, the calendrical inscription from Priene published by the Asian
League refers to the birthday of Augustus as the "beginning of good news
[*euangelia*] for the world." When word spread about Vespasian's intended
accession to the throne "every city celebrated the good news [*euangelia*]
and offered sacrifices on his behalf."[28] Contemporary with Paul is an extant
papyri from this era which said that Nero was "The good god of the in-
habited world, the beginning of all good things."[29] Immediately Paul's
gospel is conveyed in language normally used for the celebration of Rome's
emperors and their universal reign.

The title *Christos* (Messiah) in Paul has routinely been de-Judaized and
depoliticized in Pauline scholarship by those who want to show that Paul
did not have a messianic faith.[30] Yet the evidence overwhelmingly points in
the other direction with messianism forming the hub of Paul's Christology
(see Rom 9:5; 1 Cor 10:4; 15:22; 2 Cor 5:10; 11:2-3; Eph 1:10, 12, 20; 5:14; Phil
1:15, 17; 3:7). Importantly, "Messiah" implies kingship in Jewish tradition (2
Sam 7:14; Ps 2:2, 7; 89:19-21, 26-27; *Psalms of Solomon* 17.32). N. T. Wright
goes so far as to translate Romans 1:1 as, "Paul, a slave of *King Jesus*, called
to be an apostle, set apart for God's good news."[31] Now, messiahship was
political and the Romans knew it. Tacitus referred to a prediction from Israel's sacred traditions about how "at this very time the East was to grow
powerful, and rulers, coming from Judea, were to acquire a universal
empire."[32] Suetonius writes how "There had spread over all the Orient an
old and established belief, that it was fated at that time for men coming
from Judaea to rule the world."[33] Most likely, such views were acquired from
Jewish authors who mentioned Jewish messianic hopes in passing.[34] Paul
was identifying "King Jesus" with the scriptural hope for a ruler to come
from the East, and the Romans were well acquainted with the story.

Paul explicates this gospel "regarding his Son, who as to his earthly life
was a descendant of David, and who through the Spirit of holiness was appointed the Son of God in power by his resurrection from the dead" (Rom

[28]Josephus, *Jewish War* 4.618.
[29]POxy 1021.
[30]Cf. Michael F. Bird, *Jesus Is the Christ: The Messianic Testimony of the Gospels* (Carlisle, UK: Paternoster, 2012).
[31]N. T. Wright, *The New Testament for Everyone* (London: SPCK, 2011), p. 337.
[32]Tacitus, *Historiae* 5.13.
[33]Suetonius, *Vespasian* 4.5.
[34]See Josephus, *Jewish War* 6.312-13; Philo, *Life of Moses* 1.290.

1:3-4). Importantly, lineage meant legitimation. Claims to divine lineage were common in the biographies of the emperors. Suetonius wrote that Julius Caesar was a descendent of the goddess Venus.[35] Virgil narrated that Augustus was a descendent of Aeneas, the founder of Rome, himself descended from the goddess Venus.[36] Jesus is linked to the house of David, from whose house Israel's rightful king would come to fulfill the prophetic promises.[37] Yet Jesus is also the "Son of God," which is both a messianic title and expresses Jesus' unique filial relationship with Israel's God. Contra much scholarship, what we have in Romans 1:1-4 is not some primitive adoptionist Christology that still lurks beneath Paul's high Christology. These terse remarks are not about *adoption* but *accession* to the throne beside Yahweh.

Behind all of this stands a contrast between two kinds of sonship and two types of kingdoms. After Augustus's defeat of Anthony and Cleopatra at the Battle of Actium (31 BCE), Julius Caesar was deified and Augustus was declared a "son of a god" by the Roman senate. Augustus thereafter began to style himself as "Caesar, son of a god" (Latin: *filius dei*; Greek: *huios theou*) on his nomenclature in coins and inscriptions. The advent of his sonship was declared to have ushered in a golden age with prosperity and peace for Rome. Virgil wrote about Augustus, "This is he whom you have so often heard promised to you, Augustus Caesar, son of a god [*divi genus*], who shall again set up the Golden Age."[38] More contemporary with Paul, some inscriptions describe Nero as "son of the divine Claudius" and of the "divine Augustus."[39] Evidently Augustus and those emperors after him flooded their provinces with media and artwork designed to herald their divinity and accomplishments. The designation of Jesus as the "Son of God" does not follow on from the deification of his adopted father, nor is the title earned by any military battle. Jesus was rather designated the "Son of God" by resurrection from the dead. All the more significant because Roman religion did not believe in a resurrection.[40] Consider also that resurrection was politically threatening as it constituted the vindication and victory of those killed for opposing imperial rule as it is in Daniel 12, 2 Maccabees 7

---

[35]Suetonius, *Julius* 6.1.

[36]Virgil, *Aeneid* 1.286-90.

[37]Cf. Michael F. Bird, *Are You the One Who Is to Come? The Historical Jesus and the Messianic Question* (Grand Rapids: Baker, 2009), pp. 31-62.

[38]Virgil, *Aeneid* 6.791-793.

[39]Cf. Elliott, *Arrogance of the Nations*, pp. 71-72.

[40]N. T. Wright, *Resurrection of the Son of God*, Christian Origins and the Question of God 3 (London: SPCK, 2003), pp. 32-84.

and Revelation 20. Resurrection implies a reordering of power, an apocalyptic upheaval of the world, an inversion of the pyramid of privilege, so that those ruled over in fear are raised to reign in divine glory. The resurrection of Jesus to kingship means the supplanting of all kingdoms that compete with it. Paul celebrates that a person put to death by Roman authorities as a royal pretender had been brought back to life by Israel's God and is now installed as Lord of God's coming kingdom. Jesus' sonship belongs within a matrix of kingship, resurrection and kingdom that meant that everything that Rome stood for was on the precipice of annihilation (see Rom 5:21; 6:23; 7:24-25; 8:11, 38).

Romans 1:16-17. Coming to Romans 1:16-17, the central thesis of Romans, Paul declares that the righteousness of God is revealed in the gospel and that it brings salvation to Jews and Greeks through faith.

The "righteousness of God" is the righteous character of God enacted and embodied in his saving actions. Its background is primarily in Israel's Scriptures, given the close association of "salvation" and "righteousness" with connotations of God's faithfulness to his covenant promises and his intent to establish justice throughout all of creation (e.g., Is 51; Ps 98). Yet many of Paul's readers/hearers, living in Latin-speaking Rome, might well be aware of the connotations that "righteousness" (*dikaiosynē*) would have with culturally extant notions of "justice" (*iustitia*) and "fairness" (*aequitas*). The primary image of *aequitas* in Roman coinage was that of a woman holding a balance in her outstretched right hand. Alexandrian coins stemming from the third year of Nero's reign (c. 56-57 CE) show a picture of Nero on one side and on the other side a young woman holding the balance; however, the accompanying inscription reads in large Greek letters *dikaiosynē*. It seems that those familiar with Roman coinage may well have associated ideas of "righteousness" along the lines of impartiality, equality and fairness. In fact, Paul emphasizes exactly those qualities of God when he refers to salvation as coming equally to both Jews and Gentiles (Rom 1:16), his persistent focus on God's impartiality (Rom 2–3), the lack of "difference" between Jews and Gentiles in either condemnation or justification (Rom 3:22; 10:12), and God's repaying back to all as they deserve (Rom 2:6; 12:19). If so, the righteousness of God brings vindication for the faithful as well as fairness and equity to all.[41]

---

[41]Frank Thielman, "God's Righteousness as God's Fairness in Romans 1:17: An Ancient Perspective on a Significant Phrase," *Journal of the Evangelical Theological Society* 54 (2011): 35-48, esp. pp. 41-44.

The righteousness of God revealed in the gospel also results in "salvation" for Jews and Gentiles. The meaning of "salvation" (*sōteria*) is "rescue from danger" (Rom 5:9-10; 10:9-13; 11:11, 14, 26; 13:11). Interestingly enough, the Romans had a cult of "the salvation of the people of Rome" (*salus populi Romani*) which was restored by Augustus after a period of neglect.[42] Salvation was secured through the emperor executing his duties as *princeps* (first among equals) and *pontifex maximus* (high priest) over the empire, mediating between the people and the pantheon, and so bringing blessings, benefits, fortune, favor, prosperity and provision for the Roman colonies. Horace wrote in his typical sycophantic prose in praise of Augustus as defender of Rome: "As long as Caesar is safe, who would fear the Parthian, who [would fear] the frozen Scythian, who [would fear] the swarms which savage Germany breeds? Who would worry about war with fierce Spain?"[43] In addition, Roman literature often extolled the "salvation" that Rome brought to the world. Josephus describes how, "On reaching Alexandria Vespasian was greeted by the good news from Rome and by embassies of congratulation from every quarter of the world, now his own. . . . The whole empire being now secured and the Roman state saved beyond expectation."[44] Dieter Georgi infers that, "The *sōteria* represented by Caesar and his empire is challenged by the *sōteria* brought about by Jesus. Like that of Caesar, the *sōteria* of the God Jesus is worldwide."[45] Paul does not directly polemicize against the Roman *salus*, however; his gospel of salvation delivers from sin and death, and is both superior to Roman salvation in quality and is naturally contrasted with what Roman power and its political benefactors had to offer. For Paul, "Evangelical persuasion rather than political and military power is thus the means whereby the salvation of the world is now occurring."[46]

The gospel that reveals God's righteousness calls for the response of faith and faithfulness. Both trust and trustworthiness can be implied by the noun *pistis* and by the wider context of Habakkuk 2:4, which Paul cites. This entails both faith in God and fidelity to God. This evangelical "faith" can be naturally contrasted with Roman *fides*. The goddess Fides, the deity

---

[42]*Acts of Augustus* 19-21; Horace, *Odes* 3.6.1; Virgil, *Aeneid* 6.716; Ovid, *Fasti* 2.63; Suetonius, *Augustus* 30.

[43]Horace, *Odes* 4.5.

[44]Josephus, *Jewish War* 4.656-657.

[45]Dieter Georgi, "God Turned Upside Down," in *Paul and Empire: Religion and Power in Roman Imperial Society,* ed. R. A. Horsley (Harrisburg, PA: TPI, 1997), p. 152.

[46]Jewett, *Romans*, p. 141.

of loyalty and fidelity, was understood to be operative through Rome's emperors. The emperor personified Roman faithfulness to its treaties and subjects, but in return demanded reciprocal faithfulness from those over whom he ruled. The *Acts of Augustus* state that those subjugated by Rome have "discovered the *pistis* of the Roman people."[47] The Roman governor of Egypt, Tiberius Alexander, ordered "the legions and the multitude to take the oath of fidelity to Vespasian."[48] The "faith" of Roman subjects was somewhere between fealty and slavery. Roman emperors kept faith with their subjects as long as they were obedient and subservient. For Paul, faith is not fealty but a believing in and belonging to the God who calls people to himself (Rom 9:25-26). Paul will go on to say that pagan Romans have "no fidelity, no love, no mercy" (Rom 1:31), yet these are the very qualities that the God of the Messiah possesses (Rom 5:8; 8:28-39; 9:15-18, 23; 11:30-32; 12:1; 15:9).

In a nutshell, in Romans 1 we have a natural juxtaposition between two competing reigns: the house of Caesar and the house of David. There is a contrast of two divine "sons": Caesar, who achieved his divine sonship by killing his political adversaries, and Jesus, whose divine sonship is recognized by resurrection from the dead. The *iustitia* of Rome that was rife with corruption is contrasted with the *dikaiosynē* of God characterized by mercy and impartiality. The faithfulness of the emperor that demanded fealty is set against the faithfulness of God that demonstrated love. The salvation of Rome was created by violence, while the salvation of God was displayed in his offer of reconciliation. This is more than an *allusion* by Paul to political propaganda that is laden with religious language. The juxtaposition is more like a *collision* of two gospels, a confrontation between two Lords, the good news of Roman military power versus the good news of redemption through the Lord Jesus Christ. As Wright comments, "To come to Rome with the gospel of Jesus, to announce someone else's accession to the world's throne, therefore, was to put on a red coat and walk into a field with a potentially angry bull."[49]

Romans 13:1-7. The one text in Romans that says the most about the Roman governing authorities is Roman 13:1-7. Yet this passage is arguably benign in its remarks concerning Roman power. If anything, this text promotes submission to the state and complicity with its requirements by

[47]*Acts of Augustus* 31-33.
[48]Josephus, *Jewish War* 4.617.
[49]Wright, "Romans," 10:423; cf. Georgi: "If the terms chosen by Paul for his Roman readers have associations with the slogans of Caesar religion, then Paul's gospel must be understood as competing with the gospel of the Caesars" ("God Turned Upside Down," p. 152).

Christians. No surprise that this text has been controversial in its history of reception concerning church-state relationships, and various provenances have been proposed for its occasion.[50] It may also be the case that Paul's apparent subjection of Christians to Roman political power is not meant to be unchecked or unqualified.

My own view is that Romans 13:1-7 must be informed by three things. First, we must remember that Paul's terse remarks about submission to state authorities are saturated with God language with six references to *Theos* in the space of seven verses. For Paul there is no authority *except from God;* the powers are *appointed by God;* those who resist his appointed political authorities oppose the *authority of God;* political authorities preserving social order with the sword are in effect the *agent of God;* and political authorities are even *servants of God.* This is not a capitulation to pagan power but a fervent affirmation of divine authority over civil powers.[51] Second, nothing in Romans 13:1-7 compromises Jesus' lordship. However we read Romans 13:1-7, Jesus remains the one in whom the nations place their hopes. Third, we have to read Romans 13 in light of Paul's apocalyptic narrative about the overthrow of all authorities at the return of Jesus. Paul declares that the "powers," be they political or spiritual, have been disarmed and are impotent before Jesus' lordship (see Rom 8:38-39; 1 Cor 2:8; 15:25-26; Col 2:15). In fact, Paul's remarks about governing authorities in Romans 13:1-7 are relativized by his exhortation in Romans 13:11-14. Paul urges his audience with, "you know what time it is, how it is now the moment for you to wake from sleep"; and, "for salvation is nearer to us now than when we became believers; the night is far gone, the day is near" (NRSV), so that salvation is at least impending and will bring with it the dissolution and judgment of these very same authorities. Paul acquiesces to political submission for the sake of respecting God's appointed servants who genuinely benefit the city, and he recognizes that respect for authorities is a sensible way of staying under the radar of the imperial security apparatus. However, he is certain that Rome is not *Roma aeterna* (eternal Rome) because "time is short" (1 Cor 7:29), the "day is near" (Rom 13:12), and all will stand before the "judgment seat of God" (Rom 14:10).[52]

On this view, Romans 13:1-7 is still an affirmation of God's authority, Jesus'

---

[50]Cf. S. Krauter, *Studien zu Röm 13:1-7. Paulus und der politische Diskurs der neronischen Zeit* (Tübingen: Mohr/Siebeck, 2009), pp. 4-38.

[51]Stegemann, "Coexistence and Transformation," pp. 13-14.

[52]Cf. Bryan, *Render to Caesar*, pp. 81-82; White, "Anti-Imperial Subtexts in Paul," pp. 329-30.

lordship and the triumph of God through Christ over all powers at the consummation. But this passage is a footnote or qualification to what God's victory means at ground zero in Rome. Paul does not want Christians trying to effect a temporary revolution that effectively replaces one dictator with another one, nor believing that they transcend obligations to the state be it taxes or respect, nor throwing in their lot with the increasingly violent anti-Roman sentiment festering in Palestine at the time. They are in a position of vulnerability as a sect without state recognition, hence they are liable to "shame," "suffering," "sword," "accusation" and "persecution" (Rom 5:3-5; 8:18, 31-39; 12:14, 17). So he wants believers to respect authorities because even pagan authorities from Cyrus to Caesar serve an ordained role in God's purposes. Survival is one of the best forms of defiance. Yet he can say this because such kings will be held to account when they stand before the judgment seat of Christ (Rom 2:16; 14:10), and vengeance belongs to God (Rom 12:19).

Romans 15. The climax to Romans arguably comes in Romans 15:5-13, with exhortations to unity in Messiah Jesus. The most pertinent element for our study is Romans 15:12 with its citation of Isaiah 11:10:

> Isaiah says,
> > "The Root of Jesse will spring up,
> > > one who will arise to rule over the nations;
> > in him the Gentiles will hope."

The "Root of Jesse" is a messianic designation for a royal eschatological deliverer and is equivalent to the "Root of David" (1QSb 5.26; 4QFlor 1.11; Sir 47:22; Rev 5:5; 22:16). The rise of Israel's kingdom from its humiliating subjugation under foreign powers like Rome will be achieved through Messiah Jesus. It is not the case that Paul eliminates the "toxic residues of chauvinism and imperialism from the context of Isaiah 11." Instead, he sets forth the rule of the Messiah over the nations as benign and beneficial since Jesus is the object of the Gentiles' hope.[53] Jesus' reign is not militaristic, but it certainly dethrones all powers and authorities hostile to God's kingdom. Paul knows that the world is ruled by powers hostile to God's purposes, including sin and death (Rom 6:9, 14), flesh (Rom 8:7) and Satan (Rom 16:20).

If Jesus is the appointed ruler over the nations and the source of their hope, then he is precisely what many believed Rome's emperor and empire to be. The *Aeneid* asserts that Rome could achieve "sovereignty without

---

[53]Contra Jewett, *Romans*, p. 897.

limit." There was even a "gift of the nations" brought to Caesar.[54] Virgil used his poetry to teach that the Romans will "rule earth's peoples."[55] The universal reach of Rome's power in bringing other nations under its patronage is celebrated in the *Acts of Augustus*, with emphasis on the pacification of peoples, colonization of territories and the extension of Rome's empire into northern Europe, Africa and Asia.[56] Augustus even arranged for a statue of himself to be erected next to the speaker's rostrum depicting him in the nude with his foot resting on a globe.[57] But this unchallengeable Roman power is challenged by this simple citation from Isaiah 11 concerning the Root of Jesse who will regather the exiles from the "four quarters of the earth," while "Judah's enemies will be destroyed" (Is 11:11-12). For Paul, this is already a reality in the messianic community consisting of Jews and Gentiles praising God for his mercy demonstrated in the Messiah.

CONCLUSION

Romans is not a political manifesto. It is pastoral theology, albeit one not divorced from the sociopolitical realities of the Roman Mediterranean. The universal vision of Paul's gospel clearly competes with the Roman vision for its universal reign. As William Ramsay wrote, "A universal Paulinism and a universal Empire must either coalesce, or the one must destroy the other."[58]

Our survey of Romans has demonstrated that Paul's gospel has sociopolitical implications because Israel's faith was always sociopolitical. Paul clearly evokes and revises imperial concepts in his theological discourse. To be sure, Paul's principal source for his theologizing is the Old Testament and the Jesus tradition, yet he simultaneously echoes themes, language and symbols situated in the Roman imperial context. Anyone vaguely familiar with Roman coins, inscriptions, literature, votive offerings and religion could see Paul engaging in a hidden transcript of protest. It is not simply the "parallel" terminology that Paul uses like *Kyrios* or *euangelion*, but the apocalyptic and messianic narrative that such language is couched in that makes it tacitly counterimperial.[59]

---

[54]Virgil, *Aeneid* 8.715-28.

[55]Ibid., 6.1151-52.

[56]*Acts of Augustus* 26-33.

[57]Jewett, *Romans*, p. 48.

[58]William Ramsay, *The Cities of St. Paul: Their Influence on His Life and Thought* (Grand Rapids: Baker, 1979), p. 70.

[59]Contra Burk, "Is Paul's Gospel Counter-Imperial?" pp. 315-22; Kim, *Christ and Caesar*, pp. 28-30; Bryan, *Render to Caesar*, pp. 90-91.

Paul's *euangelion* is the royal announcement that God's *dikaiosynē* avails for believing Jews and Greeks, but bad news for the powers because of the concurrent revelation of God's wrath against idolatry and wickedness (Rom 1:18). Paul's letter to the Romans is delivered to the heart of the empire with a bold thesis that there is only one true Lord, Jesus Christ. The violence of Roman military power and the foolishness of Roman religion will all collapse under the weight of the kingdom of Christ. Should a Roman official have read Romans, the letter would have appeared to be the ravings of a fanatical Eastern superstition, politically malicious at best and seditious at worst.

During my childhood years, my aunt had three friendly Labradors, one of whom was named "Nero." I always thought that "Nero" was a peculiar name for a dog, especially when names like "Rover" were more common. As I think about it now, there is something fiercely ironic in that. Paul the apostle was put to death by Nero. Nero had sentenced many men and women to death, and he probably thought nothing of ordering another Jew, another religious fanatic from the East, to his death. Yet, as T. R. Glover noted, little did Nero know that a day was to come when people would call their sons Paul and their dogs Nero.[60]

BIBLIOGRAPHY

Allison, Dale C. *Resurrecting Jesus*. London: T & T Clark, 2005.

Barclay, John. *Pauline Churches and Diaspora Jews*. WUNT 1.275. Tübingen: Mohr/Siebeck, 2011.

Bird, Michael F. *Are You the One Who Is to Come? The Historical Jesus and the Messianic Question*. Grand Rapids: Baker, 2009.

_____. *Jesus is the Christ: The Messianic Testimony of the Gospels*. Carlisle, UK: Paternoster, 2012.

_____. "Letter to the Romans." In *All Things to All Cultures: Paul among Jews, Greeks and Romans*. Edited by M. Harding and A. Knobbs. Grand Rapids: Eerdmans, forthcoming.

Boda, Mark J. "Walking in the Light of Yahweh: Zion and the Empire." In *Empire in the New Testament*, pp. 54-89. Edited by S. E. Porter and C. L. Westfall. Eugene, OR: Cascade, 2011.

Bruce, F. F. *Paul: Apostle of the Free Spirit*. Rev. ed. Carlisle, UK: Paternoster, 1980.

---

[60]Cited from F. F. Bruce, *Paul: Apostle of the Free Spirit*, rev. ed. (Carlisle, UK: Paternoster, 1980), p. 5.

Bryan, Christopher. *Render to Caesar: Jesus, the Early Church, and the Roman Superpower.* New York: Oxford University Press, 2005.

Burk, Denny. "Is Paul's Gospel Counterimperial? Evaluating the Prospects of the 'Fresh Perspective' for Evangelical Theology." *JETS* 51 (2008): 309-37.

Carter, Warren. "Paul and the Roman Empire: Recent Perspectives." In *Paul Unbound: Other Perspectives on the Apostle*, pp. 7-26. Edited by M. D. Given. Peabody, MA: Hendrickson, 2010.

Crossan, John Dominic, and Jonathan L. Reed. *In Search of Paul: How Jesus's Apostle Opposed Rome's Empire with God's Kingdom.* San Francisco: Harper San Francisco, 2004.

Deissman, Adolf. *Light from the Ancient East: The New Testament Illustrated by Recently Discovered Texts of the Graeco-Roman World.* London: Hodder & Stoughton, 1927.

Elliott, Neil. *The Arrogance of Nations: Reading Romans in the Shadow of Empire.* Minneapolis: Fortress, 2008.

_____. "'Blasphemed among the Nations': Pursuing an Anti-Imperial 'Intertextuality' in Romans." In *As It Is Written: Studying Paul's Use of Scripture*, pp. 213-33. Edited by S. E. Porter and C. D. Stanley. SBLSS 50; Leiden: Brill, 2008.

_____. "The Letter to the Romans." In *A Postcolonial Commentary on the New Testament Writings*, pp. 194-219. Edited by F. F. Segovia and R. S. Sugirtharajah. New York: T & T Clark, 2007.

_____. *Liberating Paul.* Minneapolis: Fortress, 2006.

_____. "Paul's Political Christology: Samples from Romans." In *Reading Paul in Context: Explorations in Identity Formation*, pp. 39-51. Edited by K. Ehrensperger and J. B. Tucker. Festschrift William S. Campbell; LNTS 428. London: T & T Clark, 2010.

Georgi, Dieter. "God Turned Upside Down." In *Paul and Empire: Religion and Power in Roman Imperial Society*, pp. 148-57. Edited by R. A. Horsley. Harrisburg, PA: Trinity Press International, 1997.

Gottwald, Norman K. "Early Israel as an Anti-Imperial Community." In *Paul and Empire: Religion and Power in Roman Imperial Society*, pp. 9-24. Edited by R. A. Horsley. Harrisburg, PA: Trinity Press International, 1997.

Horsley, Richard A., ed. *In the Shadow of Empire: Reclaiming the Bible as a History of Faithful Resistance.* Louisville, KY: Westminster John Knox, 2008.

_____, ed. *Paul and Empire: Religion and Power in Roman Imperial Society.* Harrisburg, PA: Trinity Press International, 1997.

_____, ed. *Paul and Politics: Ekklesia, Imperium, Interpretation.* Festschrift

Krister Stendahl. Harrisburg: Trinity Press International, 2000.

_____. *Paul and the Roman Imperial Order*. Harrisburg, PA: Trinity Press, 2004.

Horsley, Richard A., and Neil Asher Silberman. *The Message and the Kingdom: How Jesus and Paul Ignited a Revolution and Transformed the Ancient World*. New York: Penguin Putnam, 1997.

Jewett, Robert. *Romans*. Hermeneia. Minneapolis: Fortress, 2007.

Kim, Seyoon. *The Gospel and the Roman Empire in the Writings of Paul and Luke*. Grand Rapids: Eerdmans, 2008.

Krauter, S. *Studien zu Röm 13,1-7. Paulus und der politische Diskurs der neronischen Zeit*. WUNT 243. Tübingen: Mohr/Siebeck, 2009.

Porter, Stanley E. "Paul Confronts Caesar with the Good News." In *Empire in the New Testament*, pp. 164-96. Edited by S. E. Porter and C. L. Westfall. Eugene, OR: Cascade, 2011.

Portier-Young, Anthea E. *Apocalypse Against Empire: Theologies of Resistance in Early Judaism*. Grand Rapids: Eerdmans, 2011.

Price, Simon R. F. "Response." In *Paul and the Roman Imperial Order*, pp. 175-83. Edited by R. A. Horsley. Harrisburg, PA: Trinity Press International, 2004.

Ramsay, William. *The Cities of St. Paul: Their Influence on His Life and Thought*. Grand Rapids: Baker, 1979.

Rock, Ian E. "Another Reason for Romans—A Pastoral Response to Augustan Imperial Theology: Paul's Use of the Song of Moses in Romans 9–11 and 14–15." In *Reading Paul in Context: Explorations in Identity Formation*, pp. 74-89. Edited by K. Ehrensperger and J. B. Tucker. LNTS 428. London: T & T Clark, 2010.

Rowe, C. Kavin. *World Upside Down: Reading Acts in the Graeco-Roman Age*. Oxford: Oxford University Press, 2009.

Stegemann, Ekkehard. "Coexistence and Transformation: Reading the Politics of Identity in Romans in an Imperial Context." In *Reading Paul in Context: Explorations in Identity Formation*, pp. 2-23. Edited by K. Ehrensperger and J. B. Tucker. LNTS 428. London: T & T Clark, 2010.

Taubes, Jacob. *The Political Theology of Paul*. Translated by D. Hollander. Stanford: Stanford University Press, 2004.

Thielman, Frank. "God's Righteousness as God's Fairness in Romans 1:17: An Ancient Perspective on a Significant Phrase." *JETS* 54 (2011): 35-48.

Wallace, Daniel R. *The Gospel of God: Romans as Paul's Aeneid*. Eugene, OR: Pickwick, 2008.

White, Joel. "Anti-Imperial Subtexts in Paul: An Attempt at Building a Firmer

Foundation." *Biblica* 90 (2009): 305-33.

Wright, N. T. "A Fresh Perspective on Paul?" *BJRL* 83 (2001): 21–39.

_____. *The New Testament for Everyone*. London: SPCK, 2011.

_____. *Paul: Fresh Perspectives*. London: SPCK, 2005.

_____. "Paul and Caesar: A New Reading of Romans." In *A Royal Priesthood: The Use of the Bible Ethically and Politically*, pp. 173-93. Edited by C. Bartholemew, J. Chaplin, R. Song and A. Walters. Carlisle, UK: Paternoster, 2002.

_____. "Paul's Gospel and Caesar's Empire." In *Paul and Politics: Ekklesia, Israel, Imperium, Interpretation: Essays in Honor of Krister Stendahl*, pp. 160-83. Edited by R. A. Horsley. Harrisburg, PA: Trinity Press International, 2000.

_____. *Resurrection of the Son of God*. Christian Origins and the Question of God 3. London: SPCK, 2003.

_____. "Romans." In *New Interpreters Bible*, 10:393-770. Edited by L. E. Keck. 12 vols. Nashville: Abingdon, 2002.

8

PHILIPPIANS AND EMPIRE

PAUL'S ENGAGEMENT WITH IMPERIALISM AND THE IMPERIAL CULT

Lynn H. Cohick

INTRODUCTION TO IMPERIALISM AND ANTI-IMPERIAL RHETORIC IN PHILIPPIANS

The subject of the Roman Empire arises naturally in a study of Paul's letter to the Philippians, for several historical and literary reasons. First, the city was a Roman colony, having the rights and privileges of a city on Italian soil. It was populated by landed Roman farmers and military veterans, perhaps sons of men who fought in the decisive battle on the nearby plains between Octavian and Marc Antony, on the one hand, and Brutus and Cassius on the other in 42 BCE (Appian, *Bellum Civile* 4.105-38). Nearby in Actium, Octavian defeated Marc Antony and Cleopatra a decade later (31 BCE), and assumed the role of sole ruler, Augustus. Second, Paul writes to the Philippians from prison, in close proximity to the Praetorian Guard, the elite force protecting the emperor. Third, Paul uses explicitly civic or political terms in Philippians 1:27 (*politeuesthe*) and Philippians 3:20 (*politeuma*), and describes Jesus as Savior, an unusual term for Paul, but more commonly found describing the emperor or a victorious general. Commentators wrestle with the implications of these disparate pieces and offer a range of interpretations. Although a few make almost no mention of either empire or the imperial cult,[1] the majority of commentators call attention to the imperial cult as a social reality present at Philippi and thus part of the historical fabric of the young church's world.

BACKGROUND OF THE IMPERIAL CULT IN PHILIPPI

A word about the imperial cult will set the stage for examining its presence in Philippi. Recent discussions about whether the living emperor was worshiped as a god or whether the living emperor's *genius* was honored have lent new vigor to the study of the imperial cult.

General background and development of the imperial cult. The prevailing view on the imperial cult's development is that it grew from the Greek ruler cult and the private worship of the *genius* (life force) of the Roman paterfamilias.[2] Most argue that Romans honored the living emperor's *genius*, much as was done in every Roman household to the *genius* of the paterfamilias or oldest male.[3] Augustus postured himself as the first citizen, *princeps*, and as the paterfamilias of the entire empire. Thus he promoted the worship of his *genius* and *Lares* (family gods) by his entire family, his empire. When a Roman family poured a libation to Augustus's *genius* at their meal, they affirmed him as the Father of the State.[4] The first-century BCE historian Nicholas of Damascus declares "Because mankind address him thus [as Sebastos, i.e., "revered"], in accordance with their estimation of his honour, they revere him with temple and sacrifices over islands and continents, organized in cities and provinces, matching the greatness of his virtue and repaying his benefactions towards them."[5] An inscription from Eresus on the island of Lesbos dated to the end of Augustus's or the beginning of Tiberius's reign declares that the community incorporated into their traditional celebrations the veneration of Augustus and his family/house. Commenting on the inscription, Price notes, "the visual expression

---

[1]Peter T. O'Brien, *The Epistle to the Philippians*, New International Greek Testament Commentary (Grand Rapids: Eerdmans, 1991).

[2]S. R. F. Price, *Rituals and Power: The Roman Imperial Cult in Asia Minor* (Cambridge: Cambridge University Press, 1984), p. 24. He cautions against drawing a neat, simplistic line from ruler cult to imperial cult, but agrees that the two share common characteristics.

[3]Lily Ross Taylor, *The Divinity of the Roman Emperor* (Middletown, CT: American Philological Association, 1931).

[4]Ibid., p. 152.

[5]Nicolaus of Damascus, *Fragmenta Historicorum Graecorum* 90 F 125; see Price, *Rituals and Power*, p. 1.

of the emperor was incorporated into the regular life of the communities through public celebrations."[6]

Addressing the consensus, Ittai Gradel argues provocatively that high-status Romans, such as senators, would not have worshiped Augustus's *genius* because such action would have been beneath their social rank; they were accustomed to receive this kind of honor, not bestow it. Instead, they worshiped the living emperor as a god. Gradel focuses on ritual and sacrifice, not on theological or philosophical treatises, because he holds that the former should not be interpreted by the later.[7] Gradel contends that Romans constructed a fluid boundary between human and divine, and the distinction was based on social status, a relative category, not on an ontological difference between humanity and divinity. The imperial cult was a privately funded cult rooted in the benefaction system. Sacrifices honored a deserving figure; they were "an aspect of the honors-for-benefactions structure found in all relationships between parties of vastly unequal power and social standing in Roman society."[8] Emperors were worshiped because they held vastly more power than any other person. In evaluating Gradel's argument, his consideration of worshipers' social status is an important observation. He is also right to point out that private worship of the emperor was extensive. However, by bracketing out most literary evidence to focus solely on the rituals of sacrifice and temple cult, Gradel artificially separates practice and theory in interpreting the ancient worshipers. Additionally, while it is likely true that a modern sociological study of Roman religion might show divine status to be a relative category, ancient Roman authors speak of divine and human in ontological terms.[9]

These discussions highlight the complexity of the imperial cult and the limitations of our evidence.[10] When considering the cult, we should note that it is an innovation that grew as the Roman Republic shifted to a monarchial form of government, but that it had continuities with pagan practices both in private home worship and in the Hellenistic ruler cult. The imperial cult promoted the emperor, but also the imperial family. The cult displayed

---

[6]Price, *Rituals and Power*, p. 3; Inscription *IG* XII Supp. 124, see Price, *Rituals and Power*, p. 249.
[7]Ittai Gradel, *Emperor Worship and Roman Religion* (Oxford: Oxford University Press, 2002), p. 3.
[8]Ibid., p. 26.
[9]D. Wardle review of Ittai Gradel, *Emperor Worship and Roman Religion*, *Scholia Reviews* n.s., 13 (2004): 19.
[10]For an engaging discussion between classicists and New Testament scholars, see *Rome and Religion: A Cross-Disciplinary Dialogue on the Imperial Cult*, ed. Jeffrey Brodd and Jonathan L. Reed (Atlanta: Society of Biblical Literature, 2011).

the military power of the emperor and also honored his euergetism (public benefaction). We should not imagine, then, that Paul's claim that Jesus is Lord would neatly parallel the claims or assumptions made when a Roman citizen or a Greek peasant said "Caesar is Savior." Indeed, perhaps the citizen and peasant would have very different expectations about their actions. Still, both individuals would interpret their actions through the lens of Roman paganism. It is to this foundational worldview structure that Paul speaks in declaring the gospel.

The imperial cult in Philippi. Philippi in Paul's day was a Roman colony refounded and established by Augustus as Colonia Augusta Iulia Philippensis. Most inscriptions were in Latin, the temples were dedicated to Roman gods and goddesses, and the city's governing structure was Roman. The city Augustus refounded was centuries earlier a Thracian city conquered by Philip of Macedon, father of Alexander the Great. Alexander became associated with the Greek god Dionysus, and around 325 BCE the city of Athens formally decreed Alexander a god, identifying him with Dionysus.[11] This connection was not arbitrary; Alexander was declared to be the son of Zeus (as was Dionysus) by the oracle of Ammon in Libya and the oracle of Apollo at Branchidae.[12] Evidence from the imperial period suggests that Dionysus was actively worshiped in Philippi. It is possible that such worship represents an ongoing form of the ruler cult that flourished in Alexander's time. If so, the imperial cult would have seemed proper and natural; with Augustus refounding the city, his worship as the city's great benefactor fit appropriately with previous customs.

First-century CE inscriptions verify that the imperial cult was present in Philippi. Archaeological excavations have unearthed several unspecified temples in Philippi, and most studies conclude that two buildings in the forum should be identified as imperial cult temples.[13] One surviving inscription from perhaps the mid-first century in Neapolis, Philippi's ancient port, identifies Cornelia Asprilla as a priestess of Livia Augusta.[14] I note this inscription for two reasons: first, it celebrates Augustus's wife, who was de-

---

[11]Taylor, *Divinity of the Roman Emperor*, p. 21.
[12]Ibid., pp. 15-16.
[13]Erik M. Heen, "Phil 2:6-11 and Resistance to Local Timocratic Rule: *Isa theō* and the Cult of the Emperor in the East," in *Paul and the Roman Imperial Order*, ed. Richard A. Horsley (Harrisburg, PA: Trinity Press International, 2004), p. 135.
[14]Peter Pilhofer, *Philippi*, vol. 2, *Katalog der Inscriften von Philippi* (Tübingen, Mohr Siebeck, 2009), pp. 2-3.

creed a goddess under the Emperor Claudius, her grandson. Often when a reader sees "imperial cult," immediately a male image comes to mind, but in the ancient world Livia was well known and greatly admired. Second, it identifies a woman priestess. Often readers assume a male priesthood for the imperial cult, but this image does not do justice to the evidence; both women and men participated in pagan cults as officials, with each cult having its own particular requirements. The imperial cult was solidly rooted in the benefaction system that linked emperor and people. The priests and priestesses who officiated in the imperial cult acted as benefactors to their cities and declared themselves friends to the imperial family.

The imperial cult cannot be abstracted from paganism generally; indeed, remains of imperial cult temples are so similar to other temples that without inscriptions identifying the building as dedicated to Roma and the imperial cult, we could not distinguish between them.[15] When Paul visited Philippi, Claudius was emperor; the senate, upon his death, declared him divine. When Paul wrote Philippians, Nero was emperor, and he did not enjoy an apotheosis (transformation to deity). Thus during Paul's lifetime, Romans (and everyone else but Jews) worshiped Julius Caesar, Augustus, Livia and Claudius in the imperial cult at Philippi. For Jews such as Paul, the imperial cult was part of the larger system of idolatry that plagued his era and that of his ancestors.

CURRENT RESEARCH ON IMPERIALISM IN PHILIPPIANS

The historical reality of the imperial cult and the ascendancy of imperial Rome have served as fertile soil to pursue modern questions about globalization and neocolonialism. From within postcolonial thought, two contradictory assertions about Paul and empire have emerged. One approach asserts that Paul is anti-imperial; he countered Roman imperial dominance with a suppressed message of resistance against Roman hegemony and emperor worship encoded in his letters. Paul writes as one oppressed, and therefore buries the message—Caesar is not Lord and Savior—in code. This perspective accepts the larger contentions of postcolonial thought, including that colonized peoples used coded communication and mimicked as well as subtly renounced the colonizer's thought and ways.[16] A second

---

[15]Gradel, *Emperor Worship and Roman Religion*, p. 81, drawing on work by H. Hänlein-Schäfer, *Veneratio Augusti: Eine Studie zu den Tempeln des Ersten römischen Kaisers* (Rome: 1985).

[16]Warren Carter, *The Roman Empire and the New Testament: An Essential Guide* (Nashville: Abingdon, 2006). See also Richard Horsley, *Paul and Roman Imperial Order* (Harrisburg, PA:

approach argues that Paul is imperialist. This position combines post-colonial and feminist hermeneutics, and maintains that Paul displays an imperial or colonist mindset, for he demands obedience from his congregations and silences dialogue while asserting a hegemonic viewpoint. The reader's responsibility, according to this perspective, is to resist Paul's colonial mindset by reading against the grain of Paul and in support of his oppressed congregations.

Not surprisingly, these two approaches arrive at quite different conclusions concerning the question of Paul and imperialism. I will argue that neither position adequately captures Paul's primary message. To tip my hand to the reader, I am not persuaded that Paul develops an explicit anti-imperial (or anti-imperial cult) program, nor do I think that the postcolonial and feminist hermeneutics convincingly establish the case that Paul exhibits colonial inclinations. Both these positions fail to engage fully Paul's Jewish theological and social environment.

PAUL'S ANTI-IMPERIAL MESSAGE IN PHILIPPIANS?

Argument for Paul as anti-imperial. Three specific texts are regularly pointed to as key indications of Paul's anti-imperialism and his desire for Christians to resist imperial Rome: Philippians 1:27; 2:5-11; 3:20-21.

Philippians 1:27: politeuesthe (exercise your citizenship). The translation of this imperative has vexed scholars, in no small part because the term is found only here in Paul (yet see Acts 23:1), although cognates are found in Philippians 3:20 (discussed later; see also Eph 2:12). The term carries the sense of participating dutifully in civic life, being mindful of one's civic responsibilities. The anti-imperial Paul perspective suggests that Paul draws on this general meaning to make a contrast for the Philippians between a civic mindset that supports the empire, and a community mindset that supports the Christian church.

Paul reframes the Philippians' duty to their city; as believers they are to live daily with new, nonimperial values and commitments.

Philippians 2:5-11: "Jesus Christ is Lord." The anti-imperial reading suggests that Paul is parodying the encomiums and paeans given to the emperor, and in so doing underscores the exalted nature of Christ over against the hegemonic claims of the imperial cult. For example, John Reumann suggests

---

Trinity Press International, 2004); and N. T. Wright, *Paul in Fresh Perspective* (Minneapolis: Fortress, 2005).

that Roman emperors serve as a foil against which the truth of Christ's lordship can be seen.[17] Erik Heen focuses on the phrase *isa theō* (equality with God) and its common occurrence in pagan panegyrics and encomiums that elevated the emperor with highest honors. He draws on James C. Scott's work that identifies public and private "transcripts," which serve to establish and maintain the elite aristocracy's grip on the culture and their city's governance. Between the private yearnings of the oppressed and the public display of praise for the elite, Heen sees a third way, namely, hymns of worship that challenge the elite's story.[18] A third interpretation suggests that Paul has in mind the Jewish Scriptures, particularly Isaiah 45:23-24, as an indirect counter to the pagan vision of a deity's coronation. As further proof of this position, N. T. Wright suggests that the injunction in Philippians 2:12 to "work out your salvation with fear and trembling" counters the position of salvation promoted by imperial propaganda, namely, that submission to Caesar as Lord will provide deliverance or salvation.[19]

Philippians 3:20-21: politeuma (citizenship) and sōtēr (Savior). The center of the anti-imperial reading of Philippians is located in these verses, particularly in Paul's use of the terms *politeuma* and *sōtēr*. Looking at Philippians 3:20, Warren Carter suggests that Paul recontextualizes the Philippians' citizenship (*politeuma*); he reorders their perceptions about everyday values and commitments from a focus on the empire to a focus on Jesus as Savior. Carter suggests Paul implicitly asks those believers who are citizens to renounce their status and privilege.[20] Wright proposes that Paul's discussion of Judaism earlier in the chapter is a coded message for the Philippians to reject their privileged status as members of a Roman colony and embrace their new status as members of God's kingdom.[21] Paul's call to imitate him is a reference to giving up social status, even as did Paul within Judaism (Phil 3:17, see also Phil 3:5-7). Paul had pride in his Jewish heritage, and according to Wright the text implies the Philippians were similarly in danger of having pride in their Roman status, and thus would miss the true

[17]John Reumann, *Philippians*, Anchor Yale Bible (New Haven, CT: Yale University Press, 2008), pp. 368-69.
[18]Heen, "Phil 2:6-11 and Resistance to Local Timocratic Rule," pp. 152-53.
[19]N. T. Wright, *Paul: A Fresh Perspective*, pp. 73-74.
[20]Carter, *Roman Empire and the New Testament*, p. 62.
[21]Wright, "Paul's Gospel and Caesar's Empire," pp. 6-7. http://ntwrightpage.com/Wright_Paul_Caesar_Empire.pdf. Building on this topic in slightly different ways, and with a bit more nuance, see Wright, "Paul's Gospel and Caesar's Empire," in *Paul and Politics*, ed. Richard A. Horsley (Harrisburg, PA: Trinity Press International, 2000), pp. 160-83.

call of the gospel of suffering and the true victory of the returning Christ. Wright asserts that Paul encourages the Philippians to hold their Roman citizenship lightly and redirect their focus to Christ as Lord and Savior. Wright reasons that because this message asks them to be disloyal to the emperor, Paul speaks in code, merely hinting at his purpose when in Philippians 3:1 he writes that he is trying to keep them "safe" in writing as he does.

A second key term in Philippians 3:20-21 is *sōtēr* or Savior. This is the only place in the undisputed Pauline letters that we find this term.[22] Most commentators note at least an echo of the claim that Caesar is Savior, as preserved in the Priene calendar inscription of 9 BCE.[23] Given the similar language, those who suggest an anti-imperial reading emphasize that Paul indirectly challenges the imperial cult and the emperor's claims on allegiance in identifying Jesus Christ as Savior.

Critique of anti-imperial theories. In placing so much emphasis on the proclamation of power underlying the imperial cult, the anti-imperial readings fail to adequately account for the prominence of benefaction that motivated worship and honor of the virtuous emperor. Moreover, the anti-imperial interpretations are at odds with other passages in Philippians. Finally, this approach undervalues the historical and theological questions that Judaism posed as Paul explained the gospel.

Benefaction in the imperial cult. The imperial cult is arguably the most prominent vehicle used to honor the one who benefited the cities. Benefaction's importance in the imperial cult highlights the relationship between the ruled and their ruler, the supreme patron who was honored through the cult. The relationship was governed by the protocols of honor that structured the social world. It was unthinkable not to honor one who gave you a gift, and if that gift was the cessation of civil war, or a land grant, or safety from outsiders, or special honors of citizenship, it was essential that proper honor be given.

Additionally, the picture drawn by modern historians of direct confrontation between two "men," Caesar and Jesus, misses the important fact that the imperial cult in Paul's day would have worshiped Livia as well. Insufficient account has been taken of the fact that Livia, Augustus's wife, was divinized by her grandson, Claudius, and the senate. Thus, when Paul arrived at Philippi, a woman was also part of the imperial cult and was worshiped

---

[22]See also Eph 5:23; 2 Tim 1:10; Tit 1:4; 2:13; 3:6. The term is used of God the Father in 1 Tim 1:1; 2:3; 4:10; Tit 1:3; 2:10; 3:4.
[23]*Orientis Graecae Inscriptiones Selectae* 458.

as a goddess. This suggests that it was the power, influence and benefaction of the family, not simply the power of the ruler, which was venerated. Therefore, Paul was not setting up a contest between "gods," Caesar and Jesus, for the imperial cult was not merely the veneration of the emperor.

Inconsistent or incomplete interpretations of Philippians. Several problems arise within the text of Philippians itself when studying arguments for an anti-imperial reading. First, the argument that Paul wrote in code is practically nonrefutable, because the argument rests only on silence. Second, the coded meanings alleged by this reading are in conflict with other statements in the letter. Indeed, the political terms need not only suggest a Roman context, but might include a Jewish community context as well.

1. Questioning the claims concerning silence. Turning to the argument on the necessity for silence, Erik Heen rightly notes that patronage was part of the civic fabric and thus was public. But he then makes an argument from silence that by definition is irrefutable. After noting the well-accepted fact that only 1-5 percent of the empire's population could be designated as elite, he postulates that very few of the remaining 95 percent of the population dared to speak out against the elite's power.[24] Underneath this statement is the assumption that the masses were outraged at their subservient treatment but also were terrified to speak. Yet we have no actual proof of their frustration, only proof of their silence.

Moreover, the elites were not all promoting the empire. A careful reading of Roman sources reveals active, open critique by senators concerning the emperor and the principate. The case of the elder Helvidius Priscus is instructive. The powerful senator navigated the reign of Nero and then the bloody year of the four emperors, finally to welcome Vespasian. Scholars debate the specifics, but his career was characterized by strong advocacy for the powers of the senate, including their freedom of speech, drawing on the precedence of Republican Rome.[25] In this he followed his father-in-law, Thrasea, who wrote on Cato (and committed suicide under Nero; see Tacitus, *Annals* 16.26.2). Eventually Helvidius was exiled and then executed under Vespasian, although Suetonius notes that Vespasian tried to stay the execution (*Vespasian* 15). With such an unpleasant end to his life, does Helvidius's experience demonstrate the ultimate power of the Princeps? Rather, does it not show that during the first century CE some senators in Rome spoke well of

---

[24]Heen, "Phil 2:6-11 and Resistance to Local Timocratic Rule," pp. 128-29.
[25]Barbara Levick, *Vespasian* (New York: Routledge, 1999), p. 87.

Republican values, especially freedom of speech for the senate? While it is true that much of Helvidius's energies were directed in avenging the memory of his father-in-law, and he was in the thick of conspiracies and intrigues that festered in the senate, nevertheless the ancient historians also note in Helvidius's case a strain of genuine political thought which lauded the Republican past. Helvidius could speak thus from the senate floor and was not immediately executed. Moreover, when he chose to withhold the title "Caesar Augustus" from his address to Vespasian, he was not summarily executed (Suetonius, *Vespasian* 15).[26] In sum, the rise of imperial rule was questioned and resisted even at the highest level, which undermines the notion that silent resistance was the only option for those who opposed imperial power.

2. Inconsistent elements of anti-imperial argument. In the first chapter of Philippians, Paul declares he is boldly proclaiming the gospel in the context of a Roman imprisonment, and apparently the gospel is spreading. He is not using code in a place where one might assume he would. Nor is he counseling others to be quiet; rather he is pleased that his situation has emboldened others. Even more, he is imprisoned in proximity to the most elite soldiers in the empire, the Praetorian Guard. These nine thousand soldiers protected the emperor, although they also permitted Caligula's murder and installed his successor, Claudius.[27] In other words, they had power. Paul, apparently, was not intimidated by that power. He writes that his gospel is known throughout their numbers and even that some believers are emboldened to speak the gospel as well.

Nor does Paul seem to imagine that the Philippians' letter (or any of his letters to churches) would be "private" in the sense that only believers would hear it. For example, Paul's declaration in 1 Corinthians 15:24 that Christ will destroy every ruler and authority and power should not be understood as something for the believers' ears only. Only one chapter earlier Paul indicates that the Corinthians' church service is open to those uninitiated,[28] and most scholars believe that Paul's letter was read to the

---

[26] Ancient historians did not judge him harshly; for example, Tacitus appears to have approved of Helvidius's opinion, even as he admits that Helvidius's antagonist, Marcellus, was more politically astute in sponsoring Realpolitik. See Jakub Pigoń, "Helvidius Priscus, Eprius Marcellus, and Iudicium Senatus: Observations on Tacitus, Histories 4.7-8," *Classical Quarterly*, new series, 42, no. 1 (1992): 246.

[27] G. Walter Hansen, *The Letter to the Philippians*, Pillar New Testament Series (Grand Rapids: Eerdmans, 2009), p. 68.

[28] Anthony Thiselton, *The First Epistle to the Corinthians: A Commentary on the Greek Text*, New International Greek Testament Commentary (Grand Rapids: Eerdmans, 2000), p. 1115.

entire church (1 Cor 14:16). Thus anyone could have heard this statement. This matches his actions before the imperial guard—boldly speaking the gospel. Much of the postcolonial argument depends on this public-private separation, which forces the oppressed to go underground and to rely on code to express their true feelings and thoughts. Yet the modern dichotomy between public and private is not found in the Roman world, with its open-door *domus* (home), wherein much business was handled. Again, the patronage system blurred lines of private and public.[29]

This point can be further illustrated by looking at other "suspicious" groups within the empire. Eastern cults at times had a hard go of it in Rome, from the Republic to Paul's day. Livy speaks in detail about the Bacchanalian controversy in 186 BCE, which at bottom seems to involve political dissension (*History of Rome* 39.8-19). More than two hundred years later, Josephus speaks of the crucifixion of a freedwoman, Ida, for crimes of aiding her former owner in an adulterous affair that also involved the priests of Isis (*Antiquities* 18.3.4-5). These examples suggest that Eastern cults in Rome itself were closely watched and condemned if their practices were determined to undermine Roman political or moral convictions.[30] However, Eastern cults, including Judaism, were allowed to establish meeting places and to openly identify themselves in Rome. Philo's *Embassy to Gaius* is instructive. He assumes a delegation could present their case and persuade Emperor Caligula of their cause's rightness; there was no need to hide or write private letters in coded message.

In view of these contextual inconsistencies with the anti-imperial readings of Philippians, better explanations can be offered for some of the key terms in the letter. Thus it is likely that by using the term *politeuesthe*, Paul intends to invoke not so much civic responsibilities but rather a sense of fidelity and duty to the local Christian community. This sense is confirmed by the term's use in Jewish sources. Markus Bockmuehl cites several contemporary Jewish sources who use the term to mean "following the Jewish way of life," a public act that often included political ramifications (see Esther LXX 8:12p; 2 Macc 6.1; 11.25; Josephus, *Vita* 12; see also Acts 23:1).[31] Again, in Philippians 3:1 the sense of the term trans-

[29]Carolyn Osiek and David Balch, *Families in the New Testament World: Households and House Churches* (Louisville: Westminster John Knox, 1997), pp. 45-54.
[30]A. N. Sherwin-White, *Roman Society and Roman Law in the New Testament* (1963; reprint, Grand Rapids: Baker, 1978), p. 79.
[31]Markus Bockmuehl, *The Epistle to the Philippians*, Black's New Testament Commentary (Pea-

lated by Wright as "safe" should be reevaluated. The Greek term *asphalēs* is used only here in Paul, and while one possible nuance of the term is "safe," when seen in the context of Paul's sentence, the other common meaning of "firm" or "safeguard" carries more weight. Specifically, Paul writes that he is not hesitating or shrinking back from writing the same things to them, for rejoicing in the Lord is a safeguard for them. Looking at the immediate context, we see that in chapter two he praised Timothy and Epaphroditus for their public witness for the sake of Christ. He asks that the Philippians rejoice in these men's faithful service (Phil 2:22-23, 28), and encourages them again in Philippians 3:1 to rejoice. Rejoicing in the spreading of the gospel will be a safeguard for their minds and hearts.

Jewish context in the anti-imperial reading. The argument that Paul uses Judaism as code for Roman status or citizenship does not stand up to close scrutiny. Paul holds that the teachings and practices of Judaism are based on the revelation of the one true God, and Paul defends this even as he argues for the surpassing revelation in Christ Jesus. However, from Paul's Jewish perspective, the ideology behind paganism and more specifically the imperial cult can lay no claim to truth in the sense of God's revelation. Thus while at a superficial level both systems presented honor to its members, in Paul's case, the honor of being a member of God's family is rooted in a true view of the world, while the honor granted a Roman citizen belongs in a different, earthly realm, part of this present age.

Additionally, this theory does not fully appreciate the pressing situation faced by Paul in his efforts to distinguish the place of the law vis-à-vis Christ. His warning that some might come to Philippi and teach adherence to the law was not a paranoid vision but a lived reality in churches in the region of Galatia, only a few days journey from Philippi. Even the Corinthians are warned that "the sting of death is sin, and the power of sin is the law" (1 Cor 15:56), and the Romans are treated to an extensive discussion on the relationship between the law and Christ's work in redemption. Paul's declaration that the church represents "the circumcision" (Phil 3:3) is best understood as proclaiming the gospel's superiority over against traditional teachings on the Jewish law, and not as code for renouncing Roman citizen status. If the issue was about citizenship, why did Paul not simply say, "hold your citizenship lightly as I do mine"? Such a claim would match Luke's portrait of Paul taking advantage of his Roman citizenship, not to get *released* from prison

body, MA: Hendrickson, 1998), p. 97.

but to be *escorted* honorably out from the jail (Acts 16:37-38).

In sum, the postcolonial perspective begins from the assumption that empire is *the* key interlocutor for Paul in Philippians. Moreover, it presupposes that this interlocutor could *only* be addressed or attacked surreptitiously and in code. It is not surprising, then, that readers using this method will find empire at the center—since they had a priori determined it to be there. Yet under closer scrutiny both the historical context and the letter itself dissuade us from thinking that Paul was making a coded anti-imperial argument in Philippians.

PAUL'S IMPERIAL MESSAGE IN PHILIPPIANS?

As we have seen, we can identify the dominant player as Rome, and the oppressed as the Christians, including Paul. But another position argues that Paul is the dominant voice silencing his congregants, enforcing hierarchy and dualistic concepts of difference, and demanding obedience to his new, foreign beliefs and practices. One application of a postcolonial hermeneutic is to advocate a reading of resistance against dominance and hegemony. This may be combined with a feminist hermeneutic that stresses a reading of suspicion and challenges assumptions of patriarchy woven within the fabric of the material and literary remains of ancient society. Some combine these two methods and conclude that Paul's thought reveals imperialist/colonialist and patriarchal tendencies that must be resisted by today's reader.

Argument for Paul as an imperialist. Joseph Marchal argues that Paul exhibits a colonialist and imperialist mindset.[32] Far from concluding that Paul's message challenges and rebukes imperialism, Marchal contends that Paul promotes universalist, sexist and hegemonic thought patterns that serve to subjugate and silence others. Paul should be read from a posture of resistance, using feminist and postcolonial analysis, argues Marchal, drawing especially from the works of Kwok Pui Lan and Musa Dube.[33] For example, he argues that feminist and queer theories illuminate Paul's patriarchal interaction with Euodia and Syntyche in Philippians 4:2-3; in demanding their obedience Paul establishes his "imperial manhood."[34] Marchal's recon-

---

[32]Joseph A. Marchal, "Imperial Intersections and Initial Inquiries: Toward a Feminist, Postcolonial Analysis of Philippians," in *The Colonized Apostle: Paul Through Postcolonial Eyes,* pp. 146-60, ed. Christopher D. Stanley (Minneapolis: Fortress Press, 2011).

[33]He cites Kwok Pui Lan, *Postcolonial Imagination and Feminist Theology* (Louisville: Westminster John Knox, 2005), and Musa W. Dube, *Postcolonial Feminist Interpretation of the Bible* (St. Louis: Chalice, 2000).

[34]Marchal, "Imperial Intersections and Initial Inquiries," p. 159.

struction of a counternarrative includes looking for places in Philippians where hints of independent thought might be discerned and finds evidence for this in Paul's discussion of his elevated status in Philippians 3:4-6.[35] Paul's viewpoint reflects his higher rank, but most Philippians do not have high status and cannot therefore completely comply with Paul's call to relinquish it. This situation, Marchal contends, reveals the fact that more than one opinion or viewpoint must be operative at Philippi, opening the way for the community to see "other possibilities for resistance both to the empire and to Paul."[36] Marchal argues that Paul used imperial language when writing to the Philippians. He is less committed to the possibility that Paul used such language to overturn the Roman Empire or the imperial cult.

Critique of the "Imperialist Paul" perspective. Marchal sees Paul's claim to authority, his call of imitation and his appeal for unity through obedience as hallmarks of an imperialist mindset; Paul accepts the underlying convictions of imperial power even if he might reject Roman claims to it. Marchal's position, however, minimizes Paul's close relationship with the Philippians, as evidenced by their prayers for him and his anxiety over Epaphroditus (Phil 2:25-30), his gratitude for their care (Phil 4:14-18) and his love for them (Phil 1:8; 4:1). Moreover, Marchal's critique of Paul's authority is too broad and thus renders even the idea of authority meaningless. For example, teachers are recognized to have authority over their students and judges over their courtrooms; such authority does not imply imperialistic attitudes or actions. In Paul's case, the Philippians are not bound to listen to him or coerced by an outside force to obey him. Their voluntary position as learners takes the teeth out of Marchal's claims of an imperialistic Paul. In the end, Marchal represents a very different, even mutually exclusive, view of imperialism, the imperial cult, the Roman Empire and Paul's place in this world than that discussed earlier by Carter and Wright.

PAUL'S ESCHATOLOGICAL, ANTI-PAGAN MESSAGE IN PHILIPPIANS

If we are not going to condemn Paul as an imperialist, and we do not see Paul as directly and consciously anti-imperial, what other interpretation of Paul and empire can be put forward? Rather than seeing Paul's primary focus as contesting the claims of the Roman Empire, a better reading recognizes Paul's concerns as located in the wider Jewish context and inner-Christian relations.

---

[35]Ibid., p. 155.
[36]Ibid., p. 158.

Indeed, *politeuma* was already in use as a term of self-identification among Jews. Philo, a first-century CE Jew from Alexandria, uses this term to describe Jewish communities living outside of Judea or Galilee (*De Gigantibus* 61; *De Confusione Linguarum* 78).[37] Paul, then, might be reflecting his Jewish heritage in describing the church as a community living outside its "homeland" and awaiting the Savior and his gift of transformed, glorious bodies.

Another interpretation suggests that Paul gives an intra-Christian argument. Because *politeuma* does not occur elsewhere in the New Testament, its specific nuance is difficult to determine. In the immediate context (Phil 3:17-21), however, Paul paints a picture of a Christian community imitating him and others who walk according to the high calling in Christ (Phil 3:14) over against those who are the enemies of the cross. Paul's warning suggests he believed the Philippians were at risk of following false Christians who rejected the message of suffering. Reumann offers a variation to this general interpretation. He submits that *politeuma* is the language of the "enemies" (Phil 3:18) who fundamentally stand against the message of the cross and its attending suffering.[38] In Reumann's argument, Paul does not choose *politeuma* because it fits his conception of the Christian community but because he wants to redeem its use. He reshapes its meaning in the opposite direction of the "enemies," refocusing the Philippians' attention toward their calling in Christ, the Savior who is to come. Reumann's assertion does not rule out the possibility that Paul's enemies used *politeuma* in an anti-imperial way; he only argues that it does not serve that function here in Philippians. Reumann's argument demonstrates that Paul's enemies need not be Rome. Moreover, he shows how language about citizenship could function metaphorically in intra-Christian disputes with little direct reference to imperial claims.

Finally, Reumann's argument highlights the important fact that Paul does not use this term outside of this letter, even though he writes to other churches located in cities with a high number of Roman citizens, including Corinth and Rome itself. I propose that Philippi's political environment was not the catalyst for Paul's use of this term but rather Paul's specific antagonist, the vaguely defined "enemies." These enemies are probably identified with those described earlier in the chapter as the "circumcision." These (false) Christians describe the church using a typical Jewish term (*politeuma*) that denotes the people of God living in community in a Diaspora

---

[37]Bockmuehl, *Epistle to the Philippians*, pp. 233-34.
[38]Reumann, *Philippians*, pp. 594-97.

setting. Paul rejects their definition of Christian community by redefining *politeuma* to have an eschatological focus.

Looking broadly at Philippians as a whole, the focus on imperial cult and Christianity has raised awareness today for Western Christians regarding the West's political power. By placing modern global Western powers in Roman sandals, the New Testament read through postcolonial eyes serves to critique Western hegemony. It is not entirely clear to me, however, that one needs postcolonial thought to arrive at this spot, given the witness in Scripture to resist oppressive human actions, whether governmental or cultural or within families. Perhaps seeing Paul and other believers as the oppressed helps restore or rehabilitate Christianity in the eyes of many today; a laudable goal, but I wonder if postcolonial thought in the end actually delivers. Moreover, postcolonial readings of Philippians fail to give full weight to the eschatological dimension of Paul's claims entailed in the conviction of Christ's return. Paul says Jesus is Lord, and the entire system of human government in whatever form is insufficient to hold all human hopes. Paul encourages the Philippians to think beyond this world and its system, even as they live in unity and community until Christ's glorious return (Phil 3:20-21).

BIBLIOGRAPHY

Bockmuehl, Markus. *The Epistle to the Philippians*. Black's New Testament Commentary. Peabody, MA: Hendrickson, 1998.

Brodd, Jeffrey, and Jonathan L. Reed, eds. *Rome and Religion: A Cross-Disciplinary Dialogue on the Imperial Cult*. Atlanta: Society of Biblical Literature, 2011.

Carter, Warren. *The Roman Empire and the New Testament: An Essential Guide*. Nashville: Abingdon Press, 2006.

Dube, Musa. *Postcolonial Feminist Interpretation of the Bible*. St. Louis: Chalice Press, 2000.

Gradel, Ittai. *Emperor Worship and Roman Religion*. Oxford: Oxford University Press, 2002.

Hänlein-Schäfer, H. *Veneratio Augusti: eine Studie zu den Tempeln des ersten römischen Kaisers*. Rome: G. Bretschneider, 1985.

Hansen, G. Walter. *The Letter to the Philippians*. Pillar New Testament Series. Grand Rapids: Eerdmans, 2009.

Heen, Erik M. "Phil 2:6-11 and Resistance to Local Timocratic Rule: *Isa theō* and the Cult of the Emperor in the East." In *Paul and the Roman Imperial Order*, pp. 125-53. Edited by Richard A. Horsley. Harrisburg, PA: Trinity

Press International, 2004.

Horsley, Richard A., ed. *Paul and the Roman Imperial Order*. Harrisburg, PA: Trinity Press International, 2004.

Levick, Barbara. *Vespasian*. New York: Routledge, 1999.

Marchal, Joseph A. "Imperial Intersections and Initial Inquiries toward a Feminist, Postcolonial Analysis of Philippians." In *The Colonized Apostle: Paul Through Postcolonial Eyes*, pp. 146-60. Edited by Christopher D. Stanley. Minneapolis: Fortress, 2011.

O'Brien, Peter T. *The Epistle to the Philippians*. New International Greek Testament Commentary. Grand Rapids: Eerdmans, 1991.

Osiek, Carolyn and David Balch. *Families in the New Testament World: Households and House Churches*. Louisville: Westminster John Knox Press, 1997.

Pigoń, Jakub. "Helvidius Priscus, Eprius Marcellus, and Iudicium Senatus: Observations on Tacitus, Histories 4.7-8." *The Classical Quarterly* New Series 42.1 (1992): 235-46.

Pilhofer, Peter. *Philippi*, vol. 2 *Katalog der Inscriften von Philippi*. Tübingen: Mohr Siebeck, 2009.

Price, Simon R. F. *Rituals and Power: The Roman Imperial Cult in Asia Minor*. Cambridge: Cambridge University Press, 1984.

Pui-Lan, Kwok. *Postcolonial Imagination and Feminist Theology*. Louisville: Westminster John Knox, 2005.

Reumann, John. *Philippians*. Anchor Yale Bible. New Haven, CT: Yale University Press, 2008.

Sherwin-White, A. N. *Roman Society and Roman Law in the New Testament*. Oxford: Oxford University Press, 1963. Reprint, Grand Rapids: Baker, 1978.

Taylor, Lily Ross. *The Divinity of the Roman Emperor*. Middletown, CT: American Philological Association, 1931.

Thiselton, Anthony. *The First Epistle to the Corinthians: A Commentary on the Greek Text*. New International Greek Testament Commentary. Grand Rapids: Eerdmans, 2000.

Wardle, David. "On the Divinity of the Roman Emperor Once More." Review of *Emperor Worship and Roman Religion* by Ittai Gradel. *Scholia Reviews* 13 (2004): 125-32.

Wright, N. T. *Paul: In Fresh Perspective*. Minneapolis: Fortress, 2005.

_____. "Paul's Gospel and Caesar's Empire." http://ntwrightpage.com/ Wright_Paul_Caesar_Empire.pdf.

9

Colossians and the Rhetoric of Empire

A New Battle Zone

Allan R. Bevere

It is my contention that the theme of empire is not central to either Colossians or Philemon. To be sure, empire can be read into both letters and indeed may have implications for empire, but it cannot be read out of both letters (Colossians and Philemon are not directly concerned with empire). In other words, Paul was not attempting to construct a counterimperial theology in the composition of either Colossians or Philemon.

Empire in Colossians?

The most thorough treatment of empire in Colossians and Philemon can be found in Brian Walsh and Sylvia Keesmaat's popular and widely read *Colossians Remixed: Subverting the Empire.* It is therefore appropriate to concentrate the discussion on their argument.

It is the contention of the authors of *Colossians Remixed* (hereafter referred to as WK) that Paul's letter to the church at Colossae is a politically subversive tract meant to challenge the totalizing claims of Caesar and his empire with the alternative affirmation of the lordship of Jesus Christ. In other words, they assert that empire is the central theme of Paul's letter and that Paul's original audience would have interpreted his words accordingly. As Matthew Lowe notes, "Paul appropriates both Old Testament and Roman imagery in order to construct a counter-imperial theology, based around the atonement: essentially, resurrected life in the face of imperial death."[1]

It is impossible in the space of this essay to deal point by point with all the issues raised in reference to an anti-imperial reading of Colossians and Philemon. Our focus must be limited to the following critical areas: the nature of the Colossian philosophy as revealed in the polemical core (Col 2:8-23), the exodus language of Colossians 1:12-14 and the Christ hymn (Col 1:15-20), and the March of Triumph in Colossians 2:15. The issue of slavery will be dealt with when attention is turned to Philemon.

In the next section I will simply sketch the argument made in support of an empire reading of Colossians and will save the evaluation of the argument for the following section.

THE NATURE OF THE COLOSSIAN PHILOSOPHY

The exact nature of the trouble at Colossae that Paul is addressing is quite difficult to discern, and the debate among scholarship continues. The range of interpretive reconstructions of the target of Paul's polemic is considerable: from the synagogue in Colossae to a Jewish form of apocalypticism, from a syncretism based in Jewish Pythagoreanism to a mix of Jewish and Platonist elements, from an amalgam of syncretistic folk religion to a critique of Cynic philosophy. WK rightly note that the certainty of these various reconstructions is elusive. For the purpose of their argument they do not wade into the continued scholarly mire of the nature of the Colossian philosophy itself. Rather, they are concerned with the "nature of Paul's attack on it."[2]

First, according to WK, it is clear from Paul's critique that the Colossian philosophy is obsessed with captivity, and thus like all "regimes of truth" it must present itself as something more as something above human construction or human tradition (*kata tēn paradosin tōn anthrōpōn* [Col 2:8]), for it needs deceit to remain in power. Also necessary for power is the limitation of freedom by intrusion, imposing restrictions commanding the church not

---

[1]Matthew Forrest Lowe, "This Was Not an Ordinary Death," in *Empire in the New Testament*, ed. Stanley E. Porter and Cynthia Long Westfall (Eugene, OR: Pickwick, 2011), p. 198.
[2]Brian J. Walsh and Sylvia C. Keesmaat, *Colossians Remixed: Subverting the Empire* (Downers Grove, IL: InterVarsity Press, 2004), p. 105.

to handle or taste or touch (Col 2:21). Moreover, the philosophy is "preoccupied with powers, rulers and authorities and employs such power precisely for the purposes of exclusion.... [S]elf-appointed umpires whose central role seems to be exercising condemnation, ruling people out (Col 2:16)!"[3]

Thus having identified the character of the Colossian philosophy without going into the specifics of exactly what it is that the philosophy promotes, WK conclude,

> Paul is convinced that evil is devastatingly real and that it is oppressing the Colossian community from without (the sheer imaginative, political and economic force of the empire) and from within (the "philosophy" that runs the risk of tearing the community apart, stripping them of their hope and enslaving them in a system of ascetic discipline).[4]

The Exodus Language of Colossians 1:12-14 and the Christ Hymn (Col 1:15-20)

WK rightly note that in the first chapter of Colossians, Paul and Timothy recall the exodus tradition in laying out their argument to the Christians at Colossae:

> giving thanks to the Father, who has enabled *you* to share in the inheritance of the saints in the light. He has rescued us from the power of darkness and transferred us into the kingdom of his beloved Son, in whom we have redemption, the forgiveness of sins. (Col 1:12-14 NRSV)[5]

Such reference to the exodus is appropriate as Israel was liberated from captivity in Egypt. Thus, their entrance into the Promised Land was received as an inheritance, and forgiveness was available to a rebellious Israel on its way to freedom. Paul's point in Colossians is that in Jesus believers have now experienced an exodus liberation from the deceitful regimes of truth embodied by empire.

---

[3]Ibid., p. 106.

[4]Ibid., p. 111.

[5]I take the position that Timothy is the writer of Colossians with Paul giving his final approval. See first E. Schweitzer, *The Letter to the Colossians*, trans. A. Chester (Minneapolis: Augsburg, 1982), and later James D. G. Dunn, *The Epistles to the Colossians and to Philemon*, New International Greek Testament Commentary (Grand Rapids: Eerdmans, 1996), pp. 35-39. See further Allan R. Bevere, *Sharing in the Inheritance: Identity and the Moral Life in Colossians*, Journal for the Study of the New Testament Supplement 226 (Sheffield, UK: Sheffield Academic Press, 2003), pp. 54-59.

It is this reminder of the exodus tradition and its anti-imperial story of rescue from the regimes of truth that leads to the "subversive poetry" of the Christ hymn of Colossians 1:15-20.[6] In the first-century Mediterranean world in which the image of Caesar dominates the landscape, Paul offers alternative poetry taking "a leaf out of the book of the ancient prophets" countering "the imperial imagination."[7]

> Rome was especially adept at shaping the imagination. Images of the emperor were as ubiquitous in the first century as corporate logos are in the twenty-first century. The image of Caesar and other Roman symbols of Roman power were literally everywhere—in the market, on coins, in the gymnasium, at the gladiatorial games, on jewelry, goblets, lamps and paintings. The sovereign rule of Caesar was simply assumed to be the divine plan for the peace and order of the cosmos. Of course, this is the way the world works. Under such conditions it becomes hard to imagine any life alternative to the empire.[8]

Thus the Christ hymn is Paul's attempt to recapture the imagination of the Christians at Colossae in poetic fashion, challenging every major claim of the empire. In this piece of subversive poetry, Paul not only challenges Caesar's divine pretensions in claiming that it is Christ who is in the image of the invisible God, but Paul also challenges the sovereign reach of the empire and in coded language rejects that peace is secured through the *pax Romana,* rather saying that through the cross of Christ all things are reconciled. As Lowe notes, "The crucified Lord is revealed as supreme."[9]

Such supremacy is revealed in that all things were created in Christ, including "thrones or dominions or rulers or powers" (Col 1:15-16). Walsh and Keesmaat note that such terminology reflects more than politics; it reveals the "very shape of life in the empire."[10] In the Septuagint, "thrones" (*thronos*) refers to kings and dynasties. They are "centralized structures of political, economic and military authorities." Dominions (*kyriotētes*) designates the sphere of rule under the control of the sovereign. Rulers (*archai*) may allude to spiritual entities that are extensions of "the normal political, military and other uses of power in daily sociocultural life." And finally

[6]WK, *Colossians Remixed*, p. 82.
[7]Ibid., p. 83.
[8]Ibid.
[9]Lowe, "This Was Not an Ordinary Death," p. 213.
[10]WK, *Colossians Remixed*, p. 92.

powers (*exousia*) refers to what Walter Wink calls the "sanctions . . . that undergird the everyday exercise of power."[11]

Thus such terminology may indeed refer to Caesar and his empire with its grip of power on its subjects day in and day out. In this piece of subversive poetry in Colossians 1:15-20, what seems to be gives way to what is real. Caesar is not Lord; Jesus is.

THE MARCH OF TRIUMPH (COL 2:15)

In Colossians 2:15, Paul writes, "He [Christ] disarmed the rulers and authorities and made a public example of them, triumphing over them in it." In understanding this verse it is critical to know the identity of the "rulers and authorities." As mentioned earlier, WK argue that they refer to the empire:

> So what is going on here? In Colossians 2:15 Paul says that Christ "disarmed the rulers and authorities and made a public example of them" on the cross, thereby exercising his sovereignty, his rule over the empire. This rule was established on the cross and confirmed in the resurrection. Rome could not keep Jesus in a grave sealed by the empire.[12]

Lowe notes that while the rulers and authorities may not refer exclusively to empire, with the other themes present in Colossians of image and sovereign rule, it would be consistent for Paul to include the imperial authorities (in Col 2:15).[13] Certainly the image of a triumphal procession after a military victory is in view, perhaps even an allusion to the Emperor Nero's victory over Tiridates in 63 CE.[14]

Thus it would appear that for WK, Jesus' death in Colossians is portrayed as the defeat of the rulers and authorities, which while not referring exclusively to the imperial authorities, specifies primarily the Roman Empire.

As Lowe notes, WK's treatment of Colossians is "definitive and imaginative," but is it too imaginative to be believed?[15] Does Paul explicitly have the imperial authorities in mind? Would the Christians in Colossae have had the empire in mind as they heard Paul's letter being read?

---

[11]Ibid., p. 91; Walter Wink, *Naming the Powers: The Language of Power in the New Testament* (Philadelphia: Fortress, 1984), p. 11.

[12]WK, *Colossians Remixed*, pp. 154-55.

[13]Lowe, "This Was Not an Ordinary Death," p. 214.

[14]Larry J. Kreitzer, *Striking New Image: Roman Imperial Coinage and the New Testament World*, Journal for the Study of the New Testament Supplement 134 (Sheffield, UK: Sheffield Academic Press, 1996), pp. 123-25.

[15]Lowe, "This Was Not an Ordinary Death," p. 212.

CRITIQUE: THE PROBLEM OF EMPIRE IN COLOSSIANS

The largest problem with WK's remixing of Colossians is that it takes the imperial implications of empire that can be legitimately read into Colossians and treats those implications as explicit pronouncements from the letter itself. In other words, according to WK, empire is to be found everywhere in Colossians by design, and that it is Paul's singular focus.

Thus, the main problem present throughout their book is the minimization of the context of the letter itself and the passages they treat. For example, the scholarly analysis of the nature of the problem being addressed in Colossians has resulted in various "interpretive reconstructions," and yet, WK seem to believe that for their purposes, such attempts at reconstruction are not necessary for the deconstruction of the letter.[16] But the deconstruction of texts is quite problematic without some attempt at reconstructing them. Such work can be a difficult endeavor to be sure, but it is a necessary one, as I hope to show in what follows. It is important to note that of the major reconstructions offered by Pauline scholars on the nature of the Colossian philosophy, not one suggests that empire is the target of the letter. Thus, while WK are certainly correct that the reconstruction of the situation that occasioned the letter to the Colossians is quite murky with little consensus, it is also the case that anti-imperial critique is not a reconstruction that Pauline scholars have considered to be an option, for good reason.

As with my analysis, my critique of Colossians and empire will focus on three matters: the nature of the Colossian philosophy, the exodus language of Colossians and the Christ hymn, and the March of Triumph of Colossians 2:15.

CRITIQUE: THE NATURE OF THE COLOSSIAN PHILOSOPHY

WK suggest that the Colossian philosophy is focused on captivity. It must therefore present itself as above human tradition, hence Paul's reference to "human tradition" in Colossians 2:8. The implication for WK is that as a "regime of truth" the empire must present itself as something more than a human creation, something that is rather divine, and Paul is calling out the empire for exactly what it is. But is that what Paul has in mind?

The phrase translated as "human tradition" (*kata tēn paradosin tōn anthrōpōn*) has a clear usage in the New Testament to refer to dietary and purity regulations of Torah observance. In Mark 7:8, Jesus uses the phrase

---

[16]WK, *Colossians Remixed*, p. 105.

in specific reference to the regulations of the Pharisees; the obvious reference here is to Isaiah 29:13. An equivalent phrase, "human commandments," is employed in Titus 1:14 (commandments; *entolē*) where the objects of such commandments are "Jewish myths" (*mythos*). Moreover, in Colossians 2:22, Paul echoes the same idea in referring to the philosophy's precepts as "according to human teaching and doctrine," which highlights the specific methodology of the teaching as "do not handle, do not taste, do not touch" (Col 2:21). And while such a methodology can be found in the practices of every religion,[17] in the context of what has been written in the polemical core of Colossians 2:8-18, it appears to refer to Jewish practices. And even if the Colossian philosophy is more of an amalgam of religious practices, in which aspects of Judaism have been incorporated, it is still quite difficult to see that Paul has imperial authority in mind as he critiques the philosophy in chapter 2. From Paul's perspective, the philosophy indeed wants to hold the Colossians captive, but it is far from clear that he has his sights set on Caesar.

When one looks at the polemical core, there are other clues that something else is afoot in the letter. There is mention of circumcision, festivals, new moons and sabbath observance, and the worship of or worshiping with the angels, none of which WK deal with at any great extent. Each must be taken in turn.

It is quite curious that WK do not deal with the subject of circumcision, since it appears in Colossians 2:11 and Colossians 3:11, other than to mention that empire imposes cultural divisions. They should have asked instead what the precise language of circumcision reveals about the nature of the Colossian philosophy itself. Indeed, the usage of the term in both instances seem to be terms of identification directed as reminders for the Colossian Christians as contrasted with a different identity. In other words, the language of circumcision refers to the standing of the Colossians "in Christ." This is significant; for such a metaphor may very well reveal the identity of the target of the letter. While there is some debate as to exactly what the "stripping off of the body of flesh" refers to in Colossians 2:11, it appears to be referenced as a contrast to the Jewish rite of circumcision. Circumcision was a critical badge of identity for the Jew as a member of God's covenant people. It bore witness to one's nationality. Such a contrast is highlighted in

---

[17]James D. G. Dunn, *The Epistles to the Colossians and to Philemon,* New International Greek Testament Commentary (Grand Rapids: Eerdmans, 1996), p. 191.

Colossians 3:11 where Paul and Timothy state that in Christ's renewal there is no longer circumcision nor uncircumcision. Clearly the contrast here with Jewish identity is obvious. If empire is directly in the minds of the writers, why is this contrast even worth mentioning?

Moreover, it is important to ask what the nature of the rituals mentioned in Colossians 2:16 possibly reveals about the nature of the Colossian philosophy—festival, new moon and sabbath observances. New moon and sabbath are clearly Jewish observances. Food and drink scruples do not necessarily have to be understood in a Jewish way, but they were significant issues in the first century CE and were important boundary markers for the people of Israel. These were a significant issue in the early church as well (Acts 10:14; 1 Cor 8–10; Gal 2:1-10). Indeed, the language of Colossians 2:16 parallels the prophets Ezekiel and Hosea:

> But this shall be the obligation of the prince regarding the burnt offerings,
> at the festivals, the new moons, and the sabbaths, all the appointed festivals
> of the house of Israel. (Ezek 45:17)

> I will put an end to all her mirth,
>   her festivals, her new moons, her sabbaths,
>   and all her appointed festivals. (Hos 2:11)

Even if those who promote the philosophy as some kind of syncretism with Jewish elements are correct, it is difficult to see how imperial authority is in the direct sight of the writers of Colossians. Indeed, the mention of angel worship in Colossians 2:18, whether it is interpreted as worshiping angels or worshiping with the angels, should raise a significant question in relationship to the nature of the Colossian philosophy, but it is absent from WK's treatment. Perhaps the reason is, however it is interpreted, it is difficult to see how it directly links to an anti-imperial critique. WK are certainly correct that the Colossian philosophers want to keep the Christians in the church captive, but upon closer inspection of the details, the captors do not appear to be the empire. If so, the polemical core of chapter two is a beside-the-point response.

CRITIQUE: THE EXODUS LANGUAGE OF COLOSSIANS 1:12-14 AND THE CHRIST HYMN (COL 1:15-20)

In reference to the exodus imagery of Colossians 1:12-14, it should be acknowledged that WK could be on firmer ground. Since the exodus story is about the deliverance of God's people from an imperial power (Egypt), empire implications at first glance appear to be more direct. But upon closer inspection of the text, and in particular how Colossians 1:12-14 sets the stage for the Christ hymn of Colossians 1:15-20, is imperial authority directly in the mind of Paul?

The emphasis on exodus in Colossians 1 is less about liberation from Egypt (and by implication, Rome) but is used instead to set the context for the liberation of the Gentiles who now share in the inheritance of Israel as Gentile believers in Christ (v. 12). This very Jewish language reminds the Christians at Colossae of what they were likely taught when they first heard the gospel: because of the liberating work of Christ, they now share in the inheritance of God's people. "Share" (*tēn merida*) and "inheritance" (*tou klērou*) are often found together in the LXX (Deut 10:9; 12:12; 14:27, 29; 18:1; Josh 19:9; Jer 13:25).[18] Thus, Paul and Timothy appropriate this exodus motif and apply it directly to the church, which includes both Jews and Gentiles. The Gentiles now share in the inheritance given to Israel by the grace of God. They now are to be numbered among those who are called "saints."

The exodus motif continues in verse 13 with the affirmation that the Colossians have been liberated from the powers that enslave them. It certainly can be stated that the empire is one of those powers, but again, is it correct to read that directly out of the text, or can it only be read into the text? Upon closer examination of the text, it appears that empire is not the direct target of the writers. Colossians 1:12-14 sets the stage for the Christ hymn of which WK make much in their argument as anti-imperial subversive poetry. In actuality, this poetry casts Jesus in the very Jewish role of God's embodied wisdom, which is directly related to Torah.

"Firstborn" (*prōtotokos*) is used in the LXX to refer to a special relationship between a father and son. In Exodus 4:22, Israel is referred to as "my beloved son" (*prōtotokos*), signifying God's special relationship with the Hebrews (cf. Mt 3:17). Moreover, the patriarchs, the Torah and the messianic king are denoted in this way, directly implying a special relationship with God. *Prōtotokos* emphasizes uniqueness. Christ is to be distinguished from the rest of creation.

Significantly related to this is Colossians 1:18, where Christ is affirmed as "the head of the body, the church; he is the beginning." In the LXX, Genesis 49:3 uses the words *beginning* (*archē*) and *head* (*kephalē*) to depict the

---

[18]See Peter O'Brien, *Colossians, Philemon*, Word Biblical Commentary 44 (Waco, TX: Word, 1982), p. 26.

firstborn as superior and as the founder of a specific people (cf. also Deut 21:17). Thus *beginning* and *head* in the Christ hymn refer to Christ, not only in the cosmological sense but in ecclesiological terms as well. To speak of Christ as wisdom is to speak of his function in creation and redemption. Christ not only helps to bring creation into being but he sustains it as well. The head (Christ) provides the body (the church) with the direction that creates unity. The Lord of the entire universe has chosen the church as the unique domain of his redemptive grace. The church is to be the microcosm of the macrocosm of creation.[19] Creation and redemption go together.

Now, many of the details of this context WK would not deny. The problem is in how this context fails to make a direct connection to their anti-imperial reading of Colossians itself. There is little doubt that Colossians 1:12-14 would have brought to the mind of the readers thoughts of the exodus, but it is doubtful that a direct connection would have been made to the empire. Indeed, in this poem the Jewish notions of wisdom, Torah and Israel are linked together. Knowing that these motifs are central for Jewish self-understanding in the first century, it would be quite odd to employ them as an anti-imperial critique. It may indeed be the case that the images of the emperor were everywhere in the Roman world, but Paul seems to have something else directly in mind in the utilization of this hymn. Whereas Torah was the wisdom of God embodied, so now Jesus is that wisdom. In contrasting Christ to the Torah, the direct distinction has something directly to do with the Judaism and not empire. Indeed, I suggest again that if empire is directly in mind, the argument that Paul and Timothy put forth is somehow beside the point. In order to directly contrast Christ with Caesar as God's image, the writers employ Jewish terminology and concepts to contrast Christ with Torah. Is this view compelling?

The Christ hymn of Colossians 1:15-20 is not only Jewish in background, it appears to be answering a problem that relates to Judaism itself. Given the argument that Christ is all-sufficient, given the Jewish nature of what is contested by the authors, and given the context of the entire letter, it appears that the Colossians were tempted to observe, at the very least, some of the more significant regulations of the Torah. Paul and Timothy employ crucial Jewish themes and motifs to respond to what I think is a critique being leveled by the synagogue against the church in Colossae. Wisdom,

---

[19]J. Gibbs, *Creation and Redemption: A Study in Pauline Theology* (Leiden: Brill, 1971), pp. 105-6.

Torah and exodus were themes intrinsic to Israel's self-understanding, and they are used to remind the Colossians that as they began their journey in Christ, they must continue their journey in Christ. They do not need to become Jews to be Christians. As people in Christ they can "bear fruit" (a very Jewish expression) "in every good work" (Col 1:10; cf. Jer 1:9-10; 18:7-9; 24:6; 31:28; 42:10). Nothing else needs to be added. Thus while Colossians 2:15 may imply vaguely to a Roman march of triumph, the emphasis is soteriological—that when Jesus was crucified, his public shame resulted in the shame of the "rulers and authorities," which released the Colossian Christians from the badges of Torah identity, which is likely the writers' point in referring to the "handwritten document" (v. 14). One may read an anti-imperial message out of this, but considering the Jewish nature of the practices surrounding verse 15, it is likely not directly anti-imperial.

Thus the echoes present in Colossians 1 are clear and distinct, but they are not distinctly the sound of anti-imperial critique. That is tangentially implied at best.

Empire in Philemon?

WK are indeed correct to note that what Paul is calling for in his letter to Philemon is a fundamental reordering of relationships in the life of the early church. But is Paul's request of Philemon in reference to Philemon's slave Onesimus directly anti-imperial?

Those who believe so point to Albert Harrill's work on slavery in the New Testament, taking note of his account of the hierarchy of Roman society.[20] He shows that an

> examination of Rome's hierarchical society shows that a *personalized* understanding of power was integral to the empire: the relative qualities of honor (*dignitas*) and mastery (*auctoritas*) that distinguished the master from his slave were the same traits that sustained the role and governance of the emperor, as when Augustus was "proclaimed the ultimate guarantor (*auctor*) of peace and stability after decades of civil war." That is, the empire's societal structure and the integrity of the *pax Romana* itself were subject to the same rules as master and slave: a distinctively Roman ideology of mastery.[21]

---

[20]J. Harrill, *The Manumission of Slaves in Early Christianity*, Hermeneutische Untersuchungen zur Theologie 32 (Tübingen: Mohr, 1995).

[21]Lowe, "This Was Not an Ordinary Death," p. 224 (Lowe is summarizing Harrill).

The implications of this for Philemon appear obvious. The manumission of slaves threatened the unity and very fabric of the empire. Thus, Paul's implicit way of asking Philemon for Onesimus's freedom was a way of avoiding trouble for Paul and for Philemon with the imperial authorities precisely because his request was politically subversive.

But it is not at all clear what is happening in this short epistle of twenty-five verses. The sources we have for understanding slavery in the Roman Empire of the first century are problematic. It is not easy to know how to employ the Roman legal texts we do have: First, the Digest of Justinian, our main source for Roman law, is not necessarily an accurate indicator of the legal aspects of slavery in the first century. Second, legal texts do not necessarily indicate what was practiced socially. Roman slavery was not a monolithic institution. Third, what laws in reference to slavery were implemented in what provinces in the empire and which ones were not is quite thorny in nature.

Additionally, it is not clear from the letter that Paul is asking Philemon to free Onesimus. In verses 15-16, Paul writes, "Perhaps this is the reason he [Onesimus] was separated from you [Philemon] for a while, so that you might have him back for ever, *no longer as a slave but as more than a slave, a beloved brother*—especially to me but how much more to you, both in the flesh and in the Lord" (emphasis added). The first clause in italics alone would directly suggest that Paul is asking for Onesimus's release, but the next clause, "but as more than a slave," may suggest that Paul is asking that Philemon receive Onesimus as a brother in Christ while they maintain the master-slave relationship. As Thompson notes, "While it is not clear that Paul is asking that Philemon manumit Onesimus, Paul does underscore the changed situation: Onesimus must now be considered first and foremost not as a slave, but as a brother and, by virtue of being a brother in Christ, beloved."[22]

Perhaps Paul, in his vagueness, is leaving both options open to Philemon, but the main thrust of Paul's point is clear—Onesimus is now Philemon's brother in Christ. Whether Philemon frees him or whether he remains a slave in his household, their relationship has fundamentally changed. It should be noted that in the house code in Colossians, Paul does not indicate that masters should free their slaves, but that they treat them in accordance to what it means to be in Christ (Col 3:22–4:1).

---

[22]Marianne Meye Thompson, *Colossians and Philemon*, Two Horizons New Testament Commentary (Grand Rapids: Eerdmans, 2005), p. 219.

Thus, while slavery in the Roman world had implications for empire, it does not appear to be directly on the mind of Paul. What he is much more concerned with is how Onesimus's conversion has fundamentally reordered his relationship with Philemon—master and slave—and Christian brothers. Thus WK are correct in how this little letter gives us a model for that reoriented life in the church, but its existence as an anti-imperial tract is much less obvious.

Finally, it should be noted that Paul's language here concerning Philemon is not all that implicit. He directly suggests the possibility of manumission in verse 16. Any Roman authority reading this little letter would have understood that clearly. Paul is hardly being secretive.

CONCLUSION

The thesis that Colossians is an anti-imperial tract is quite difficult to sustain. Walsh and Keesmaat have written a creative assessment in their book *Colossians Remixed*, which certainly is to be commended for mining how the gospel is related to the powers of this world. More should be made of the important issues they raise and the questions they ask. But the book falls short as a convincing portrayal of the letter as an explicit critique of empire in which Paul has the imperial authorities foremost in his mind as he writes. Whether the nature of the Colossians philosophy is Jewish (as I believe) or an amalgam of Judaism and other pagan religious aspects, there is no direct connection between what the writers are combating in the letter and imperial pretensions.

As well, Paul's letter to Philemon is directly about the changed relationship between a master and a slave, as the slave is now a beloved brother in Christ. Paul seems to suggest that Onesimus's manumission is an option that he holds before Philemon, but more than that, even if he retains Onesimus as a slave, their identity as followers of Jesus must transform their relationship as master and slave. Paul is clear about this. He does not seem to be secretly coding his language in fear of the authorities who have him imprisoned.

So while empire can be read into both letters and both letters have implications for empire, anti-imperial sentiments cannot be directly drawn out of either Colossians or Philemon. To say that Jesus is Lord is to affirm that Caesar is not. But Paul seems to have more pressing concerns in these two epistles.

BIBLIOGRAPHY

Bevere, Allan R. *Sharing in the Inheritance: Identity and the Moral Life in Colossians.* Journal for the Study of the New Testament Supplement 226. Sheffield: Sheffield Academic Press, 2003.

Byron, John. *Recent Research on Paul and Slavery.* Sheffield, UK: Sheffield Phoenix Press, 2008.

Dunn, James D. G. *The Epistles to the Colossians and to Philemon.* New International Greek Testament Commentary. Grand Rapids: Eerdmans, 1996.

Harrill, J. Albert. *The Manumission of Slaves in Early Christianity.* Tübingen: Mohr, 1995.

Porter, Stanley, and Cynthia Long Westfall. *Empire in the New Testament.* Eugene, OR: Pickwick, 2001.

Thompson, Marianne Meye. *Colossians and Philemon.* Two Horizons New Testament Commentary. Grand Rapids: Eerdmans, 2005.

Walsh, Brian, and Sylvia Keesmaat. *Colossians Remixed: Subverting the Empire.* Downers Grove, IL: InterVarsity Press, 2004.

10

Something Old, Something New

Revelation and Empire

Dwight D. Sheets

An empire-critical analysis of the book of Revelation is unique among other New Testament writings because there is little debate about whether Rome is identified with much of the work's symbolism. Much could be made of John's "coded language," but most scholars readily admit that the average first-century reader would have easily identified the code with the activities of Roman rule. Most also agree that the clearest anti-empire themes in the New Testament writings are found in Revelation. This idea is not new. From the earliest era of church history commentators have recognized Rome as the referent behind Revelation's visions. One might question the necessity of this analysis; is it even necessary considering the widespread agreement on John's anti-Roman themes?

The answer is a definite yes. Empire criticism brings something to the table that is distinctly new. Empire critics interpret the text through the lens of a political ideology.[1] Although a tip of the hat is given to John's Hebrew background, the symbolism in Revelation reflects the political

---

[1] Richard A. Horsley notes that "'Apocalyptic' texts are not about the end of the word but the end of empires" (*Revolt of the Scribes: Resistance and Apocalyptic Origin* [Philadelphia: Fortress Press, 2009], p. 1).

world of Roman imperial rule. Moreover, John's opposition to Rome becomes paradigmatic for present-day resistance to modern empires. The
anti-empire approach allows the modern interpreter to apply the text in
ways that extend beyond most traditional applications. Resistance to *empires* is its paramount lesson. Horsley's suggestion that "the *pax Americana*
has come to replace the *pax Romana*" is applied by numerous writers who
suggest that patriotism, the Pledge of Allegiance, participation in a capital-
istic system and accumulation of wealth are activities John would have
likened to those in league with the beast.[2] Whether the United States is the
new Roman Empire is not a consideration of this essay. The purpose of this
study is to understand John's underlying reasons for writing the Apocalypse, and to determine whether he presents a paradigm for resistance to
all empires.

A DISTURBANCE IN THE FORCE?

In some ways the book of Revelation reads like the Star Wars trilogy. The
beast or anti-Force emperor Palpatine rules from his imperial capitol, the
Death Star "Babylon," imposing loyalty through his false prophet Lord
Darth Vader and the priestly Sith lords. True believers, the Rebel Alliance,
resist the empire, aided by John and his Jedi band of prophets. Is there any
wonder where George Lucas got his story line? Without a doubt, when we
enter into Revelation, there has been a disturbance in the force. Things have
changed from other New Testament writings. Nothing of the likes of
Romans 13 is to be found. Rome has no benevolent purpose. It is not a
servant of good; it is a purely evil entity. No one can know if John held this
point throughout his life or whether circumstances necessitated it. Israel
had a long history of occupation by empires, some of which conducted
themselves in relative peace and even benevolence. At other times this was
not so. Many believe the rule of foreign tyrants in Israel gave birth to the
Jewish apocalyptic tradition, which includes a literary form that makes up
much of the book of Revelation. A number of recent studies have concluded
that the apocalypses were resistance literature.

John clearly wants believers to resist the activities of the empire. Not
clear is whether his reasons included the same political sensitivities as the
modern reader. Did he advocate resistance because he believed that one

---

[2]Richard A. Horsley, introduction to *In the Shadow of Empire: Reclaiming the Bible as a History of
Faithful Resistance*, ed. Richard Horsley (Louisville: Westminster John Knox, 2008), p. 178.

empire's exercise of authority over another involved oppression, cultural pollution and relinquishing of self-determination? How would John have responded to a Roman rule devoid of its emperor cult and lavish opulence? One might expect that if he were against *empires* in general, he would have avoided the use of empire language in describing his own eschatological hope. He does not. John regularly reinvests the domination language of empire with even greater intensity in his description of the kingdom of God. The opulence of Rome is exceeded only by that of the New Jerusalem. This suggests that John was not against empires so much as he was against the Roman Empire.

Why John would be against the Roman Empire seems to be a very easy question. He opposes Rome because of its opulence, periodic harsh rule and emperor cult that claimed the prerogatives of God alone. It is, however, very possible that John saw these elements of Roman rule as symptoms of something much more serious. Certainly he was opposed to the empire's activities, and yet his main concerns may have had little to do with imperialism or oppression. These activities may be in the periphery. The case can be made that John's concerns were *chiefly* eschatological. He was against Roman rule not because it was an empire or even because it did evil things, but because, like other empires in Israel's history, its activities were fulfilling traditional eschatological expectations. John perceived these events as a fulfillment of prophecy.

The elephant in the room. An unavoidable subject in the discussion of Revelation that is often ignored or explained metaphorically is that the work exhibits a strong sense of imminence. John believed that Jesus would return; he believed it would happen soon. The nearness of Christ's return is not a peripheral issue. But for some it has become the elephant in the room that has a difficult time finding its place at the table. The warning of Jesus' return occurs three times in chapter 1 (Rev 1:1, 3, 19) and five times in chapter 22 (Rev 22:6, 7, 10, 12, 20), effectively bracketing the message of the book. Warnings occur within the messages to the churches (Rev 2:16; 3:11) and as well at key moments toward the end of the three vision cycles (seals, Rev 6:11; trumpets, 10:7; 11:14; bowls, 15:1; 16:15; 17:10). The lure of the Roman system, the rise, popularity and threat of the emperor cult and the accommodation of believers to the system could easily fit within early Christian traditional eschatological expectations. John may have interpreted these events as fulfillments of prophecy, a phenomenon that has a significant role

in the rise of apocalyptic expression. It indicated to John that Jesus' return
was near. If John's concerns are chiefly eschatological, it becomes more difficult to assume that Revelation is a paradigmatic program of resistance to
empires. Revelation becomes primarily a warning to the churches that Jesus
was coming soon and that participating with Rome would disqualify them
from participating in the kingdom of God.

PAINTING EVERYTHING WITH THE SAME BRUSH?

This view differs from the scholarly consensus that apocalyptic thought originates from and primarily addresses social/political environments marked
by some form of deprivation—commonly referred to as "deprivation theory."
"Deprivation theory holds that apocalyptic groups arise among people who
are marginalized, alienated, or at least feel deprived of what is essential to
their well-being."[3] By various means over the last century, scholars have
come to link the concept of deprivation to the rise of all apocalyptic literature and movements. A classic description is seen in D. S. Russell, who
states that the genre "is essentially a *literature of the oppressed* who saw no
hope for the nation simply in terms of politics or on the plane of human
history."[4] For these groups apocalyptic thought and expression functioned
as a coping mechanism. It brought hope for those to whom it seemed that
God's will on earth was failing. Otto Plöger's work *Theocracy and Eschatology* traced the rise of apocalypticism in Israel to the postexilic inner-
Israelite tension between the controlling priestly theocratic party and marginalized prophetic groups.[5] Paul Hanson developed beyond Plöger's work with
a sociological framework for the study of the postexilic period.[6] Hanson
concluded that the impulse giving rise to apocalyptic eschatology existed
among those who held most strongly to the prophetic promises of Yahweh's
restoration of Israel but at the same time witnessed the nation falling to its
adversaries. The prophetic promises were not coming to fulfillment. Apocalyptic theology and literature presented a symbolic universe that exposed
the demonic origin of those in power and presented a scenario that traced

---

[3]Stephen L. Cook, *Prophecy and Apocalypticism: The Postexilic Setting* (Minneapolis: Fortress
Press, 1995), p. 2.
[4]D. S. Russell, *The Method and Message of Jewish Apocalyptic: 200 BC-AD 100* (Philadelphia:
Westminster Press, 1964), p. 15, emphasis added.
[5]Otto Plöger, *Theocracy and Eschatology*, trans. S. Rudman (Richmond, VA: John Knox
Press, 1968).
[6]Paul Hanson, *The Dawn of Apocalyptic: The Historical and Sociological Roots of Apocalyptic
Eschatology*, 2nd ed. (Philadelphia: Fortress Press, 1979).

their soon-coming end. God would come and change the present situation, bringing judgment upon the wicked and blessing for the righteous.

Hanson's theory was given further definition by the work of Robert Carroll.[7] Carroll accounted for the rise of apocalypticism by combining the sociological theory of cognitive dissonance to Hanson's focus on the failure of prophecy and tension between various parties in Israel. According to Carroll those involved in apocalyptic movements are overcome with cognitive dissonance because their prophetic expectations had not come to pass. Although observable deprivation may not be evident in a number of apocalyptic movements, Carroll concluded that it was not needed; a *perceived* deprivation was adequate. Cognitive dissonance alone could be considered deprivation adequate to elicit an apocalyptic response.

The work of D. F. Aberle defined the deprivation theory even further with the concept of "relative deprivation." *Relative deprivation* is defined "as a negative discrepancy between legitimate expectation and actuality."[8] Deprivation could now be defined as "not getting what you hoped for" even though your life situation experienced no adversity. The concept of relative deprivation made it possible to define deprivation as the inner subjective mental experiences of the individual alone without any objective evidence.

Today the deprivation theory is considered a given in the study of apocalyptic literature and movements. Most studies of Revelation assume this setting for John and his churches. Some hold to the traditional belief that Revelation is a response to objective deprivation, its purpose being to give hope to the reader; in some cases it is believed that the reading alone acted as a sort of therapy. Others have seen John's focus as the conflict that existed between the Jewish and Christian communities. For others, John writes to deal with inner-community church conflicts and tensions between those who accommodated to culture and those who believed in separation. Still others reject the view that Revelation has a setting of objective deprivation, preferring to explain the setting as one of relative deprivation. These works concentrate their attention on the seer's own inner beliefs. Along these lines

---

[7]Robert Carroll, *When Prophecy Failed: Reactions and Responses to the Failure of Old Testament Prophetic Predictions* (London: SCM Press, 1979).

[8]D. F. Aberle, "A Note on Relative Deprivation Theory as Applied to Millenarians and Other Cult Movements," in *Millennial Dreams in Action: Essays in Comparative Study*, ed. S. L. Thrupp (The Hague: Mouton, 1962), p. 209. Aberle's work was a development of the studies of L. Festinger, H. W. Riecken, S. Schachter, in *When Prophecy Fails: A Social and Psychological Study of a Modern Group That Predicted the Destruction of the World* (New York: Harper & Row, 1964).

some posit that John's rhetoric worked as an agent to create opposition to the church. Others take the position that cognitive dissonance led John to a radical, even pathological, reaction against the empire.

Historical and theoretical approaches to empire criticism fit within this trajectory. Deprivation is located within the relationship that exists between the colonized and colonizer; it is the universal experience of the colonized. Although using the tools of the historical and sociological disciplines, empire criticism is a movement beyond both models. Undergirded by a progressive political and ideological worldview, colonialism itself is deprivation, and John's main purpose is anti-empire rhetoric.[9]

The problems involved with the deprivation model in apocalyptic research are also inherent in the empire-critical approach. When a theory becomes too broad and all-encompassing, it loses much of its explanatory power. Without objective data it can be teased out as the setting for any group simply by virtue of their social/political setting. The converse effect is that other more promising explanations are a priori ruled out of consideration. Certainly one of the more promising approaches would be to explore the historical situation of first-century Asia Minor on its own terms, and then attempt to understand how John would have interpreted the situation in light of his inherited eschatological traditions. To do this the first step is to explore the nature of the relationship between the Roman colonizer and the colonized in first-century Asia Minor. The second step is to consider how John interpreted this relationship in light of his eschatological tradition. This will move us much closer to understanding the central focus of Revelation.

ROMAN RULE IN ASIA MINOR: A CARROT OR A STICK?

Research on the setting of the Apocalypse has traditionally concluded that it reflects difficult relations between believers and the Roman state. Scholars usually came to this conclusion via the traditional ancient sources for Domitian's rule. These sources present an account that is almost without exception negative. Domitian is characterized as a tyrant, demanding divine prerogatives, inept, unjust and so on. Leonard Thompson believes that in general these sources have not been critically examined.[10] He sug-

---

[9]"Standard scholarly interpretation does not necessarily deny that the texts are concerned with oppressive rule and the resistance to it among teachers or the enlightened. But its conceptual apparatus tends to block the recognition that *these are the focal concerns of the texts*" (Horsley, *Revolt of the Scribes*, p. 4, emphasis added).

[10]For the following, note the description of Domitian's reign in Leonard Thompson, *The Book*

gests that the negative portrait was not given by neutral observers but rather by those who shaped Domitian in order to draw favor with Emperor Trajan. Domitian was made a tool for praising Trajan—Trajan's foil. He served as the binary contrast to the new regime and was used as an aide for propagandizing a "new era."

Recent studies have shown that "the seer and his audience did not live in a world of conflict, tension, and crisis."[11] These studies posit that John and his churches lived in relative peace and quiet not much different than anyone else in the provinces of Rome. It is said that during Domitian's reign the provinces prospered financially, and the wealth seems to have benefited all classes. The evidence also shows that the social status of Christians was not confined to the lower strata of society. Western Asia Minor under Domitian reflects stable political, economic and social relations. The provinces flourished under his rule. They were provided with more and better services, heightened status and economic prosperity. This is reflected in the buildings, coinage and private donations. The trend toward stronger imperial control of the provinces resulted in better administration, less waste and less taxation of the people. Domitian was known for supporting and granting favors to the provinces. The period is marked by greater justice and equality among the provinces, being seen in Domitian's demand for justice in the treatment of the poor and weak, action to curb the cost of living and prohibition of the abuse of citizens by traveling dignitaries. Domitian seemed concerned to protect the people from the abuses of both government and the upper class, and to minimize tension between the groups. Of Domitian's governors in the provinces Suetonius comments, "At no other time were they more honest and just" (Domitian, *Lives of the Caesars* 8:2).

Stephen D. Moore comments that in Asia Minor Roman rule was not by invasion but rather by invitation. Roman rule was that of hegemony, or domination by consent. Emperor worship was welcomed and thrived in the cities of Asia Minor because of their strong connection with the Greek pantheon and history of sovereign worship. It was an important means for the emperor to be represented. Honor of the emperor flowed both to Rome and also from Rome. Cities that had built and maintained an imperial temple

---

of Revelation: Apocalypse and Empire (New York: Oxford, 1990), pp. 95-170. Note that in Revelation deprivation is commonly linked to the rule of Emperor Domitian, but some also place it in the time of Nero. It may be the case that Revelation was compiled from sources having their origin in both reigns.

[11]Ibid., p. 95.

could receive the special honor of being named *neokoros* (temple warden), a title held with pride. Among the seven cities of the Apocalypse "five . . . had imperial altars (all but Philadelphia and Laodicea), six had imperial temples (all but Thyatira), and five had imperial priests (all but Philadelphia and Laodicea)."[12] John wrote to cities that had been a hotbed of emperor worship for over a century.

The practice would always have been objectionable to John; however, little clear evidence exists that Domitian demanded divine prerogatives more than any other emperor. The greater problem for early Christians was their rejection of traditional religious cults into which the emperor cult had been integrated. Their rejection of sacrifice of any kind was to the locals primarily an affront to the traditional cult and only secondarily to the emperor. John confronts the great temptation for believers to accommodate to the local religious practices. He also sees a trajectory into the future that involves the apostasy of believers as homage to the emperor becomes more and more compulsory.

Likewise, the book of Revelation offers little evidence that Christians were under any economic or social hardship. It is true that Revelation contains the language of conflict, and this leads many to conclude that it reflects an actual situation. It is important to make a general observation about the language of the apocalypses. Conflict language is characteristic of the apocalyptic genre and should not be overemphasized in one's attempt to find the historical setting. This is especially true of judgment language, which is typically hyperbolic metaphor.

Granting this, it is still necessary to address a few passages that are believed to indicate an adverse relationship between believers and the state. For instance, John refers to his present situation as being in the "tribulation" (Rev 1:9 KJV). It is certainly true that John believed that he was in the "tribulation." The earliest church interpreted "the sufferings of the Messiah . . . [to be] the inauguration of the messianic travail."[13] Jesus' "tribulation" was the beginning of his follower's "tribulation." D. C. Allison traces this idea to early Palestinian Christianity, where John probably originated. It makes sense that he would use tribulation language to describe his present experience, and yet, in Revelation 3:10 he draws a distinction between his present situation and the greater

---

[12]Thompson, *Book of Revelation*, p. 159.
[13]D. C. Allison Jr., *The End of the Ages Has Come: An Early Interpretation of the Passion and Resurrection of the Jesus* (Philadelphia: Fortress, 1985), p. 80. Allison holds that Revelation reflects a situation of objective deprivation (ibid., p. 70).

tribulation he believed was soon to come. Clearly, his expectations were of a future situation far worse that he was presently experiencing.

John was on Patmos "because of the word of God and the testimony of Jesus" (Rev 1:9). Many interpret this phrase to mean that he was banished to Patmos because of his preaching of the gospel. There is no evidence that Patmos was a penal colony. Considering the fact that John refers to the entire revelation as "the word of God and the testimony of Jesus" (Rev 1:2), one could conclude that he went to Patmos simply to write the apocalypse. John also refers to the martyrdom of a certain "Antipas," which seems to have been due to his belief in Christ, but no other details are given (Rev 2:13). The phrase, "in the days of Antipas" certainly gives the impression that it was a long past event.

To be sure, John mentions martyrs in Revelation 6:9-11. The souls under the altar are believers who, from John's perspective, had been killed for the proclamation of their faith. Clearly, believers had experienced martyrdom in the first half-century of the church's existence. However, less clear is the question of whether these martyrs were victims of a recent persecution. The plea "how long" (v. 10) implies that their martyrdom had taken place, at the very least, over a long period of time. These martyrs may well make up the sum total of those who over many decades had died due to their proclamation of Christ.

ROMAN RULE IN ASIA MINOR: "THE SIGNS OF THE TIMES"

If the preceding accurately describes the experience of early believers, the question arises as to how John would have understood the situation in light of his eschatological tradition. Allison is correct that people "interpret their experiences in terms of previously established categories and prior expectations."[14] There is good reason to hold that the primary factor behind the rise of apocalyptic expression is a group's interpretation of its social/political environment through the lens of its eschatological tradition. Rather than *social/political conditions*, it is the *religious tradition* of the community that prompts a response to the various stimuli. How the group interprets its present experiences becomes not only the impetus but also the emphasis of their response.

Rather than responding to the negative factors of deprivation, failure of eschatological expectations and colonialization, apocalyptic expression de-

---

[14]Allison, *End of the Ages*, p. 142.

rives from positive factors—excitement and even optimism—produced by the perceived *fulfillment* of eschatological expectations as they are interpreted through the eyes of the group's traditional beliefs. Cognitive dissonance was not part of John's mental process. The advantage of this approach is that it can account for the rise of apocalyptic movements from a broad spectrum of societal conditions and social classes. It also explains the theme of imminence, so commonly found in apocalyptic literature. Perceived fulfillment of expectations was the single greatest reason for apocalyptic imminence, but even partial fulfillment allowed for apocalyptic writers to reinterpret earlier tradition for new situations, keeping an imminent hope alive. The following will explore this phenomenon in Revelation in relation to three early Christian eschatological motifs: apostasy of believers, the appearance of an eschatological adversary and the destruction of the temple in Jerusalem. These events were considered to be harbingers of the very imminent coming of God's kingdom.

The belief that the coming of Jesus would be preceded by widespread apostasy of believers is clearly seen in John's letters to the seven churches. The letters of Revelation 2–3 do not reflect communities struggling with existence under the rule of the Roman state. For the most part they reflect people experiencing its every benefit. The fact that Roman rule was not by force but by invitation, along with the many benefits it provided to the provinces, created an overwhelming attraction for believers. John was not pleased with the Nicolaitans in Ephesus, the followers of "Balaam" in Pergamum and of "Jezebel" in Thyatira. These promoted accommodation to urban society and were probably like-minded with those in Laodicea and Sardis in their rejection of boundary systems of John's minority. They were probably successful both socially and economically. For John this kind of intermingling with the culture was unacceptable, but the major issue was that it caused believers to lose sight of the imminence of Christ's return. He may have felt that the harassment that those in Philadelphia and Smyrna were receiving was more typical of those who follow Christ. Even for these John is concerned that the difficulties they were experiencing would lead some to fall away.

Apostasy of believers is a prominent eschatological expectation in Old Testament, Second Temple and New Testament literature.[15] John inter-

---

[15]The later redaction of Zech 1–8, as well as additions to Zech 9–14; Jews who sided with Antiochus IV in the historical apocalypses of Dan 7–12; Joel 2:12ff; *1 Enoch* 89:73ff; *Testament of Moses* 8:6; *4 Ezra* 5:2; 12:25; Mt 24:12, 2; Thess 2:3; 1 Tim 4:1; 2 Pet 2:1ff; 1 Jn 2:18; 4:3; Jude 14.

preted the spiritual decline as well as the harassment in these communities as a fulfillment of the traditionally expected apostasy of believers. His warnings to the churches take a strongly eschatological tone (Rev 2:16 [cf. 19:15], 23 [cf. 20:13], 25; 3:3, 11, 20). These developments heightened his sense of eschatological imminence; Christ's return was near because "the apostasy comes first" (2 Thess 2:3).

A second motif involves the eschatological adversary and his activity in the destruction of the temple in Jerusalem. A development of the theme begins in the seals cycle of Revelation 6 and is further developed in Revelation 13. Although John's four horsemen have Old Testament parallels, the Synoptic apocalypse is the most important source for the first cycle.[16] This is not a new observation. Many commentators have recognized the parallels between the two. John sees partial fulfillment of the Synoptic tradition but also delay that will require reinterpretation.

Seals one through four fit the tradition of "the signs of the end of the age," but which are not "the end" (Mt 24:4-6 and pars.). Believers had experienced wars, famines, false teachers and earthly catastrophes at various times. In the Synoptic tradition, following these events "the desolating sacrilege" would appear and defile the Jerusalem temple, bringing great suffering that would find relief in the coming of the Son of Man. Seal five, however, breaks this pattern. Here martyrs under the heavenly altar cry "how long?" until their blood is avenged in judgment. The question expressed by the martyrs was certainly a reflection of John's own concerns. How could the Synoptic tradition warn that the coming of "the desolating sacrilege" and the destruction of Jerusalem would immediately bring the coming of Christ, and yet twenty years after the event there had been no fulfillment? Moreover, the Jerusalem temple was not destroyed in the manner described in the Synoptic tradition. The expectation was that it would involve an anti-God figure profaning the temple similarly to Antiochus IV (see also 2 Thess 2:4). These instances of partial fulfillment raised John's eschatological enthusiasm, but also made it necessary for him to explain the delay.

How John reinterprets the role of the eschatological antagonist is partially seen in Revelation 13. Jerusalem had been destroyed, but the historical drama took unforeseen turns. In response John moves the center of the

---

[16]Note Zech 1:8-15; 6:1-8; and Ezek 14:12-23. The Synoptic apocalypse is referred to as the "Olivet Discourse" and is found in Mt 24, Mk 13 and Lk 21. Matthew and Mark fit earlier expectations but Luke has reinterpreted earlier expectations much like that seen in Revelation.

drama west to Rome; now the anti-God figure sits not in the Jerusalem temple but in his own temple via the emperor cult. The beasts of chapter 13 are John's reinterpretation of "the desolating sacrilege." The complexity of chapter 13 is caused not only by the fact that the beast is a multipersona, but also because his traditional role as the eschatological antagonist has been divided. John does this by means of mythical tradition and by reason of historical necessity. The beasts from the sea and the land allude to the Canaanite mythical combination Leviathan and Behemoth. According to a legend inspired by Genesis 1:21, on the fifth day God made the sea monsters but ordered chaos by separating the female Leviathan from the male Behemoth, giving the latter rule of the land.[17] The rise of these two from their appointed place symbolizes a return to chaos.

What John does with the myth is brilliant. Various expectations existed in Jewish and Christian literature with regard to the eschatological adversary of God and his people.[18] Some of these expectations were: committing blasphemy or declaring himself to be divine,[19] deceiving and leading people astray,[20] performing miraculous signs[21] and setting up an image to himself or being worshiped.[22] All of these themes occur in Revelation 13, but instead of attributing them to one figure, John divides them between the two beasts. By means of the Leviathan-Behemoth myth John divides the function of the "desolating sacrilege" into two figures. The reinterpretation was necessitated by the fact that in the late first century two contemporary historical realities filled the role of the eschatological antagonist. The beast from the sea is the blasphemous one who claims divine honors

---

[17]"And you separated one from the other, for the seventh part where the water had been gathered together could not hold them both. And you gave Behemoth one of the parts that had been dried up on the third day, to live in it, where there are a thousand mountains; but to Leviathan you gave the seventh part, the watery part; and you have kept them to be eaten by whom you wish, and when you wish" (4 Ezra 6:50-52; see also 2 Baruch 29:4; Job 41:1-34; Ps 104:25-26).

[18]Recent studies have shown that a developed "Antichrist" tradition was most probably a distinctly Christian phenomenon. Christian writers picked up antecedent themes from diverse and independent strands of Jewish tradition (cf. Dan 11:36-39; 1 Macc 1:20-61; 2 Macc 5:11-6:11). Note the various New Testament titles for this entity: "the Antichrist" (1 Jn 2:18; 2:22; 4:3; 2 Jn 1:7); the "false prophet" (Mt 7:15; Mk 13:22 [par Mt 24:24]); "the man of lawlessness" (2 Thess 2:3; Ascension of Isaiah 4:2-14).

[19]Dan 7:25; 8:11-12, 25; 11:36-37; 2 Thess 2:4; Ascension of Isaiah 4:6; Mk 13:6, 22; Lk 21:8; Didache 16:4.

[20]Mt 24:10, 24; Mk 13:22; Ascension of Isaiah 2:7; 2 Thess 2:10-12.

[21]Mt 24:24; Mk 13:22; Ascension of Isaiah 4:4-5, 10; 2 Thess 2:9; Didache 16:4; Sibylline Oracles 2:167-8; Apocalypse of Peter 2:13; Apocalypse Elijah 3:7.

[22]Ascension of Isaiah 4:11; 2 Thess 2:4; cf. Dan 3:4-5.

and is worshiped as god. He represents the Roman Empire as manifested in its successive leaders. The beast from the land represents the emperor cult as it was promoted in the imperial priesthood. Since these prominent local officials fulfilled a role traditionally associated with the eschatological antagonist, they are also attributed with his character.

John alone may have fashioned a scenario in which the eschatological antagonist becomes two different entities. The scenario is based on both his eschatological expectations and his own historical reality. The persecution referred to in Revelation 13:15 refers to trends John saw in the direction of emperor cult worship. The demands of the second beast were the growing pressure of the local civic leadership in favor of the emperor cult. The seer saw in the growing pressure to conform a perilous trajectory that would lead either to confrontation or the falling away "even of the elect."

Conclusion

Revelation 6 and Revelation 13 display fulfillment, reinterpretation and prediction. John's purpose was to warn the churches of the soon coming of Jesus by showing how prophecy was being fulfilled, some in unexpected ways made known via the seer's prophetic reinterpretation. John was concerned with the emperor cult; he was concerned that believers had accommodated themselves to its way of life; he was concerned with the fact that participation with the emperor cult was more and more becoming a matter of compulsion. But Revelation is not primarily about whether empires are evil or even whether it is wrong for them to impose their authority on other peoples. These developments were primarily important for John because they pointed to the soon coming of Jesus. Through reinterpretation John presents a traditional portrait of the actions expected by the eschatological empire opposed to God—a portrait not unlike empires past and present— but he does not intend to offer a program of resistance for future generations. If John's primary concern was the nearness of the return of Jesus, if the spiritual situation of the church and the rise of the emperor cult were indicators of this fact, then the view that Revelation is a paradigm for subversive anti-imperialism must be seen as an issue that reflects more the modern reader's concerns than the author of the apocalypse. One may be more true to the message of Revelation by seeking to understand the ways in which the concerns of accommodation and spiritual apostasy are part of the church's contemporary experience.

BIBLIOGRAPHY

Friesen, Steven J. *Imperial Cults and the Apocalypse of John: Reading Revelation in the Ruins.* Oxford: Oxford University Press, 2011.

Frilingos, Christopher A. *Spectacles of Empire: Monsters, Martyrs, and the Book of Revelation.* Divinations: Rereading Late Ancient Religion. Philadelphia: University of Pennsylvania Press, 2004.

Horsley, Richard A. *Revolt of the Scribes: Resistance and Apocalyptic Origins.* Minneapolis: Fortress Press, 2009.

Howard-Brook, Wes, and Anthony Gwyther. *Unveiling Empire: Reading Revelation Then and Now.* Maryknoll, NY: Orbis, 1999.

Kraybill, J. Nelson. *Apocalypse and Allegiance: Worship, Politics, and Devotion in the Book of Revelation.* Grand Rapids: Brazos, 2010.

Moore, Stephen D. *Empire and Apocalypse: Postcolonialism and the New Testament.* The Bible in the Modern World. Sheffield, UK: Sheffield Phoenix Press, 2006.

Schussler Fiorenza, Elisabeth. *The Power of the Word: Scripture and the Rhetoric of Empire.* Minneapolis: Fortress Press, 2007.

Thompson, Leonard. *The Book of Revelation: Apocalypse and Empire.* Oxford: Oxford University Press, 1990.

CONCLUSION

Scot McKnight and Joseph B. Modica

If I had a hammer . . .[1]

We are all familiar with the oft-cited maxim (expressed in many ways) of Abraham Maslow: If the only tool you have is a hammer, you tend to see every problem as a nail. This maxim does not discourage the use of a hammer when one is attempting to nail two pieces of wood together, but it cautions one not to use a hammer when tightening a door hinge. Although a valid and useful tool, using a hammer for every situation is simply an ill-fated strategy. Forty-plus years ago Morna D. Hooker prophetically warned of this sort of thing occurring in biblical studies: "the answers which the New Testament scholar gives are not the result of applying objective tests and using precision tools; they are very largely the result of his [or her] own presuppositions and prejudices."[2] The conundrum that Hooker wrestles with is when a scholar overconfidently uses an interpretative tool when, in actuality, it may be the wrong one for the task at hand. So, if all one sees is the Roman Empire while reading the New Testament, then everything becomes empire criticism. This is not to suggest that those we interact with in

---

[1]From "If I Had a Hammer (The Hammer Song)," with apologies to Peter Seger, Lee Hays and the folk group Peter, Paul and Mary.

[2]Morna Hooker, "On Using the Wrong Tool," *Theology* 75 (1972): 581. The contributors to this volume are not blinded to their presuppositions. We all have them. In the final analysis, however, we think our presuppositions explain the evidence better.

212 JESUS IS LORD, CAESAR IS NOT

the book always do just that. But sometimes they appear to do so.

Biblical studies, much like other fields, has the proclivity to sway to extremes. This book is an attempt to strike a balance between a postcolonial reading of the New Testament and one that recognizes the contributions of such a reading, yet posits a very different view of the concept of "kingdom of God."[3] Our title clearly offers our perspective: Jesus is Lord, Caesar is not. To make the claim "Jesus is Lord," one does not make specific sociopolitical allegiances; rather the claim forthrightly involves repentance and following Jesus. Hence, the New Testament writers affirm that Jesus is Lord, not with the sole intent of debunking Caesar and his empire, but to offer a stark contrast between the kingdom of God and the kingdom of Satan.

Let us make this point crystal clear: We believe that the New Testament writers do indeed address the concerns highlighted by empire criticism. But we also strongly suggest that this is not their primary modus operandi. The New Testament writers are cognizant of Roman occupation, aware of Roman customs and laws, but they fundamentally understand Jesus' inaugurating of the kingdom of God in direct opposition to and in contrast with the kingdom of Satan (see Mt 12:26; Lk 11:18). The kingdom of God exemplifies redemption and life; the kingdom of Satan exudes sin and death. Kim aptly notes: "Jesus fights the kingdom of Satan and redeems the sick out of it, but he does not fight the Roman imperial system and does not redeem the victims of its evil rulers."[4]

A FEW BRIEF OBSERVATIONS

1. The reality of the Roman Empire needs to be reckoned with in the New Testament. Thus the discipline of empire criticism (vis-à-vis postcolonial interpretation) has something unique to offer the field of New Testament interpretation. There is no denying that the New Testament writers were quite cognizant of Roman rule. Moreover, the New Testament writers seem to do two things simultaneously: (1) affirm the reality of the imperial influence of the Roman Empire, and (2) adroitly demonstrate that Jesus' mandate of the kingdom of God stands in direct opposition to the principalities and powers (i.e., kingdom of Satan). We must not succumb to the temptation of "binary confusion," namely, where a "both-and" exists,

---

[3]What is also implied here is the phrase "kingdom of Heaven."
[4]Seyoon Kim, *Christ and Caesar: The Gospel and the Roman Empire in the Writings of Paul and Luke* (Grand Rapids: Eerdmans, 2008), p. 123.

one might be tempted to see an "either-or." When the kingdom of God is used in the New Testament, it appears to be a "both-and": Jesus and his followers are certainly aware of the ideological and idolatrous nature of the Roman Empire; yet, Jesus ultimately establishes a fundamentally different, one-of-a-kind kingdom—one "not from this world" (Jn 18:36).

2. The purpose of the kingdom of God is not to replace, so to speak, the Roman Empire; rather it is to overcome the kingdom of Satan. Let us not forget that in a first-century cosmology, the New Testament writers see the world championed not by Caesar but by the "Ruler of this World," Satan (Jn 12:31; 14:30; 16:11). This cosmology developed during the intertestamental period. First Enoch, perhaps the most significant piece of Jewish literature from this period, aptly purports this cosmology: "Overall, [the various sections of *1 Enoch*] express a common world view that characterizes this present world and age as evil and unjust and in need of divine adjudication and renewal."[5] So, any discussion of empire by Jews and Christians emerged from this kind of cosmology, where empire and idolatry would have been closely tied together.

There is no denying the numerous power encounters between Jesus and Satan in the Gospels.[6] Jesus is tempted by Satan, exorcises demons and even is labeled Beelzebul by his opponents.[7] Simply, Jesus' kingdom, as presented by the Evangelists, is not "in conscious antithesis to the imperial ideology of Rome."[8] Bryan rightly observes, "I think that the biblical tradition challenges human power structures not by attempting to dismantle them or replace them with other human power structures but by consistently confronting then with *the truth about their origin and purpose.*"[9]

3. The New Testament writers show the earliest followers of Jesus how to live in the "already but the not yet" day-to-day realities of the empire. One must critically evaluate Rome, but does the New Testament always view it as oppressive or negative? Bryan observes that there were many "tangible

---

[5]George W. E. Nickelsburg, *1 Enoch: A New Translation* (Minneapolis: Augsburg Fortress, 2004), p. 1.
[6]See Susan R. Garrett, *The Demise of the Devil: Magic and the Demonic in Luke's Writings* (Philadelphia: Fortress Press, 1990).
[7]See the excellent essay by D. Sheets in *Who Do My Opponents Say That I Am? An Investigation of the Accusations Against the Historical Jesus*, ed. Scot McKnight and Joseph B. Modica (New York: T & T Clark International, 2008), pp. 27-49.
[8]Kim, *Christ and Caesar*, p. xiv.
[9]Christopher Bryan, *Render to Caesar: Jesus, the Early Church, and the Roman Superpower* (Oxford: Oxford University Press, 2005), p. 9.

benefits" afforded by the empire (e.g., harbors, water supplies, road systems).[10] Jesus seems to suggest that even paying the appropriate taxes to Rome has benefits to its citizens (see Mt 22:15-22). Perhaps this motivates the apostle Paul to write, "Let every person be subject to the governing authorities; for there is no authority except from God, and those authorities that exist have been instituted by God" (Rom 13:1 NRSV). Again, we don't want to paint a rosy picture of the ancient Roman Empire, but we want to avoid, as Bryan puts it, "a colonizing attitude *to the past*."[11]

Finally, we must listen to the New Testament documents themselves. The New Testament conviction that Jesus is Lord, Caesar is not, is not a direct assault on the Roman Empire or even a veiled attempt to usurp it. Rather, to claim that Jesus is Lord is to place oneself in the servitude of an Emperor of a radically different kingdom—one which has no equal, now and forever (Phil 2:9-11).

---

[10]See ibid., p. 120.

[11]Bryan wants to remind his reader that New Testament interpreters are often tone deaf to the text because of their blaring agendas (ibid., pp. 122-23).

CONTRIBUTORS

Andy Crouch (M.Div., Boston University School of Theology) is an editor-at-large at *Christianity Today* and the author of *Culture Making: Recovering Our Creative Calling*. He is executive producer of *This Is Our City*, a multi-year project featuring documentary video, reporting and essays about Christians seeking the flourishing of their cities. His writing has appeared in *The Wall Street Journal* and in several editions of *Best Christian Writing* and *Best Spiritual Writing*.

David P. Nystrom (Ph.D., University of California) is provost and senior vice president at Biola University. A specialist in New Testament and Roman history, he is the author of many works including *James* in the NIV Application Commentary and, with Bradley P. Nystrom, *The History of Christianity*.

Judith A. Diehl (Ph.D., University of Edinburgh) is an instructor of New Testament and hermeneutics at Denver Seminary. She has written numerous journal articles, including a series on anti-imperial rhetoric in *Currents in Biblical Research*.

Joel Willitts (Ph.D., Cambridge University) is associate professor in biblical and theological studies at North Park University. Among Joel's several publications on Matthew's Gospel are *Matthew's Messianic Shepherd-King: In Search of the Lost Sheep of the House of Israel* and "Matthew and Psalms of Solomon's Messianism: A Comparative Study in First-Century Messianology."

Dean Pinter (Ph.D., Durham University) is rector at St. Aidan Anglican Church, Moose Jaw, Saskatchewan. His doctoral research related to the areas of divine and imperial power in the writings of Paul and Josephus.

Christopher W. Skinner (Ph.D., The Catholic University of America) is assistant professor of religion at Mount Olive College in North Carolina. He has published many articles and books, including *John and Thomas: Gospels in Conflict?*, *What Are They Saying About the Gospel of Thomas?*, *Characters and Characterization in the Gospel of John* and, with Kelly R. Iverson, *Unity and Diversity in the Gospels and Paul*.

Drew J. Strait is a Ph.D. candidate in New Testament at the University of Pretoria, South Africa. He is an adjunct lecturer in biblical and theological studies at North Park University and North Park Theological Seminary. His research interests include Luke-Acts, the speeches of Paul in Acts, Greco-Roman religion and rhetorical strategies for critiquing deified rulers in early Judaism.

Michael F. Bird (Ph.D., University of Queensland) is lecturer in theology at Ridley College in Melbourne, Australia. He is the author of many publications including *The Saving Righteousness of God*, *A Bird's-Eye View of Paul* and *Colossians and Philemon*.

Lynn H. Cohick (Ph.D., University of Pennsylvania) is professor of New Testament at Wheaton College in Wheaton, Illinois. Her interests include the Greco-Roman cultural and social world and how Jews and Christians negotiated that environment. Her publications include *Women in the World of the Earliest Christians* and, with Gary M. Burge and Gene L. Green, *The New Testament in Antiquity*.

Allan R. Bevere (Ph.D., Durham University) is a professional fellow in theology at Ashland Theological Seminary and the pastor of Akron First United Methodist Church. He is the author of *Sharing in the Inheritance: Identity and the Moral Life in Colossians*. His interests include the ecclesial nature of politics and the church's witness.

Dwight D. Sheets (Ph.D., Fuller Theological Seminary) is associate professor of New Testament at Evangel University in Springfield, Missouri. His expertise is in the area of Jewish and early Christian apocalyptic literature. The research of his dissertation *The Sitz im Leben of The Apocalypse: Realized Eschatology and Apocalyptic Expression* provided the basis for the views expressed in the present work.

Subject and Author Index

Scripture Index